THE ART OF RIDING STRESS WAVES
Self-help psychology for an anxious age

THE ART OF RIDING STRESS WAVES
Self-help psychology for an anxious age

Dr Wayne R. Somerville

CREEK'S BEND
Kyogle, Australia

2025

Creek's Bend
Kyogle, NSW, 2474, Australia

First published by Dr Wayne Robert Somerville 2025.

Copyright © Dr Wayne R. Somerville 2025

All rights reserved. Without limiting the rights under copyright reserved above, no part of this publication may be reproduced, stored in or introduced into a retrieval system, or transmitted, in any form or by any means (electronic, mechanical, photocopying, recording or otherwise) without the prior written permission of the publishers of this book. Every care has been taken to trace and acknowledge copyright. Please let the author know of any accidental infringement and it will be addressed.

The Art of Riding Stress Waves is educational material designed to inform and entertain. The information in this book is made available on the understanding that the author is not providing any form of specific legal, medical or psychological advice relevant to any individual reader's circumstances. In all cases, readers should consult appropriate professionals for legal, medical or psychological advice and treatment. The author shall have neither liability nor responsibility to any person or entity with respect to any loss or damage caused or alleged to be caused directly or indirectly by the information contained in this book. If you do not wish to be bound by the above, you may return this book to the publisher for a full refund. If you have questions about this disclaimer, please contact the author.

Typeset in Garamond 12.4/22 by the publishers
Layout and design by Performingdesign

A catalogue record for this book is available from the National Library of Australia

Creator: Somerville, Wayne, author.

Title: *The Art of Riding Stress Waves: Self-help psychology for an anxious age*/ Wayne Somerville.
ISBN: 978-0-6480628-7-5 (paperback)
ISBN: 978-0-6480628-8-2 (e-book)
ISBN: 978-0-6480628-9-9 (audiobook)

Please leave your honest review on an Amazon books website.

For everyone who wants to make their life
and the world better.

Contents

ILLUSTRATIONS xii
ACKNOWLEDGEMENT xiii
PREFACE xiv

INTRODUCTION   1
   About This Book   2
   What's in This Book   7
      Mental Exercises and Thought Experiments   7
      Stories, Studies and Drawings   8
      References   9

PART 1: WHAT YOU NEED TO KNOW   11

Chapter 1: Riding Waves   13

Chapter 2: Stress and Stress Responses   17
   What are Stress and Anxiety?   17
   The Fight-Flight-Freeze Response   19

Chapter 3: The Structure of Mind   23
   The Executive Mind   24
   The Deep Mind   27

Chapter 4: Avoidance Strategies   31
   The One-thought Solution   32
   When Avoidance Causes Trouble   34
      Separation Anxiety Disorder   37
      Avoidant Personality Disorder   38
      Specific Phobia Disorder   39
      Obsessive-compulsive Disorder   41
      Social Anxiety Disorder   42

    Agoraphobia and Panic Disorder   42
    Posttraumatic Stress Disorder (PTSD)   44

Chapter 5: The Engage Strategy   51
  A Brief History   53
  Mental Processing   57
  The Basic Formula for Riding Stress Waves   60

PART 2: TOOLS, TIPS & TECHNIQUES   63

Chapter 6: Using Your Toolkit   65

Chapter 7: Attitudes and Beliefs   69
  Self-Efficacy   69
  Learning and Making Mistakes   70
  Optimism and Pessimism   72
  Stress Responses   73
  The Need to Keep a Stress Reaction   74
  Other People and the World   77
  Health and Healing   79
    Physical Pain   79
    Chronic Illness and Disability   80
    Addictive Substances   82

Chapter 8: Emotions   85
  Fear and Anxiety   86
    The Stress Scan   87
    Rationing Emotional Energy   89
    Letting Go of Unnecessary Anxiety   91
  Anger   92
  Depression   93
  Guilt and Shame   94
  Courage   98
  Fear of Death   100
    Liberation in Dark Times   102
    The Unity of All Things   103
    On Acceptance   105

Grief   107
   The Importance of Ceremony   107
   Resolving Grief   109

Chapter 9: Language   113
Troublesome Words   114
   Generalisations   114
   Hope and Try   114
   Must and Should   115
   Negative Language   117
   Motivation Style   119
Names and Labels   120
Talking About Stress   125
Writing About Stress   127

Chapter 10: Thinking and Reasoning   129
Thinking Styles   129
The Fallacy of Hindsight and the 'What Ifs'   130
Flawed Reasoning   131
Reasoned Thought   132
Holistic Thinking   134

Chapter 11: Attention and Awareness   141
Meditation   141
Contemplation   142
Metacognition   142

Chapter 12: Perception   143

Chapter 13: Memory and Imagination   149
Controlling the Emotional Impact of Imagery   151
   Changing Perspective   157
   Adjusting Brightness and Colour   158
   Varying Distance   159
   Altering Size   160
   Adjusting Volume   160
   Adding Support   161

　　　　Using Humour　161
　　　　　　Positive and Negative Self-Statements　162
　　　　　　Enhancing the Memory　162
　　　Resolving Stress Memories　162
　　　　　Transferring Adult Resources　163
　　　　　Rescripting Memories　165
　　　　　Working with Good Memories　168
　　　Crafting the Future　169
　　　Guided Imagery　170
　　　Media Stress　172

Chapter 14: Sleep, Dreams and Daydreams　175
　　　Sleeping Well　177
　　　　　Temperature and Noise　178
　　　　　Sleep Apnoea　178
　　　　　Insomnia　179
　　　The Natural Trance　181
　　　The Magic Theatre of Hypnagogia　183
　　　Rapid Eye Movement Dreams　185
　　　To End a Recurring Nightmare　189

Chapter 15: Intuition　191
　　　Setting Up Signals　192
　　　The Technique of Respectful Communication　193
　　　Mental Processing Without Conscious Awareness　194

Chapter 16: Therapies for Traumatic Stress　199
　　　Shared Processes in Therapy　200
　　　Medications　202
　　　Hypnotherapy　203
　　　Systematic Desensitisation and Exposure Therapy　203
　　　Cognitive Therapy and Cognitive Behaviour Therapy　206
　　　Imagery Rescripting Therapy　207
　　　Emotional Freedom Techniques　209
　　　Eye Movement Desensitisation and Reprocessing　210
　　　Somatic Psychotherapies　211

    The Evidence-Based Approach   213
    Cautionary Cases   214
    Choosing a Therapy   216

PART 3: ART IN ACTION   219

Chapter 17: Dealing with the Past   221
    A Personal Case Study   222
    A Generation's Shared Stress   225

Chapter 18: Healing Nature   229
    Luck and Improbable Events   230
    Costs and Benefits of Solutions   231

Chapter 19: Facing the Future   235
    The Avoidance Option   237
    Taking Care of the Home Front   238
    On Hope   240

Chapter 20: Bringing It All Together   245

REFERENCES   249

Illustrations

The Fright Response   21
The Key Mental Processes   25
A One-carriage Train of Thought   32
Hypervigilance   45
Optimism vs. Pessimism   72
Circles of Concern and Influence   89
Scales of Perceived and Real Danger   91
A Cranky Cow   92
The Yin-Yang Symbol   104
A Systems Model of Forest Dieback   136
Logs on Road Illusion   145
Woman Illusion   145
Chequerboard Illusion   146
Good Sleep   178
Insomnia   180
Taking a Break   182
Sweet Dreams   185
Exposure for Fear of Heights, Spiders, Snakes & Storms   204

Acknowledgements

I acknowledge the Githabul traditional owners of the Country where Susan and I live. We need the wisdom of their elders, past, present and future if we're to live gracefully on this land and pass on a worthwhile future to our descendants.

To Susan, my chief editor, muse and wife, thank you for a lifetime of love, support and inspiration.

I want to thank Rebecca Hendershott, Suzanne Evans, Brendan Shoebridge, Denise Lego, Murray Smith, Meg Nielsen, Greg Somerville, Paula Martin, Juliet Smith, Lucie Smith and Peter Nielsen for reviewing and editing earlier versions of this book.

A special thanks to Paula Martin and Greg Somerville for the cover design.

I also wish to thank Bradley Duniam for sharing his knowledge of the ocean with me and Stephanie Shoebridge for giving me my first opportunities to present these ideas to live audiences.

I am grateful for all my teachers. Everything I know was built on the foundations they laid for me.

Preface

During my near-forty-year career as a clinical psychologist, I have helped my clients deal with anxiety, stress and trauma. But times have changed. Communities worldwide now face an uncertain future and an ever-growing array of threats.

In this hyper-anxious age, psychologists cannot provide personalised consultations to meet the demand for mental health services. This self-help book, *The Art of Riding Stress Waves*, with its associated presentations and workshops, is my response to this challenge.

Drawing on insights gained from 70-plus years of life, much study and decades of clinical practice, I want to help you manage the stress in your life with style and joy.

May you benefit from this book.

Dr Wayne Somerville B.A.(Hons), M.Clin.Psych., D. Psy
Clinical Psychologist
Kyogle, NSW, Australia

drwaynesomerville@gmail.com
www.ridingstresswaves.com.au

Introduction

MACBETH. How does your patient (Lady Macbeth), doctor?
DOCTOR. Not so sick, my lord, as she is troubled with thick coming fancies, that keep her from her rest.
MACBETH. Cure her of that. Canst thou not minister to a mind diseased, pluck from the memory a rooted sorrow, raze out the written troubles of the brain and with some sweet oblivious antidote (medication) cleanse the stuff'd bosom of that perilous stuff which weighs upon the heart?
DOCTOR. Therein the patient must minister to himself.
(Macbeth, Act 5, Sc.3)
William Shakespeare (1564–1616)

IT'S GETTING HARDER TO LIVE a happy, healthy and satisfying life. As well as the usual challenges, we face cascading crises the likes of which humanity has never seen before. Through media, we bear impotent witness to great suffering as stories of war, social decay and political turmoil stream into our homes and minds. Meanwhile, human activity degrades our planet's life-support systems, destabilises the climate and drives plant and animal species to extinction. And the stress waves keep rolling in.

Like ocean swells, the stress comes in sets. As one wave crashes over us, the next forms before we've fully recovered from the previous hit. About five years ago, severe drought culminated in firestorms that devastated Eastern Australian communities, forests and animals. Then, with memories of fire still raw, the COVID-19 pandemic struck. In the Northern Rivers region of New South Wales, Australia, where my wife, Susan, and I live, people still struggle with the impact of these disasters and the two record-setting floods that followed. Such circumstances are not unique; disasters are becoming common. Meanwhile, the grind of coping with anxiety and stress drives up prescription rates of psychoactive medications.

Nothing can cocoon us from life's stresses; you won't find a quick fix to soothe frayed feelings here. This book offers something of greater value: the knowledge and skills you need to deal effectively with all the stresses — from the everyday to the lethally dangerous — that come your way.

About This Book

The Art of Riding Stress Waves is a self-help psychology book; it's not about medical treatments for mental health problems. I focus on the mind, not the brain. The distinction matters, and it profoundly affects the way we respond to stress and anxiety.

Tell a medical practitioner or a psychiatrist that you're on edge or are feeling down, and they'll probably prescribe a medication for you. This is the standard, front-line medical response; each day, about one in seven Australians take prescribed anti-depressants and about one in six use anti-anxiety medications. And every discovery of an association between a mental state and a brain process comes with the promise of new drug treatments for psychological problems down the line.

The thinking that underpins the medical model of mental health goes like this: when we become anxious or depressed, our brain and body change, so taking a substance to counter these physiological effects should relieve our emotional distress. Take the right pill, and voilà, we've fixed the problem with a quick, easy solution that doesn't involve psychologists or much time and effort.

The way we perceive and think about things that happen to us clearly affects our body as well as our mind.

If were to meet someone who appears friendly and engages us in polite, social conversation, our muscles would likely relax, and we'd probably smile and feel pleasant emotions. This effect would be enhanced if the person reminded us of someone we liked and trusted.

But if an angry person was to unexpectedly act aggressively and attack us verbally, we'd likely experience an instantaneous surge of adrenaline and our heart rate and blood pressure would rise. Such a stressful event could leave us with a lingering sense of unease and make us feel anxious and on guard for a considerable time after the encounter. This distressing effect would be intensified if the person reminded us of someone who seriously harmed us in the past.

There's no doubt that our brain and body react when we feel threatened. But does it follow that our best option for dealing with such a persisting stress reaction is to take a medication to counter our physiological responses? Or would it be better to think about why we reacted to the offensive person as we did, learn what we can from the experience and work out how we can better protect ourselves in similar stressful situations in the future? I'm for the latter option.

Doctors and psychiatrists consider anxiety to be a 'symptom' of 'mental dysfunction', while I, as a clinical psychologist, understand anxiety to be a natural, healthy stress response that serves an important protective function. For me, anxiety is not a symptom; it's a signal. Anxiety is the emotion that lets us know there's danger present.

Using medication to counter anxiety is like putting masking tape over a warning light that blinks on your car's dashboard. The tape relieves your immediate stress of seeing a flashing light, but if you investigate no further, you'll never know what the signal meant, at least not until your engine breaks down.

There are other practical, scientific and philosophical reasons why this book is about the mind and psychology rather than the brain and physiology.

As we'll discuss later, psychoactive medications and psychedelics can be used as tools for riding stress waves, but there's no medication that, by itself, effectively treats a problematic stress response. Sure, some substances can ease distress while a patient takes them. But when they stop using these medications, the patient's anxiety, depression or anger returns. Doctors and psychiatrists tend to see this outcome as a 'relapse' (a deterioration in health after some improvement) and recommend further courses of medication. When this happens, a patient can come to believe that they're unable to self-manage stress, so they go on taking the medication, perhaps for the rest of their lives.

Further, the medical model of mental health, with its focus on the brain and physiology, makes no good sense; it relies on misunderstandings about the relationship between mind and brain and what's referred to as 'levels of explanation'.

Consider, for example, the everyday experience of deciding to have a cup of tea.

The thought 'I'll make a cuppa' initiates brain processes that, with little to no further mental input, lead to an interaction of nervous and muscular systems that ends with you sitting down to enjoy a break. If we look deeper into our brain, nerves and muscles, we can see that they are also composed of ever-smaller cellular, molecular, atomic, subatomic and, ultimately, quantum field systems.

Each level of systems that make up our mind and body operates in its own way and requires a specific type of explanation. Understanding how subatomic particles form atoms tells us nothing about how our nervous system moves a muscle. Knowing about the chemical and electrical processes in our muscles cannot explain how we know when we've poured the right amount of tea into a cup.

If we could monitor every physical process in our brains and bodies, we'd be none the wiser about why we do what we do. To explain why we thought to have that cup of tea, we have to take into account social, cultural and psychological factors. Perhaps a friend dropping by or a host of other experiences, thoughts, beliefs, attitudes, memories, motivations, plans and other psychological processes played a part.

To understand even so simple an act as deciding to make a cup of tea, our explanations must consider the mind. But the medical model of mental health does not go there; it avoids thinking about mental factors and confines itself to physiology. The underlying philosophy of physicalism (the doctrine that the real world only consists of physical things) assumes that the mind arises from the brain and mental processes can be explained in physiological terms. From this, it follows that mental health problems can be treated with medications.

The mind and the brain are intimately linked, but they're not the same thing.

Physical substances can affect our mind. For example, drinking alcohol can make us feel braver, ingesting a benzodiazepine medication blocks anxiety and taking 100 millionths of a gram of LSD-25 — the barest mote of psychedelic — can profoundly alter our sense of identity and reality.

We also know that thinking about or remembering happy and sad events can induce our bodies to smile or shed tears. From neuropsychological case studies, we understand that stroke and other brain injuries can leave patients with startlingly specific deficits, such as a dairy farmer who forgot only the names of his cows and other folk who lost just the ability to understand pronouns or conjunctions.

Thinking about computers can help us understand the mysterious relationship between the mind and the brain.

When our computer works, we don't care what its 'hardware' (the physical makeup) does; we're more interested in the 'software' (the data and programs that run the machine).

Programs consist of an ethereal flow of symbols and instructions for manipulating information. We might store them on a disk, memory stick or in the cloud, but programs are not physical things and they have nothing to do with wires, currents or atoms.

If you had superhero vision and could see through the casing of your laptop, tablet or phone, down into every circuit, even to the atomic and quantum levels, you still wouldn't know how the thing works. For this, you need to understand the machine's software.

In the 'human bio-computer' analogy, the mind corresponds to the computer's software, while the brain represents the hardware. A computer's programs determine how information is moved, stored, retrieved and processed to produce the observed performance. In we humans, thoughts, images, beliefs and other mental processes initiate and control our body's emotional, behavioural and physiological responses.

If you want to learn how to ride stress waves, understanding brain activity is no more useful than knowing which electronic components are involved when you use your computer.

The bio-computer analogy only takes us so far; it can't account for consciousness and our awareness of ourselves and the world around us. Again, an analogy to a different technology can help. The intriguing concept of 'fields' (a region in space-time in which each point is affected by a force) gives us another way to think about the relationship between mind and brain.

We live in a world awash with information transmitted across fields. Except for visible light, we can't directly perceive the electromagnetic fields that surround and flow through us. But if we've got the appropriate knowledge and technology, we can tune into the messages being transmitted via radio, television, Wi-Fi and cell phone fields. With the right SIM card and phone number, we can select one telephone conversation from billions, and with our tablets and phones, we can tune into the internet at the speed of light. But if we didn't have the technology to receive this information, we'd never know it existed: we couldn't see, feel or decipher it.

No informed modern person thinks that the information they receive on their phones and computers mysteriously emerges from, or is in any way explained by, the materials that make up the device. Accordingly, some contemporary philosophers of mind liken the brain to a receiver that enables us to tune into a 'mind/

consciousness field' that permeates our lives.

My clinical psychologist's perspective informs everything you'll read in this book. Most people assume that external events determine their thoughts, feelings and actions. But for a psychologist, it's not so much what happens to us as what goes on in our psyche that matters. When we practice the art of riding stress waves, all the relevant action takes place in our minds, not our brains.

Swallowing a pill is easy, but learning to control your mind and ride stress waves is a better investment; you get to keep your new skills with no ongoing costs or negative side effects.

What's in This Book

This book has three parts.

Part 1: What You Need to Know sets out the essential information you need to practise the art of riding stress waves. I give you new ways to think about anxiety and stress and how we respond to life's threats and challenges. This knowledge underpins the book's practical, self-help advice.

Part 2: Tools, Tips and Techniques provides a guide to psychological insights and methods for working with your mind and resolving stress.

Part 3: Art in Action presents three case studies of the art of riding stress waves applied in the real world.

Mental Exercises and Thought Experiments

Throughout the book, I use the symbol Ψ (the Greek letter 'psi' that the Romans transformed to 'psyche') to mark off mental exercises, imaginal experiences and thought experiments.

Before you undertake any exercise, check with your intuition that it feels all right to work this way. Trust your gut feeling to identify the exercises and experiences that are relevant for you.

Sometimes, I'll ask you to think about, say or imagine certain things. You might find that a requested scene comes clearly to your mind's eye or, perhaps, the image will be vague or absent. Whatever happens, it doesn't matter. You can benefit by just reading the instructions.

In some exercises, I ask you to rate your feelings on a scale. There are no right or wrong answers, and no correct or incorrect way to rate your reactions. You are a unique individual and can take from these experiences what's relevant to you.

To help you follow the processes, I've numbered the steps in most exercises and experiments.

Stories, Studies and Drawings

This non-fiction book is based on actual events, scientific research and my personal and professional life. Stories and dialogues are sometimes reconstructed to protect identities and privacy. I'll flag when I'm using a pseudonym by placing double quotation marks around the initial presentation of a name.

For examples and stories, I've drawn on my experiences as a clinical psychologist, farmer, bush regenerator and environmental activist. I've lived on the land most of my adult life, and as a young man, I bred, trained and worked draught horses. In my clinical practice, I specialise in gentle therapies for trauma survivors. Over 25 years as bush regenerators, my wife, Susan, and I developed a treatment for a dieback disease that's devastating eucalypt forests across Eastern Australia. To protect our farm and community, I became an activist against the gas field industrialisation of rural Australia.

What I know about surfboard riding comes from lazy summer days watching from a headland as surfers practise their art and, second-hand, from listening to my surfer-friend Bradley's stories.

My now-adult daughter drew the 'cowtoons' that brighten the pages of this book when she was 14 years old.

References

The Art of Riding Stress Waves is a practical, self-help guide for troubled times. It's no academic treatise. I could cite research for almost every sentence you'll read here, but you won't find many references. The citations that go with the superscript numbers in the text can be found at the end of the book. And, of course, for further information, you can Google any topic.

Part 1

What You Need to Know

Chapter 1

Riding Waves

You can't stop the waves, but you can learn to surf.
John Kabat-Zinn (1944–)

WHEN WORD OF A GOOD break spreads, surfers gather to watch the ocean and 'read' the conditions. If they judge the waves unsuitable or the 'rips' (powerful, narrow currents that pull out to sea) too dangerous, they might stay around for a while to see if conditions improve, or they'll spend the day on shore. But when the surfers decide that water and wind are favourable, they wax their boards and hit the surf. Being able to swim and get a surfboard out beyond the 'breakers' (heavy sea waves that break into churning foam) are essential skills. When they get to that special place, where the swell gently rises and falls, the surfers sit on their boards, scan the horizon out to sea and wait.

If the surfboard riders see a wave coming that appears to have the right form and power, they work with Nature's forces to best position themselves and paddle hard to catch the wave before it breaks. As they're propelled forward, the surfers spring to their feet and ride the wave as skilfully as they can. And so the cycle goes; surfers execute the same basic routine of getting out beyond the breakers, waiting as swells go by until they find a wave that'll take them on what, I imagine, is an exhilarating ride. As with any complex skill, surfers can never perfect their art, but with each ride, that's what they strive to do.

An accomplished surfer possesses the knowledge and skills needed to practice their art. They've got the basics; they know how to swim in rough seas, they can stand and balance on a flighty board and, by shifting position and weight, they can manoeuvre where they want to go. But these practitioners of the surfing art know more than that, and at times, they pull off remarkable feats.

Most avoid strong rips, but sometimes, a surfer, like my friend Bradley, will let the lifeguards at the beach know what they're up to before they 'ride the rip' out to sea and then up or down the coast, depending on which way the current turns. Bradley grew up with the ocean and knows you never swim directly against a rip; doing so is exhausting and risks drowning. Rather, Bradley uses the energy of the flow to pull him along, and when he decides to do so, he angles across the current to exit the rip. These rides can take Bradley kilometres away from where he entered the water. Like other accomplished surfers, Bradley even takes being pinned underwater by a wave as an opportunity to relax, calm his mind and enjoy one of the edgier experiences that his sport offers.

The stress-wave metaphor in this book's title is apt. The image of ocean waves coming in sets suggests the never-ending sequence of threats and challenges that life throws at us. Like ocean waves, stress often peaks before it crests and resolves. Furthermore, the broader analogy that links surfboard riding to how we respond to stress highlights some fundamental features of all skilled endeavours.

To practice any art well, there are things to learn, skills to develop and routines to follow. And practice is the appropriate word. We never perfect our art, though that's what we aim to do.

A surfboard rider has to know when darker water and a flattened section of wave indicate the presence of a rip. If they don't know how to apply wax properly, they'll slip off their boards. Being able to swim powerfully and stand on a surfboard are necessary skills. Notably, the art of surfing is not all about action; it entails lengthy periods of considered inaction as the surfer sits and waits for the next suitable wave. Surfboard riding is demanding and, at times, dangerous, but surfers pursue their art for the joy, satisfaction and good health it brings them.

Similarly, we practice the art of riding stress waves not just to manage or cope with anxiety and stress. Instead, we aim to live happy, healthy and productive lives as we deal with each stress wave effectively and efficiently. And, as it is for any art, if we're to ride stress waves well, we need certain knowledge and skills. We have to understand how our human mind deals with stress. Crucially, we must learn how to harness all our mental abilities to the task. And like the surfer waiting for their next ride, we have to judge when it's time to engage with stress and when it's better to let it go by.

The art of riding stress waves involves an exploration of our mind and our abilities to think, reason, imagine, remember, plan, believe, learn and dream. As students of the art, we can only ever be 'works in progress'; this is a lifetime practice, not an occasional performance. With each encounter, we learn and strive to do as well as we can with what life presents us.

When people consult a clinical psychologist, their therapeutic adventure begins with them feeling anxious and despondent and ends when they're able to control their thoughts, emotions, memories and behaviours. Dear Reader, as you explore this book, I'll show you how you can change your mind and life for the better. Self-help psychology is real. But it's for you to decide whether you'll take up the art of riding stress waves.

The remaining chapters in *Part 1* outline what you need to know about stress, stress responses and the human psyche. Then, in *Part 2*, you'll find the tools, tips and techniques to help you pursue your art.

Chapter 2

Stress and Stress Responses

It's not stress that kills us, it's our reaction to it.
Hans Selye (1907–1982)

TIMES ARE TOUGH, BUT so are we. Each of us, and every other living creature, has an unbroken line of ancestors that goes back about three and a half billion years to the first life on Earth. Over the past two and a half million years, our relatives from the *Homo* genus survived endless ages of ice, wars, climate upheaval, pestilence and much more. Through deep time, evolution prepared us for coping with life's challenges, from the everyday need to eat to the rarer trial of surviving a life-threatening disaster. Our being here is proof that our inbuilt, natural coping responses work pretty well, and anxiety is a key component in the strategies Nature gives us for dealing with stress.

What are Stress and Anxiety?

We all know what stress and anxiety feel like. Both can come with psychological reactions of fear, irritability and a sense of dread, as well as physiological responses such as fatigue, sweating, digestive upset and an elevated heart rate. I'll use the term 'stress' to refer to the tension that our body and mind experience when we encounter anything that warrants attention and possible action. And anxiety is the emotion triggered by higher levels of stress that we perceive to be dangerous.

Both threats and challenges can cause stress. Successfully navigating a challenge, such as moving house, going to university or getting a new job, can be satisfying, rewarding *and* stressful. These potentially positive experiences call on us to pay attention and expend energy, and we can never be sure that things will work out as we hope. And taking on a threat is likely to be stressful even when we ultimately eliminate the danger.

Stress and anxiety make us uncomfortable, but they play positive roles. Stress pushes us to respond and adapt to what's happening in and around us. The stress of being too hot or cold prompts us to seek comfort. The stress of needing to work gets us out of bed in the mornings. And in hazardous situations, stress triggers ancient survival mechanisms to protect us. Anxiety is a signal; it tells us that there's a threat or challenge we need to take account of and possibly do something about.

Stress can be good or bad for us. Good stress drives us to resolve a threat or successfully respond to a challenge. When we've done that, our bodies and minds can return to balance. Good stress has a practice effect. The more often we succeed, the better we become at riding stress waves. Conversely, a lack of practice from having too little stress in our lives can leave us unprepared for the more severe threats and challenges that come our way. It's the unremitting stress that's bad for us. If we don't adequately address a threat or meet a challenge, we can be left with a chronic, uncomfortable reaction that undermines health.

Stress waves can come at us from the past, the present or the future. Stress can arise from repetitive echoes of an earlier threat or challenge that we did not adequately resolve or meet. Stress can also arrive in real time as a wave that breaks over us. It can also come from the future as a yet-to-occur event that we see forming in the distance.

Stress takes many forms and comes in varying degrees of

intensity. At the lower end of the stress scale are everyday experiences such as feeling thirsty or tired. Around the mild stress level are circumstances such as changing schools, going on holiday and copping a traffic ticket. Incidents likely to provoke moderate stress include taking on a mortgage, a child leaving home, changes in living conditions and troubles at work. At about the moderately severe level are events such as marriage, divorce, separation, being fired, retiring from work, pregnancy, sexual difficulties, health problems and changes in one's financial state.

The stress reactions known as 'eco-anxiety' (the chronic fear of environmental doom), 'solastalgia'[1] (existential distress caused by environmental change) and environmental grief over the loss of ecosystems fall towards the severe end of the scale. The terms 'trauma' and 'traumatic stress' are reserved for potentially life-threatening incidents.

A trauma is defined as an event that exposes a person to actual or threatened death, serious injury or sexual violence.[2] Common traumas include direct or indirect contact with accidents, natural disasters, interpersonal violence, illness, sexual assault and medical emergencies. If you've experienced a trauma, you're not alone. Researchers estimate that 50 to 75 percent of Australians suffer a trauma during their lifetime.[3,4,5] And every survivor of such an event knows what the 'fight-flight-freeze' stress response feels like.

The Fight-Flight-Freeze Response

If we meet a dangerous stress wave, a protective response known as fight-flight-freeze automatically kicks in. We share this survival mechanism with all other animals, and when it operates, the fight-flight-freeze response profoundly affects our minds and bodies. In an instant, our mind and sympathetic nervous system give us the attitude and drive to take on the stress. A mild case of fight-flight-freeze wakes us up and gets us moving. But when the stress response is strong, it feels like we're prepared to fight or run for our lives. Sometimes, when the danger is overwhelming and we can't escape, 'freezing', a kind of playing dead, becomes a third option. If all goes well and we satisfy the need or resolve the threat, our minds and parasympathetic nervous system return us to equilibrium.

When strong fight-flight-freeze takes hold, a cascade of stress hormones readies our bodies for intense, sustained muscular effort. Breathing and heart rate quicken, digestion slows, blood pressure rises and vessels constrict to redirect circulation to core organs. To protect us if we're wounded, our blood clotting ability increases to counter excessive blood loss. Pupils dilate to enhance vision by letting more light into our eyes. At the mental level, we scan intently for signs of threat, lose interest in sex and become hypersensitive to the facial expressions, words and actions of others. A surge of powerful emotions can manifest as deep gratitude for people who help us, or as intense anger, even hatred, for those we perceive to be uncaring or hostile. This is a time for heroism, not just horror; a time when we can confront both the best and the worst in ourselves and others.

The fight-flight-freeze response is similar for humans, our mammalian cousins and even our distant reptilian relatives. Susan and I live surrounded by forests, paddocks and animals. As we walk around our farm, most domesticated sheep, cattle and horses pay us little attention, while a few flighty lookouts remain on alert and scan for danger. These guard animals stand out in any mob, flock or herd; they're the ones who stop grazing, lift their heads and watch intently as we walk by. If we glance at them or walk in their direction, they promptly stir up the others and move them away. As you'd expect, native animals are touchier than domestic stock. The big jack wallabies might hop once or twice before they go back to grazing, but the female jills are more skittish; if we even look in their direction, they bounce away.

When I come across a snake, it's usually an instant two-way flight response. Before I'm even aware of its presence, I let out my distinctive snake squeal and jump backwards. At the same time, the startled serpent usually springs up and then slithers away. My response is just as strong and immediate when, out of the corner of my eye, I see a stick that resembles a snake. With snakes, I nearly always prefer flight over fight or freeze. The flattened, raised head and defiant posture of a big snake in the mood for a fight sends a message all mammals understand.

The Fright Response

I had my most recent dose of fight-flight-freeze during the 2019–20 bushfires. For me, fleeing or freezing were not options. On our property, I could see signs of danger everywhere: choking smoke for days on end, charred leaves falling from the sky, tragedy playing out on the media and helicopters buffeted by fierce winds as they flew over our house to fight nearby fires. I felt strong and was up for the fight — to the death if it came to that. I've known the feeling before; I think of it as my 'warrior mode'. At the conscious level, I was keenly focussed on what I had to do to prepare for the coming fire. Then things took a turn for the worse.

My wife, Susan, fell deathly ill, and I feared that I could lose her. When the pressure eased a bit — Susan's surgery was successful — my fight-flight-freeze superpowers began to falter.

While alone on our property, I made mistakes for the first time since the fires started. The state of high alert that had served me well now caused problems. That morning, I backed my tractor into our ute. Later that day, I ran across the yard wearing thongs, stubbed my foot on a metal stake and flew headfirst into a gate. I should've listened to the advice I give my clients: after severe stress, be careful because your concentration and judgement will be impaired. We can only remain in fight-flight-freeze for so long. We need more than this automatic response to sustainably manage protracted periods of high stress.

For Susan and myself, once the immediate danger passed, the challenge was to feel normal again in what now seemed like a more dangerous world. When an acute threat abates and flight-fight-freeze is no longer needed, we have to choose between two fundamental strategies that Nature gives us for dealing with stress. And the choices we make have profound implications for our mental health. But to appreciate the nature and significance of these alternative responses to stress, you first need to know more about how our mind works.

Chapter 3

The Structure of Mind

The conscious mind may be compared to a fountain playing in the sun and falling back into the great subterranean pool of subconscious from which it rises.
Sigmund Freud (1856–1939)

WE KNOW OURSELVES AND the world around us through our subjective experience. But without us being aware of what it's doing, our mind also automatically manages many essential psychological and physiological processes.

Can you recall how intensely you had to concentrate when you learnt to drive a car? To get the vehicle moving smoothly, you listened carefully to your instructor, paid close attention to coordinating your hands and feet while, with your eyes, you scanned what was going on around you. But now, what was so difficult has become easy and automatic. Driving is a reliable, habitual skill that you perform safely without much thought or effort.

I never saw it; luckily, Susan did. Susan was driving us into Hobart, Tasmania's capital, when a sheet of tin flew through the air towards our car. As Susan recounts the incident, in a flash, before she knew what was happening, she identified the flying obstacle as a sheet of tin rather than plastic or cardboard.

Susan then swerved to avoid the tin, taking account of nearby cars. Susan says that even now, a long time after the incident, she can vividly visualise the scene. Her mind responded appropriately to this novel threat and has laid down a memory of the incident that she will not soon forget. Experiences like Susan's tell us that some part of our mind protects us even when we're not aware of, and don't control, what it's doing. These hidden components of our psyche monitor what's going on inside and around us, and when they're required to keep us safe, they can initiate and control subtle, sophisticated behaviours.

Sigmund Freud and Carl Jung contrasted what they called the 'conscious' and 'unconscious' minds. I'll give you my take on the distinction between what I call the 'executive' and the 'deep' mind. We'll also discuss the operation of the 'key mental processes' that enable us to practice the art of riding stress waves.

The Executive Mind

The executive mind represents the familiar territory of our conscious awareness, the reality we perceive and live in. The executive mind is where, from the perspective of our unique self, we think, believe, remember, imagine, make decisions, plan and dream. This part of our psyche is in touch with external and internal realities. It can reason, but that doesn't mean it's always rational or well-informed. Here, at the executive level of mind, we recall the past, navigate the present and imagine the future.

We live in a kind of zone of sentience, existing in our island universe of subjective experience that only we can directly access. Like an orchestra that we enjoy without being aware of how the sounds of diverse instruments meld to produce the music we hear, our conscious reality is stitched together from the unnoticed, synchronous operation of a suite of mental abilities.

Consider what goes on as you read the single word 'regret'. You instantly know what regret means because you have a definition of the word stored in the internal lexicon you built up

THE STRUCTURE OF MIND

as you learnt to speak and read. But the word has more than a literal meaning attached to it. Just saying 'regret' and lingering with the word can elicit sad feelings, poignant memories, a resolve to do better or even beliefs about what kind of person you are and the fairness of life. The word might trigger an inner dialogue about things you wished you'd done differently and future events you'd like to avoid. And even when you're no longer consciously thinking about it, hearing or reading the word regret can affect you intuitively and even work its way into your dreams.

In real time, as we hear and read single words embedded in phrases, sentences and paragraphs, our minds automatically process enormous amounts of information generated by our key mental processes. And this is only the mental activity involved in understanding language.

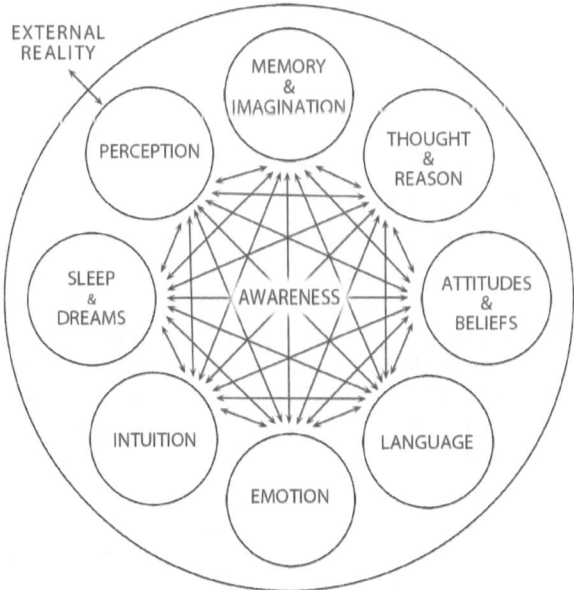

The Key Mental Processes

In the realm of conscious awareness, we remember events from the past as well as the facts, skills and insights we picked up along the way. We also draw on beliefs and knowledge built on life's lessons to imagine and anticipate what's coming in the future. As impressive as all this is, our awareness is quite limited; its focus is narrow, and its capacity is restricted. When awake, we're only aware of whatever we pay attention to at that moment. There are strict constraints on how much information we can receive, process and remember at any time: about seven, plus or minus two, bits of information.[1] It doesn't take much to fill our executive mind, and there's only so much we can attend to at any time.

Sentience is not like daylight, which illuminates everywhere. Conscious awareness is more akin to a spotlight that we shine on this or that, aiming it at things we're interested in. The beam of light is only so wide, and when we point it at something new, what we were previously attending to recedes into shadow. No matter how carefully we pay attention, there's much more going on than we know about.

The next thought experiment illustrates how attention works. Notice what goes through your mind as you read on.

Ψ

1. Are you aware of your breathing?
2. You are now because I asked you about it. But before I did that, your mind automatically monitored your breathing, even though you weren't aware of it doing so.
3. Focus on your breathing. Notice the way that your body likes to breathe. Each time you inhale, bring in a good feeling. And as you breathe out, let go of some muscle tension. Bring in a good feeling. Relax with each out-breath.
4. Now notice the sights and sounds around you. What can you see and hear? What's in front of you? What colour is it? Does it trigger any thoughts or memories for you? Can you hear any noise outside?
5. Shift your attention to the sensations in your left leg. Focus on the back of your knee. Can you feel any pressure there? Is your skin touching clothing or perhaps a chair?
6. Are you still aware of your breathing?

7. I know you are now because I mentioned your breathing again.

Ψ

As you shifted your attention from breathing to the sights and sounds around you and then to your knee, did you notice the 'spotlight effect' of what you were attending to slip away as you focussed on something new?

Our conscious, executive mind decides what we pay attention to and how long and intensely we focus on it. The executive mind directs much of what we think about and do, and crucially, it determines how we respond to threats and challenges. Your executive mind is a lead player when you deal with stress; it decides if you're going to read this book and it chooses the lessons you'll absorb. And as the executive mind focusses on thoughts, feelings and perceptions, the deep mind monitors a bigger picture, taking in a broader band of information.

The Deep Mind

In the following familiar experiences, we can see the deep mind at work.

Have you ever set your clock for an early morning get up only to wake a few minutes before the alarm sounds? If so, while you were asleep, some part of your mind accurately judged the passage of time, was willing to cooperate with your executive mind's plans and was able to wake you on schedule.

Perhaps you've had the experience of sensing that something was not quite right, but you couldn't say what was bothering you until later when you suddenly realised what was amiss. Or maybe you've given up on trying to recall someone's name, only to have it pop into your mind later on. If so, you know what it's like when you've consciously abandoned a task, but a part of your mind goes on searching and lets you know when the elusive information is located.

Our Western culture has adopted Freud's insight that 'ego-defence mechanisms' operate unconsciously to protect us from becoming aware of things about ourselves that would make us uncomfortable. If someone accuses us of 'projecting', we know that they mean we're attributing our undesirable feelings, actions or traits onto someone else. When we're said to be 'repressing', we understand this to mean that we're unconsciously blocking ourselves from thinking about upsetting things.

And we all know about habits. After we've used our executive mind to learn something, the deep mind establishes a habit which, from then on, will automatically control how we think and act in certain situations. Habits are efficient and essential. Life would grind to a halt if, every morning, we had to relearn how to brush our teeth, tie our shoelaces or hold the spoon as we eat breakfast.

Beyond our conscious awareness, rational, sophisticated mental processes work to protect us. Our deep mind can respond to threats and demands before we're even aware of them, and it can access all our key mental processes. The deep mind understands us, and even though it can't express itself by speaking, we can communicate with this part of our psyche through intuition and with specific hypnotic techniques.

My analogy for the relationship between the executive and deep mind likens it to that between the pilot and crew of a large aeroplane. The pilot represents our conscious awareness, while the aeroplane's crew corresponds to the deep mind. To keep the plane flying safely, the pilot and crew have to share the same goal, trust each other and be able to communicate. The pilot decides what's to be done, sets the course and flies the plane to its destination, while the crew attends to the many essential things that navigators, engineers and flight attendants do.

Just as the pilot and the crew have to work together to keep the plane flying safely, our executive and deep minds need to coordinate if they're to effectively protect us. When we're dealing with severe stress, we cannot rely solely on the executive or the deep mind. Rather, our success will depend on the synchronised efforts of both aspects of our psyche; after all, they *are* us, our complete Self. Working in concert, our executive and deep minds give us the means to change our lives and deal artfully with any stress wave that comes our way.

We'll now return to our earlier discussion about the strategies we can implement when we confront stress.

Chapter 4

Avoidance Strategies

> Pain in this life is not avoidable, but the
> pain we create avoiding pain is avoidable.
> R.D. Laing (1927–1989)

WE HAVE TWO BASIC options for responding to stress. When any living organism — from a single-celled amoeba to a human — encounters something that warrants its attention and possible action, it has to decide whether to engage with the stress or seek to avoid it. Neither strategy is inherently superior to the other, and both have a role to play when we ride stress waves.

Avoidance is a protective response that's worked well through the ages. There are many times in life when, like the surfboard rider waiting for a good wave, it's better to conserve our energy and let a stress pass by.

Australians have a saying from the game of cricket, 'Let it go through to the keeper', to describe a skilful, considered choice to avoid, rather than engage with, a threat or challenge. In cricket, a batsperson is 'out' and has to leave the field of play if a bowled ball gets past them and hits their 'wicket' (three upright stumps topped with two horizontal sticks known as 'bails'). When a batsperson judges that a ball is too good to score off but doesn't threaten their wicket, they can pull their bat out of the way and let the ball go safely through to the 'wicketkeeper' (catcher) who stands behind the stumps. Similarly, there are many stresses, such as a partner's bad mood, a huffy email or an upsetting news item, which we can appropriately decide to do nothing about.

I disagree with the advice to 'get straight back on the horse that bucked you off'; at least, not until you've worked out how to prevent yourself from being thrown again. At such times, considered avoidance is the right choice.

One step up in complexity from just ignoring stress, there's a simple, specialised avoidant strategy that allows us to think that we've resolved a problem when we haven't done much at all; I call it the 'one-thought solution'.

The One-thought Solution

The one-thought solution can come into play anytime we confront stress. When we use this train of thought with just one carriage, our executive mind only has to develop a simple image or thought that's true (or true enough). The feeling that this true statement engenders gives us the impression that we're dealing with the stress when, in fact, we're avoiding it.

A One-carriage Train of Thought

The one-thought solution relies on what psychologists, hypnotists and salespeople call the 'yes effect'. When a client or potential customer accepts a series of statements as true, they're more likely to give credence to the next thing you tell them. I'll illustrate this with how hypnotherapists use the yes effect.

Hypnotherapists construct sentences that pair undeniably true statements with the suggestions that they want their client to follow. For example, they might join 'As you listen to my voice' with 'You will relax more deeply'. There's no rational, causal connection between hearing a therapist's voice and relaxing. Still, the yes set established by the first, true observational phrase makes it more likely that the client will accept the subsequent suggestion to relax.

To induce trance, a traditional, authoritarian-style hypnotherapist might ask a client to stare at a spinning watch. It's not easy to focus on such a thing for long, and when the therapist notices that the client wants to blink their tired eyes, they link the undeniably true statement 'As you look at the watch' to the likely true suggestion 'Your eyelids will feel heavier and heavier'. If you buy the idea that the hypnotist somehow controls how your eyes feel, you're on your way to more interesting suggestions.

One-thought solutions powered by the yes-set effect can work well for everyday decisions that are of no real consequence. It often doesn't matter if we don't thoroughly think things through or we end up with a less-than-ideal outcome. For instance, there's little risk in basing our choice of colour for a new car on the true thought 'I like blue' without considering factors such as the cost, availability, visibility in poor light, heat absorption in sunlight, ease of keeping clean and cost of repair of different tints.

Avoidant one-thought solutions can sometimes resolve more important stresses, but they're unlikely to produce optimal results. For instance, if we pair the true thought 'I can't stand this job' with the conclusion 'I should quit', that outcome becomes more likely even though it might not be the best way to resolve our stress.

During the 2019–20 Australian bushfires, then-Prime Minister Scott Morrison used a one-thought solution to resolve his stress when journalists asked why he was on holiday in Hawai'i. Mr Morrison felt he'd excused himself when he explained, 'I don't hold a hose'. It was true that he didn't hold a hose — at least it was plausible that he never had — and, from the ex-PM's perspective, this true statement was sufficient to justify his decision to go on holiday. Unfortunately, citizens could see that, with a bit more thought, the then-PM might have found something helpful to do at home during this crisis.

At the high end of the stress scale, with challenges that could affect our health and well-being — or even the future of humanity and life on Earth — ignoring threats, one-thought solutions and other forms of avoidant thinking have no legitimate role to play. And yet, such shallow thinking is commonplace in political discourse and government policy.

Some politicians refuse to acknowledge the big stress waves coming our way; they'd rather court disaster than deal with complex challenges. Other politicians, who want to appear as if they're managing risk, justify damaging developments such as gas mining with nothing more than simple — albeit true — statements that 'people need jobs' and 'we use gas for our barbecues'.

Avoiding stress can work, but when it's used for personally significant stress waves, the strategy can compromise mental health and even result in an unjustified psychiatric diagnosis.

When Avoidance Causes Trouble

> Classifying thoughts, feelings and behaviours as diseases is
> a logical and semantic error, like classifying whale as fish.
> *Thomas Szasz (1920–2012)*

Throughout our lives, we build up networks of emotionally related autobiographical memories; Carl Jung called them 'memory complexes'.[1] Childhood experiences of being loved, encouraged and succeeding can bolster our adult sense of self-worth and confidence, while memories of being unloved, criticised and failing can undermine how we respond to stress. Such recollections shape our personalities and can support a life-long strategy of avoiding similar situations. But this does not necessarily cause trouble if we think of the habit as a preference rather than a problem.

If you feel anxious about speaking or performing in public, I suspect that, sometime in the past, you were embarrassed in the company of others. I remember being singled out as a disruptor of harmony in front of the class in primary school. My teacher, "Miss Dowdy", abruptly called on us students to stop singing. She then had me sing alone before she cut me off to announce that I was 'tone-deaf'. Miss Dowdy publicly excused me from all future singing and gave me a job in a storage room. I was a nine-year-old who usually listened to teachers, so I grew up believing that I was, in fact, tone-deaf. Miss Dowdy was surely right that I couldn't sing in tune, and my executive mind was not mature enough to question her diagnosis or to think about what I might do about it.

I feel no unpleasant emotion when I recall this event, and I've never felt short-changed by having to lip-sync 'Happy Birthday' and 'Advance Australia Fair'. I just avoided singing and was happy enough to do so until I came across a YouTube video that tested your musical ear. It turns out that I have an average perception of pitch and harmony, but I've never practised sustaining a note in tune, so how would I have ever learnt to sing? I grew up in a family that was not musical. We never sang together, and none of us played instruments, at least not for pleasure. My now-adult executive mind has rethought things, and I've let go of the false belief that I'm tone-deaf. I now enjoy singing, though still not usually in company.

My not singing is but one example of the many preferences based on past experiences that develop during our lives. When someone feels anxious about and avoids an activity, their executive and deep minds typically protect them by conjuring up thoughts and images of past or possible future failure and embarrassment. These avoidant stress responses might limit what we do, but there's nothing essentially wrong with responding this way. Such avoidance protects us and is usually considered to be a preference which we accept as an aspect of our personality. But sometimes, our minds adopt an avoidant strategy that can attract an unwarranted, potentially dangerous diagnosis of a 'mental disorder'.

The current edition of the *Diagnostic and Statistical Manual of the American Psychiatric Association (DSM-5)* describes patterns of mental processing, emotional experience and behaviour which, if they cause 'clinically significant distress or impairment in social, occupational or other important areas of functioning', are classified as mental disorders.[2] These syndromes are assumed to arise from 'dysfunction in the psychological, biological, or developmental processes underlying mental functioning'.[2] Here, the explicit but dubious assumption is that if a stress response results in severe anxiety, then there's something wrong with an affected person's mind. I disagree with this way of thinking.

Over the years, a kind of classification creep has seen more and more normal human reactions to stress attract diagnoses of mental disorders and recommendations for medications. Of chief concern are stress responses that the DSM-5 classifies as 'anxiety', 'trauma-related' and 'dissociative' disorders. The central issue is whether these syndromes are due to mental dysfunction or whether they are, in fact, healthy, though sub-optimal, psychological strategies for coping with stress.

Avoidance can work well when a stress wave is short-lived, the experience is readily forgotten and there's not much risk of future harm from a similar threat. However, in certain circumstances, adopting an avoidant strategy can inadvertently cause great suffering and compromise mental health. The risk of such adverse outcomes increases when a significant threat remains unresolved because the executive mind is unable or unwilling to think about what happened. Under these conditions, to keep us safe, the deep mind responds to signs of imminent danger by generating intense anxiety and a strong urge to escape. We'll explore variations on this type of avoidant strategy in which the deep mind creates anxiety to protect us.

Our response to a stress wave is influenced by the nature and severity of the threat and the strengths and abilities available to us at that time. Coping responses that generate recurring episodes of intense, involuntary anxiety and avoidance take distinctive forms depending on whether the original, precipitating stress involved abandonment, physical threat, embarrassment, ridicule, panic or trauma. And it matters how old we were when the initial stress occurred.

As adults, if we feel afraid, we can react in various ways. We might reassure ourselves, physically remove the danger, diffuse tension with a joke, walk away, try to forget the scene or ignore what happened. But if a young child feels fearful, what can they do about it? They can try to ignore it. They're unlikely to confront the threat by themselves. Perhaps they'll just cry. And what options does an infant have when it confronts severe, intractable stress?

Separation Anxiety Disorder

Infants cry and throw their little arms and legs about to let others know that they're upset and need care; there's not much else they can do in response to stress. But if a child, aged five years or younger, becomes afraid when left alone, they might subsequently respond to the threat of again being left alone by worrying a lot, refusing to leave their oh-so-important carer and by not going to sleep in case they're abandoned in the dark. These are the defining features of the stress reaction known as 'separation anxiety disorder'.

For a child diagnosed with separation anxiety, there's a risk that a doctor or psychiatrist will prescribe a recommended antidepressant (such as clomipramine or imipramine) or an anti-anxiety medication (such as buspirone). These medications have side effects, including blurred vision, difficulty urinating, increased heart rate, hypotension, chest pain, shortness of breath, headache, dizziness, drowsiness, insomnia, nausea and, yes, feeling nervous. What's the chance that, if side effects develop, these will be diagnosed as symptoms of an even more complex mental disorder? Is the risk of using drugs that have deleterious effects on the body and mind justified when a child is terrified of being left alone because they've been left alone before?

I don't think that a young child should be diagnosed with a mental disorder when they're exhibiting an understandable, age-related, avoidant stress response. These children need love and reassurance that the adults in their lives will keep them safe and not again abandon them. To my mind, there's no good reason for prescribing potentially harmful medications that mask the underlying problem and get in the way of the child learning effective coping skills.

Avoidant Personality Disorder

Psychiatrists use the term 'personality disorder' to indicate that a person's 'dysfunctional' stress response results from lifelong psychological defects. Personality disorders are assumed to be severe conditions that are difficult to treat.

Infants and young children who suffer trauma, abuse, neglect, rejection and a lack of emotional warmth from caregivers sometimes adopt a stress-management strategy that attracts a later diagnosis of 'avoidant personality disorder'. Their executive mind focusses on their perceived shortcomings, and they avoid friendships and other relationships in which they might be rejected.

The next example of an involuntary, anxiety-provoking, avoidant stress reaction initially occurs at about the age of seven years.

Specific Phobia Disorder

The intense, sudden anxiety and desire to escape that defines a 'specific phobia' is triggered when the affected person comes upon, or anticipates meeting, a situation or thing that frightened them or someone else in their presence earlier in their lives. 'Situational phobias', such as fear of tunnels, bridges, flying, enclosed places and driving, are the most common, followed by 'natural environment phobias' involving such things as storms, heights and deep water. Next come 'blood-injection-injury' and phobias of animals like snakes, dogs, spiders and birds. As you'd expect, in specific phobias, we see a more sophisticated avoidant strategy for dealing with stress than that which operates in the younger child diagnosed with separation anxiety.

When a seven-year-old is frightened, they have response options beyond the crying, worrying and clinging available to the young child, but they do not yet have an adult's ability to deal with the stress. Consequently, the child defaults to an avoidant strategy in which their deep mind assumes responsibility for protecting them, and their executive mind scans for danger and gets on with life. As the years go by, whenever the affected person comes upon a similar threat to the one that frightened them earlier, their deep mind instantly propels the original fear and urge to escape into conscious awareness. They typically do not remember the initial stress event itself. Instead, they just feel out of control — like a terrified child — and have no insight into why they feel that way.

Few people with phobias seek treatment. Most manage their anxiety by structuring their lives to avoid the things they fear. If you fear heights, you avoid high places and working on rooftops. If you fear enclosed spaces, you don't apply for a job in an office building with elevators. But some folk do seek psychological treatment for their phobic stress reactions.

In the late 1980s, I used a brief, low-stress technique in a treatment program that relieved clients' phobias by working with their memory of the first time they encountered their fear.[3]

"Joan", a 40-year-old businesswoman, sought help for a phobic fear that overwhelmed her whenever she walked across the ramp onto the Manly Ferry. She faced this ordeal every day she went to work. Joan was usually confident and in control of her emotions. Still, when she saw deep water, she felt helpless and was only aware of her intense fear, a desperate need to escape and little else other than vague thoughts about personal weakness. Joan was ashamed that other commuters had seen her quivering like a frightened child.

During therapy, Joan recalled an incident she hadn't thought about for many years. Joan remembered being six years old when her brother held her head under the bath water, and she believed that she was drowning. With a process I'll describe in *Part 2*, I asked Joan to review, from an adult's perspective, her memory of what happened all those years ago. With guidance, after some 34 years of fearing deep water, Joan learnt what she needed to learn from the experience and worked out how to protect herself from similar threats in the future. Joan could then let go of the old, now-out-of-date stress response that had protected her for so long.

To me, it makes no sense to call a phobia a mental disorder. What was dysfunctional about Joan's stress reaction? When she suffered a near-drowning at six years of age, Joan's psyche did the best it could to protect her, given the resources available at that time. Years later, in therapy, Joan updated how she dealt with the stress of seeing deep water.

It's important to recognise that Joan's old avoidant strategy had done a good job of protecting her. Since her long-forgotten bathtub ordeal at six years of age, Joan had never again come close to drowning. How can a phobic reaction be due to a disordered or dysfunctional mind when a fear of heights reduces the risk of injury or death from falling and a fear of storms reduces the likelihood you'll be outside when lightning strikes?

Specific phobias make good evolutionary sense; they

characteristically involve things and situations that are potentially dangerous in the real world. Our minds and bodies have been 'biologically prepared' to develop a phobic stress reaction if we confront just one instance of a specific kind of threat at a particular stage of life.[4] In our ancestors' world, children who didn't learn to avoid deep water after nearly drowning, or who played near cliffs, or who went back to explore holes along the creek after their mother warned them about the poisonous snakes that lived there were less likely to pass on their genes.

Obsessive-compulsive Disorder

Distressing thoughts are common at times of threat, but for some people, their inability to control their stress response results in a diagnosis of 'obsessive-compulsive disorder' (OCD). The more these folk try to avoid their unwanted thoughts or feelings, the stronger their compulsion to do something to ease their anxiety becomes. If their fear relates to possible contamination from dirt, germs, poisons or other substances, they might repeatedly wash their hands and clean things. If they fear harm from illness or accidents, they can be hypervigilant about protecting themselves and others. If they're concerned that they've done something incorrectly or left something important undone, they might respond by making lists, checking their work or repeatedly ensuring that things are safe. Their yearning for certainty and control can manifest as seemingly unnecessary rules for such everyday activities as walking, opening a door or placing objects on a desk. They might repeatedly touch or move things, ask questions or repeat words or numbers. Such attempts to avoid things that trigger anxiety can snowball until it becomes difficult for them to enjoy their lives.

Not surprisingly, the avoidant obsessive-compulsive coping strategy usually develops after a person is exposed to severe stress at a young age. As with other problematic stress responses, during treatment, the affected person reviews their memory of the initiating event, learns what they need to learn and works out how they'll respond differently in the future. The OCD stress reaction demonstrates that the affected person is disciplined, diligent and caring, which are all worthwhile traits. However, to achieve optimal mental health, in addition to those existing strengths, they need to add more discerning and flexible strategies for keeping themselves and others safe from danger.

Social Anxiety Disorder

Humans are socially dependent creatures. Rejection can threaten our very survival, and adolescence is a time in life when we're extra sensitive to the opinions of others. The supposed mental disorder, 'social anxiety', usually arises between eight and fifteen years of age when a young person is embarrassed or humiliated in a social situation. After the initial stress, the child's executive mind allocates much of its limited processing capacity to thinking about humiliation, and it scans for hints of negative opinions in other people. Meanwhile, the deep mind injects a surge of anxiety and the fight-flight-freeze response whenever it seems that other people could be nasty or critical. In this way, the psyche does its best, given the resources available to it at the time, to protect the young person.

Agoraphobia and Panic Disorder

With the so-called mental disorder of 'agoraphobia', an episode of sudden, intense anxiety combines with catastrophic thoughts to set up another example of a habitual, avoidant stress response. Agoraphobia is not the fear of open spaces, as the name suggests, but is instead the fear of becoming anxious or panicky in a public place. A person typically adopts this protective strategy after an event in which their executive mind interprets panic symptoms — such as shortness of breath, chest pain and feeling dizzy — as proof that they've lost control, are going crazy or are dying. From then on, they avoid public situations where they might panic and feel trapped.

Agoraphobia highlights the role that catastrophic thoughts, beliefs and imaginings play in setting up problematic stress reactions. A disrupted pattern of breathing can trigger intense anxiety without our being aware of why we feel that way. If you've been skin diving, you know that to get fresh air into the snorkel, the in-breath has to be deeper, and the out-breath more pronounced, than in normal breathing. Breathe shallowly while you're snorkelling, and you'll soon feel light-headed and unwell because rebreathing the exhaled air in the snorkel disrupts the balance of oxygen and carbon dioxide in your blood. The human windpipe from mouth to lungs is like a snorkel, and protracted shallow breathing when you're on dry land also creates unpleasant physical effects. Throw some inflammatory, mistaken thoughts along the lines of 'I'm going mad' or 'I'm dying' into the mix, and you've got the ingredients for a panic attack. The executive mind concludes that death is imminent, so it has no time or inclination to think about much else. Hence, the deep mind adopts the avoidant strategy of inducing fear and an urge to escape whenever the person confronts a potentially dangerous situation.

The agoraphobic stress response becomes debilitating if the affected person avoids such important places as their workplace, school, shops or transport. My client "Robert" believed that he was going insane. When he first came to see me, Robert's breathing was chaotic, but he wasn't aware of that. He dreaded driving, so he'd quit his job, and his life was unravelling. Robert had his first panic attack while he was lost in thought on the way to a funeral and he suddenly realised that he was driving across a bridge over a deep valley. Robert's breathing was rapid and shallow, but when he thought that he was having a heart attack, his anxiety shot off the scale, and he suffered his first episode of full-blown panic. With help, Robert retrained his breathing and learnt what he needed to learn from his initial encounter with this stress. He could then craft new ways of thinking, feeling and acting that helped him let go of the old avoidant stress response.

We'll wrap up our review of deep mind-driven, avoidant strategies by examining the protective stress response known as 'posttraumatic stress disorder' (PTSD).

Posttraumatic Stress Disorder (PTSD)

Recovering after severe or traumatic stress is never easy. It can be a rough ride as our mind and body slowly exit the hormone high of the fight-flight-freeze response that helped us survive. But for some folk, their acute stress response never abates, and they remain in a persistent state of hypervigilance and near-constant anxiety and arousal. This stress reaction can get diagnosed as post-traumatic stress disorder (PTSD).

High levels of anxiety characterise the PTSD stress response. The affected person tries to avoid anything that can trigger their frequently recurring thoughts, memories, flashbacks and nightmares about the trauma. Some develop partial or total amnesia for what happened. Fearing their nightmares, some resist falling asleep. Over time, as they lose confidence in their ability to control their minds, affected folk cut themselves off from their own emotions and sensations, and they're left feeling empty and numb. Distorted, negative beliefs about what's wrong with them and why they feel the way they do intensify suffering and further impede the person's ability to learn from the stress. They feel trapped by their past.

When the PTSD strategy operates, the executive mind remains hypervigilant, and over time, the potential threats balloon into an extensive list of to-be-avoided memories, sensations, images, thoughts, emotions, people, places and things. For example, bushfire survivors check constantly for the smell of smoke and fear summer days, and flood victims scan weather forecasts and panic when it rains. The Herculean task of trying to avoid everything that might trigger anxiety consumes much of their executive mind's attentional capacity, leaving little energy for other cognitive functions. Consequently, they lose interest in things and activities that they once enjoyed, and they have problems concentrating and remembering. The avoidant strategy effectively rules out any prospect that the affected person will engage with their stress memories, learn what they need to learn and work out how to better protect themselves.

Hypervigilance

PTSD is an evolved coping mechanism that was forged in our ancestors' encounters with life-threatening situations. This avoidant response develops after exposure to potentially harmful or lethal stress, and it protects the individual from similar dangers that they might encounter later on. As distressing as PTSD can be, it arises from the protective but clashing impulses of the executive and deep mind. The executive mind is preoccupied with the impossible task of trying to forget an event that is, in reality, unforgettable. At the same time, the deep mind ensures that the experience will not be forgotten.

In severe traumatic stress reactions, communication between the executive and deep mind breaks down. The deep mind understands that the executive mind cannot think about what happened and, therefore, can't learn from the past or do anything to make the future safer. In our aeroplane analogy, the pilot is far too distracted to even talk to the crew. With a coordinated effort ruled out, the deep mind monitors internal and external reality. If it detects any hint of a threat, it compels the executive mind to remember the initial stress event and fires up the fight-flight-freeze response.

The intrusive, stress-related thoughts and memories that the deep mind projects into awareness are disturbing, but they do not arise from any mental dysfunction or pathology. In our aeroplane analogy, the crew must do this when the pilot isn't paying attention and can't fly the plane safely. It's not ideal and it creates much anxiety, but when the crew detects a sign of danger, they give the pilot a 'jab' to wake them up to the imminent threat.

I'll give you a couple of cases to illustrate the protective nature of PTSD and related stress reactions.

"Jim", a war veteran, would never have seen me if his doctor hadn't ordered him to do so. Like many survivors of extreme violence, Jim felt ashamed when he was diagnosed with PTSD; he figured this meant he was crazy. During the Vietnam War, Jim was the forward scout on his first day on patrol in the jungle. Many years had passed since then, but in his mind, Jim had never really come home.

Every day, Jim relived memories of an intense firefight in a rubber plantation. As his wife, "Claire", explained, in restaurants, 'Jim has to sit facing the door with his back to the wall' and 'it takes him forever to park in town; he keeps driving around and around'. Jim knew it seemed strange, but he felt compelled to keep looking for a parking spot that he could identify as safe from ambush and crossfire. Jim's stress response was out of place in his current life in regional Australia. Still, there was no doubt that hypervigilance and his deep-mind strategy of scanning for signs of ambush had not only helped him survive the war but still protected him in restaurants and parking lots back home.

When I first met "Jane", she was a 38-year-old teller whom I assessed following a violent bank robbery. Screaming threats and brandishing shotguns, the criminals had ordered Jane and her fellow tellers to lie flat on the floor. In the immediate aftermath, when the robbers had fled, Jane stood out as someone who comforted others and appeared to be coping. When I assessed Jane some weeks after the robbery, she was doing well enough, but in my report, I recommended that she receive further counselling support. I sensed that Jane's initial, apparently satisfactory coping could falter, and a delayed post-trauma stress reaction might develop. A couple of years passed before I next saw Jane.

The second time we met, Jane was referred to me because her employer was concerned about the accounting errors she was making. Jane had been a meticulous teller, but now her competence was being questioned, and she was at risk of losing her job. Jane couldn't explain her mistakes; she just said she struggled to concentrate. Jane denied that she was troubled by any thoughts or memories of the robbery, but a clue to the source of her problems emerged later in the session.

Jane was hesitant to describe an obsessive habit that she'd developed. Jane couldn't stop looking at people's socks when she was out in public. Jane had no idea why she was doing this until I had her review — not relive — her memory of the bank holdup. Lying on the floor as she and her fellow workers were being threatened, Jane could only see the robbers' lower legs under a desk partition, and her attention focussed on their socks. Now, years later, with no conscious insight, Jane's deep mind protected her by scanning for signs of impending danger, which was seeing anyone whose socks resembled those the robbers wore. Unfortunately, this protective process consumed Jane's executive mind's attentional capacity, leading to her making accounting errors that threatened her job.

The fact that some traumatised people can function for decades — at least well enough to stay alive, work and raise a family — is consistent with the notion that PTSD is essentially a natural, protective stress response. The strategy makes us feel awful, but from an evolutionary point of view, the repeated triggering of intense fear and anxiety makes it less likely that we'll fall victim to another threat similar to the one we faced in the past. The deep mind is trying to protect us, not hurt us. We need to work with and respect the wisdom of the deep mind, not fear it.

Nonetheless, the avoidant PTSD strategy is sub-optimal because it entails much anxiety, trouble and exhaustion. The good news is that, no matter how long or severe the suffering, when affected folk safely re-engage with their stress memories, learn what they need to learn and take action to make themselves safer, their executive and deep minds can let go of the old stress response. With the appropriate groundwork in place, they can update their old, habitual stress response quickly, gently and effectively. I've witnessed this rapid shift during work with hundreds of clients who, even after decades of suffering, were able to engage with their trauma memories, restart their healing journey and achieve emotional balance.

In this chapter, we've examined some of the avoidant coping strategies that people adopt to deal with stress at various times in their lives. Avoiding stress can work well, and the strategy sometimes manifests as preferences that shape our personality. However, avoidant strategies can also cause serious trouble and result in diagnoses of mental dysfunction or personality disorder. We also could have looked at other stress responses, outside of the anxiety disorder grouping, that the DSM-5 deems to be mental disorders (e.g., body dysmorphic disorder, hoarding disorder, dissociative identity disorder, dissociative amnesia, depersonalisation/derealisation disorder and illness anxiety disorder), but a similar analysis applies. All these stress responses arise from the reasonable attempts of the affected person's mind to deal with stress waves and to protect the individual from future danger.

Avoidance is a practical, time-honoured strategy for responding to stress; it frees us from the immediate effort of having to think or do something. Avoidant strategies can work well for less severe stresses when ignoring the threat doesn't increase the risk of later harm. But when the stakes are higher, and we face personally significant stress waves and threats that could inflict real damage, engaging with the stress wave is the better option.

Chapter 5

The Engage Strategy

*The greatest weapon against stress is our ability
to choose one thought over another.*
William James (1842–1910)

IT'S UP TO US whether we avoid stress or take it on, and our decisions have consequences. If we ignore a threat or challenge, we save ourselves from having to think and act, at least in the short run. But if we engage with stress, we have work to do now for an uncertain payoff in the future.

Being able to make considered choices to avoid or engage with a stress wave is an essential skill in our art. To develop this ability, we first have to take account of the 'opportunity costs' of our decisions. These are the alternative possibilities that taking one option rules out. For instance, if I turn left, I miss out on whatever might have happened if I'd turned right. If I do 'this', I won't experience 'that'. I'd like to work outside on this sparkling day, but if I did, I'd be no closer to finishing this book. We negotiate such dilemmas whenever we confront a threat or a challenge. I'll give examples to illustrate the trade-offs in choosing one stress-management strategy over another.

Most people manage the stress of public speaking by simply not doing it. They never volunteer, decline all invitations to say a few words and, if pressured, they find a reason why they can't attend the event. Their avoidant strategy protects them; the threat is eliminated, and there's no need for any anxiety. However, the choice entails a cost because they forgo an opportunity that could enrich their life. And if they rise to the challenge, their executive mind has work to do. It's not easy to prepare and deliver a gratifying speech, and there are those butterflies in the stomach to contend with.

Engaging with the stress of feeling hungry by eating food seems an easy decision. Still, as the presenting stress becomes more complicated, choosing between engaging or avoiding becomes more difficult. For instance, if we're prone to 'comfort eating' and have trouble keeping our weight under control, an artful response to the stress of hunger would require us to work out why we use food this way and what we might do differently.

And, to revisit an earlier example, if we decide to quit a job because we don't enjoy it, our avoidant response might work, but our chances of achieving the best possible outcome improve if we think more deeply and ask such questions as 'What makes the job so distasteful?', 'Could I improve things?' and 'What would be the consequences of leaving?' And if, after asking such questions, we decide not to leave the job, we'd be less likely to regret our decision to stay.

In the previous chapter, we examined avoidant strategies for dealing with stress. We'll now explore what's involved in the alternative approach of engaging with threats and challenges. By the end of this chapter, you'll have basic guidelines for practising the art of riding stress waves.

You won't find the ideas and principles we discuss in this chapter elsewhere. Consequently, I need to explain where the fundamental elements come from and how I arrived at this formulation. The art of riding stress waves principally derives from research into the avoidant stress response known as posttraumatic stress disorder. The story spans about 130 years and begins with the hypnotic recall of traumatic memories.

A Brief History

In the 1890s, years before he developed his fanciful 'psychoanalytic theory', Sigmund Freud and his colleague, Josef Breuer, hypnotised patients suffering from 'hysteria' (a stress response that today would be diagnosed as PTSD, 'conversion disorder' or other trauma-related conditions).[1]

When Freud asked his hypnotised patients to recall memories related to their problems, many relived vivid, distressing incidents of childhood sexual assault, interpersonal violence and other traumas. To Freud and Breuer's 'great surprise', after their patients relived their trauma and talked about what had happened to them, their symptoms 'immediately and permanently disappeared'.[1] In addition to this therapeutic process, which they dubbed 'abreaction' or 'catharsis', Freud and Breuer described a second, less demanding path to healing. In what they called 'the process of association', a problem-causing stress memory can be changed when it comes 'alongside other experiences' or ideas that 'rectify' or 'contradict' it.[1]

For the first time, Freud and Breuer highlighted the essential roles that engaging with memories and cognitive processing play in resolving severe, avoidant stress reactions. As Breuer and Freud put it, 'The psychical process which originally took place must be repeated as vividly as possible; it must be brought back to its status nascendi (as at birth) and then given verbal utterance'.[1] It's noteworthy that the rapid, lasting therapeutic effect they described belies the notion that severe stress reactions arise from a mental disorder; it seems unlikely that reliving and talking about a trauma would be sufficient to mend a seriously dysfunctional or disordered mind.

Apart from John G. Watkins' use of Freud's hypnotic abreaction therapy to treat 'war neuroses' in World War II[2], little more was written about traumatic stress until thousands of Vietnam War veterans presented to their doctors with similar problems and, in 1980, PTSD was added to psychiatry's diagnostic manual.

Few American psychologists knew about Freud's work with hypnosis and trauma memories; most of them adhered to a doctrine known as 'behaviourism'. These psychologists ignored the psyche and weren't interested in the mind. The behaviourists considered fear and anxiety to be learnt responses which, in therapy, needed to be unlearnt through a process of 'habituation' (the weakening of learnt behaviour when it's repeated often without being reinforced).

In the 1950s, behaviourists developed phobia treatments that exposed clients to their feared situation either 'in vivo' (in reality) or in imagination until the anxiety subsided. You might have heard of people with phobias being asked to touch snakes: that was in vivo exposure. If they imagined that they were touching snakes, it was 'imaginal' exposure. When the diagnosis first appeared, these 'exposure' therapies were used to treat posttraumatic stress disorder (PTSD).

In exposure therapy, traumatised clients relive their stress memories for extended periods; the recommended dozen or more 90-minute long sessions are tough going for both client and therapist. Behavioural psychologists held that engaging with the trauma memory was essential for recovery. But, unlike Freud and Breuer, their therapy was lengthy and did not require clients to talk about what had happened to them. Nonetheless, practitioners soon recognised the crucial therapeutic role that cognitive processing plays in exposure therapy. As a client repeatedly relives their traumas, they inadvertently learn to control their stress memories in a way that enables them to 'more rationally' assess 'the future risk of threatening events recurring'.[3] The clients also self-correct dysfunctional cognitions and beliefs.[3] As Edna Foa put it, 'By confronting the trauma, the patient learns that the memory does not control her. She controls the memory'.[4]

New ideas about traumatic stress abounded. In 1986, Edna Foa and Michael Kozak proposed that PTSD was relieved when the client engaged with their trauma memories and added new information 'so that a new memory can be formed'.[5] In 1993, Mardi Horowitz argued that, after a trauma, the repeated, involuntary recall of stress memories is normal and beneficial because it allows the affected person to learn from what happened and helps them to develop new, more beneficial ways of thinking about themselves, other people and the world around them.[6] And it became clearer why, post-trauma, some people develop PTSD while others don't.

Researchers discovered why some individuals engage with trauma memories and gradually recover their emotional and physical balance, while others avoid such recollections and remain in a near-constant state of fight-flight-freeze. The things that promote suboptimal avoidant responses include various coping strategies, thinking styles, personal narratives and an array of beliefs about the self, emotions and other things. Most of these blocks to thinking things through operate as habits that run automatically. Some serve a protective function in an avoidant strategy adopted to cope with an earlier event. Others reflect faulty thinking and dodgy logic or arise from a lack of necessary knowledge or skill. These obstacles can trap us in dead-end lines of thought, consume our capacity to process information and hinder communication between our executive and deep minds. A few derail us before we even engage with a stress wave, while others induce us to give up long before we resolve the threat.

By the late 1980s, it was clear that engaging with stress memories and learning new ways of thinking and acting were essential for resolving PTSD and other avoidant stress reactions. And Freud and Breuer's assumption that working with trauma memories had to be stressful was being challenged.

In the 1990s, new insights into the causes and treatment of traumatic stress became personally relevant when I confronted one of my biggest challenges: how to alleviate the suffering of war veterans and other survivors of trauma. My private clinical practice flourished as members of the local veterans' community learnt that I specialised in treating PTSD. Until I began my practice, a psychiatrist, who worked hundreds of kilometres away, was their closest source of mental health support.

I knew that counselling, by itself, would not resolve my clients' traumatic stress reactions, and there were fixed constraints on how I might take on this task. I had to find a way to safely, reliably and efficiently ease my clients' intrusive memories, flashbacks and nightmares within the confines of the clinician's traditional 50-minute consultation. I usually skipped the 10-minute break between clients, but I couldn't run too much overtime because another client or family was waiting to see me. I worked in a group medical practice but didn't have the backup available to practitioners who run exposure therapy programs in hospitals. I had to deal with whatever emerged during a session, and ensure that the client was emotionally stable before the consultation ended.

Freud's cathartic method and other high-stress interventions, such as exposure therapy, were out of the question. But I had a lot of new ideas to work with. At the time, a treatment known as 'eye movement dissociation and reprocessing' (EMDR) showed that trauma-related stress reactions could be alleviated quickly and effectively. Still, I was looking for a more reliable way to manage the intense emotional distress that can unexpectedly emerge when traumatised people recall horrific events. I found what I was looking for elsewhere.

Before training as a specialist clinical psychologist, I practised as a hypnotherapist during a golden age of innovation in psychotherapy. The work of Milton Erickson (1901–1980), an Arizona-based psychiatrist, fostered what was known as the 'new hypnosis'. Erickson offered a practical wisdom that was at odds with traditional thinking.[7,8,9] He respected the rationality and intent of the deep mind, understood the protective function of stress reactions and looked for gentle solutions to wicked problems. Erickson's work inspired a raft of therapies, including 'neuro-linguistic programming', 'solution-focused therapy', 'systemic family therapy', 'Ericksonian hypnotherapy' and much more. Erickson explained that a therapist's job is to offer ideas that liberate the deep mind's creativity and enable clients to bring their memories, knowledge and abilities to bear on their problems. For clients, psychotherapy became a process of learning about who they are, what they're capable of and how they can improve their lives.

For the published research component of my Master of Clinical Psychology degree, I'd integrated aspects of Erickson's work, Edgar Barnett's 'analytical hypnotherapy'[10] and neuro-linguistic programming into a brief, gentle therapy for locating and resolving phobia-related memories.[11] Building on this work, I found what I needed. Over the coming decades, I helped hundreds of traumatised clients successfully resolve their stress reactions. I never asked anyone to relive the past. Some clients cried, but these were the 'cooler' tears of relief and resolution, not the 'hot' crying of catharsis and abreaction. These experiences inform what I'm teaching you about the art of riding stress waves.

Mental Processing

In 1980, Jack Rachman coined the term 'emotional processing' to describe what happens when a person resolves their problematic stress reactions.[12] Back then, most mental health practitioners believed that emotional re-living of memories was essential; hence, the tag 'emotional' processing. But those times passed, and twenty years later, Rachman recommended that emotional processing be 'accomplished in a calm, safe and reassuring environment' where the client can engage with their past in a 'predictable' and 'controllable' way that fosters self-mastery and corrects problematic beliefs.[13]

I prefer the term 'mental processing'. All our key mental

abilities have a role to play, and while therapy can be challenging, it doesn't have to be emotionally distressing. I wish I had a better name for what goes on in our minds when we successfully take on a big stress wave. 'Mental processing' is an abstract, sterile-sounding label, but I haven't come up with a better term for the wonderfully creative ways the human psyche deals with stress.

When we successfully ride a stress wave, our executive and deep minds work in sync as they tap into our key mental processes of attention, perception, thinking, reasoning, memory, imagination, beliefs, language, intuition and dreaming. Our executive mind seeks solutions, while the deep mind provides insights, intuitions and resources. This work goes on during the day as we reflect on and think about what happened, and importantly, it continues through the night as we sleep and dream. In our aeroplane analogy, the pilot and the crew cooperate and talk to each other.

We now know what factors contribute to the successful mental processing of stress. The therapist gives the client a credible explanation of their suffering and a motivating account of what can be done about it. Any beliefs, thinking styles or coping strategies that hinder the client's ability to mentally process stress must be challenged and changed. The positive, protective nature of anxiety needs to be understood.

Mental processing transforms a client's relationship to their stress reactions. Through experiences of 'enactive mastery', the client learns that they can control intrusive thoughts, memories and imagery. Then, with that preparation under their belt, the client has to find the courage to engage with their stress so they can learn what they need to learn and work out how they're going to resolve the threat and make their future safer. And, of course, none of this is easy when we're dealing with powerful, dangerous stress waves.

Unless we've been there ourselves, it's impossible to comprehend the courage and strength that survivors of war, childhood sexual abuse and natural disasters draw on as they work through their stress reactions. Big stress waves can rattle our assumptions, but mentally processing traumatic stress can force us to recast the very meaning of our lives. In its wake, a brush with death poses profound questions: Is this where we should be? Are we in control of our lives? What does how we behaved say about us? Can we trust other people? Is it possible to find peace in a place where we could have been killed? How are we to let go of our grief for the people, places and prospects we've lost? Can we come to terms with the now-undeniable realities of suffering and death? We have to work out what's truly important and decide what we'll do with our lives from then on.

Susan and I were fortunate during the 2019–20 bushfires: our farm and forests survived that awful season. Thanks to heroic firefighters, our property, community and the nearby rainforests didn't burn. Still, it wasn't easy to work out how we would live safely, stay well and enjoy farm life as we grow older in an increasingly perilous world. The stress pushed us to adapt, and now, years after the fires, Susan and I have changed the physical nature of where we live to make it safer. We've adjusted how we think about life, death and living on the land. Thanks to good luck and much thinking, talking, planning, remembering, imagining and dreaming, I feel no unpleasant emotions when I tell you our story. I've picked up some new scars — real and metaphorical — and I can never be the person I was before the drought, bushfires and pandemic. Nonetheless, Susan's and my sense of emotional balance has returned, as we and the world around us changed.

The benefits of mentally processing stress endure. Once we've learnt what we need to learn and done what we need to do to be safe in the future, there's no reason to again think about the original stress event. When the job's done, we no longer need to feel anxious. The issue becomes 'old hat'; we could remember what happened, but why would we want to?

The Basic Formula for Riding Stress Waves

Stress waves come at us from different directions in time, but we always feel the tension and anxiety in the present. Sometimes, the stress is linked to memories of an earlier threat we never resolved. Stress can also be generated in real time, as a breaking wave that sends us tumbling. Some stress comes mainly from the future, as a threat we see forming in the distance. Stress also often arises from the combined effect of memories, present threats and imagined future dangers.

When stress is generated by an old, avoidant coping response that we've lived with for a while, we can take a more considered approach. But the need to respond becomes more urgent when a big stress wave breaks on us. At such times, the fight-flight-freeze response gives us the strength and focus to do what we have to do to survive. When anxiety warns us about a future stress wave, we still need to engage with the threat, but this can be difficult when the danger is yet to materialise. We might be tempted to distract our executive mind, but this can cost us dearly if the threat is realised and our lack of preparation results in serious harm. In such circumstances, it's better to take timely action while our prospects of success are greatest and we can minimise the impact of the developing stress.

Regardless of where in time your stress originates, the task at hand is to deal effectively and efficiently with every threat and challenge that comes your way. The aim is to ride stress waves, not fight them. We want to channel the energy that stress generates into new solutions that make us safer, stronger and more resilient. As we tailor our approach to the unique events and circumstances we confront, the basic principles for practising the art of riding stress waves stay much the same.

Resist the natural urge to escape discomfort, at least long enough to decide whether you'll engage with the threat or try to avoid it. If you take on the stress wave, the next step is to explore what your anxiety is telling you. Then learn from the experience,

THE ENGAGE STRATEGY

and work out how to resolve the threat to make the future safer and more satisfying. When the executive and deep minds agree that this work is complete, your anxiety will dissipate and emotional and physical balance will return.

The groundwork is in place. You have the essential knowledge. You understand that stress and anxiety protect us, and you've learnt how the executive and deep minds work together to keep us safe. We've examined the two basic strategies for dealing with stress and discussed when it's safe to let a stress wave go by and when the better option is to take on the threat. We'll now build on this foundation by adding the skills you need to practice the art of riding stress waves.

Part 2

Tools, Tips and Techniques

Chapter 6

Using Your Toolkit

*The expectations of life depend on diligence;
the mechanic that would perfect his
work must first sharpen his tools.*
Confucius (trad. 551–479 BCE)

IN PART 2, YOU'LL FIND tools, tips and techniques for working with stress and anxiety. Each tool serves a specific purpose, and together, they constitute the essential skills for riding stress waves. There are tools for deciding which stresses you can avoid and which you need to address, tips for countering things that interfere with mental processing and techniques for working with all your key mental processes.

The tools and techniques are not a rehash of psychological treatments for stress and anxiety. They're based on the psychological literature and my clinical experience, but to my knowledge, these methods have never been grouped together and discussed as they are in this book. They're usually isolated in distinct schools of practice that have little to no contact with each other. This makes this book a unique resource.

In no particular order, I've arranged the tools, tips and techniques into chapters based on the key mental processes. I did this for clarity and convenience, but the separation is artificial.

Once you've acquired the basic skills, you'll bring them together in a seamless, artful performance. When we ride stress waves, our executive and deep minds simultaneously tap into all our mental abilities.

If we were face-to-face, I'd guide you to interventions that I thought might help you with your specific challenges. But here, there's no way to know beforehand which tools, tips and techniques you'll find most useful; that's for you to discover. You could find that one technique works well for different stresses, or you might adapt and combine different methods for a particular task.

You can work with the tools and techniques by yourself, but for longer procedures, you might find it easier if a friend reads the instructions to you step by step.

When an exercise asks you to imagine something, allow the images to form in your own way and in your own time. And it doesn't matter if images don't come to you at all. You can use these tools and techniques even when you only read about them, or if you just make-believe that you're seeing and hearing the things I describe.

Be patient with yourself. Remember that it usually takes a few weeks of practice before a new way of thinking or doing things becomes automatic. As you work with these methods, your confidence will grow. You can't know where your self-help journey will take you. Be curious, open and flexible. With experience, you'll discover which tool or combination of tools works for you.

Let your intuition guide you when you're selecting a tool for a task. Inspiration and solutions may appear in unexpected forms; a dream can fix faulty thinking, rational thought can resolve emotions and our deep mind can sort out issues even when we have no idea what it's doing. If something doesn't work, try something else. When practising the art of riding stress waves, there is no failure, only information and inspiration for further practice.

To gauge how therapy's progressing, I usually just ask my clients how they're doing. If they say they're feeling a bit lighter or calmer, things are going well. These are the subtle signs that they're successfully working through their stress. But I never know precisely why things improve for them. The crucial intervention could have occurred during a dream that they can't remember. Perhaps the breakthrough insight came from something they thought about or someone said. It doesn't matter if I or my client don't know how the beneficial change came about. As it is for me, my clients and for you, progress and an easing of anxiety and stress are all we need to confirm the value of our work; insights are optional.

We begin with tools, tips and techniques for working with the key mental processes of attitudes and beliefs.

Chapter 7

Attitudes and Beliefs

> They can because they think they can.
> *Virgil (70–19 BC)*

OUR BELIEFS, THE IDEAS we hold to be accurate, cluster around broader attitudes that determine how we think, feel and act. Beliefs and attitudes can limit or liberate our mind, guaranteeing failure or powering us to success.

We can't determine what stress waves come our way, but we can choose how we react to them. Beliefs and attitudes powerfully affect the way we respond to life's challenges. By becoming aware of these notions, we open them up for change. And then, with our executive and deep minds on the job, we can work out new, better ways of thinking and going about things.

We'll begin with some important beliefs and attitudes about the learning process, ourselves and other people.

Self-Efficacy

Do you believe you can change how you think, feel and act? Our 'self-efficacy' beliefs (automatic ideas about our ability to act and succeed) set rigid limits on what we achieve. When we confront the hypervigilance and emotional turmoil that comes with a powerful stress wave, it's easy to doubt ourselves, and we're vulnerable to certain crippling beliefs.

The next imaginal exercise explores the impact of self-defeating thoughts.

Ψ

1. Silently or out loud, repeat the following phrases a few times: 'I'm weak. I can't control my thoughts. I'm going crazy.'
2. Notice the feelings that come with those statements.
3. Now rate how confident you feel about taking on a new threat or challenge using a 0–10 scale, where 0 indicates no confidence at all and 10 indicates very confident.
4. When you've done that, clear your mind and repeat the following statements a few times: 'I'm strong. I can control my mind. I'll be all right.'
5. Notice the feelings that come with these statements and use the above 0–10 scale to rate how confident you now feel about your prospects of being able to ride the next stress wave that comes your way.

Ψ

When we're preoccupied with limiting ideas, mental processing of stress becomes impossible; if we believe that we can't do something, why would we even try?

If deep down, you believe that you can't succeed, it'll take more than my words or reciting affirmations to bolster your confidence. A 'can-do' attitude and the belief that we can change things grow out of positive experiences, observing others who succeed and giving things a go.

Learning and Making Mistakes

> Failure is the foundation of success,
> and the means by which it is achieved.
> *Lao Tzu (Circa 5th century BC)*

Certain beliefs about learning stymie our desire to ride stress waves before we even get started. Not understanding that achieving anything worthwhile takes time and effort can lock us

ATTITUDES AND BELIEFS

into a fixed mindset that prevents us from pursuing our art. 'I bought a guitar and practised for a week, but it was too hard, so I gave up.' 'I tried to change a bad habit but kept returning to my old ways.' These folk didn't understand that it takes effort to gain new knowledge and skills; their beliefs about learning guaranteed failure.

Learning anything new is challenging at first, but it becomes easier with practice. That's how it was for me when I learnt to ride a bicycle and drive a car. And being prepared to make mistakes is essential. You can't learn to ride a bike unless you're willing to wobble. You can't master a manual gear shift without a few kangaroo hops. We learn by doing things we've never done before and trying out options that won't necessarily work. Or, as Thomas Edison famously described his efforts to invent the light bulb, 'I have not failed. I've just found 10,000 ways that won't work'[1].

Learning about learning helped my client "Rachael" resolve her longstanding avoidant attitude towards life. Rachael couldn't understand why she kept responding to stress in the same old, ineffective way. Whenever she looked inside for a solution to a problem, nothing came to her and her mind would 'go blank'. Rachael assumed that insights should come to her fully formed; like 'manna from heaven' was how she put it. But when Rachael realised that learning new skills takes effort, she persevered and was able to change how she dealt with stress.

Some of my clients are taken back if I recommend that they attend regular consultations for an extended period of time. They ask, 'Do I really need to see you for that long?' I reply, 'If you see me for an hour each week for six months, we'll spend about 24 hours working together. That's a bit more than half a working week. It's up to you whether what you want to achieve is worth the time and effort it'll take'. The same applies when you're working with this book. Remember that accomplishing anything worthwhile requires effort, but it's worth it.

Optimism and Pessimism

> We can complain because rose bushes have thorns,
> or rejoice because thorn bushes have roses.
> *Abraham Lincoln (1808–1865)*

When you take on a demanding task, do you believe you're more likely to succeed or to fail? Do you expect the worst or the best to happen? Such attitudes and beliefs matter. The belief that things always turn out for the worse can make us think that there's no point in taking on a threat or a challenge.

Optimism vs Pessimism

Our next imaginal exercise explores the impact of optimistic and pessimistic beliefs.

Ψ

1. Imagine there's a big stress wave coming your way. Then say a few times, silently or out loud, 'The threat is too big. The challenge is so tough. I can't deal with this'.
2. Notice the feelings that come when you say these things.
3. Now rate how enthusiastic you feel about taking on the stress on a 0–10 scale, where 0 indicates no interest and 10 indicates very enthusiastic.
4. Clear your mind. Then say to yourself, 'The threat is real. It's a big challenge, but I'm up for it. I can cope with this stress'.

ATTITUDES AND BELIEFS

5. Notice the feelings when you say these things, and then use the above 0–10 scale to rate how enthusiastic you now feel about taking on the stress.

Ψ

Did you notice any difference in the impact of the optimistic and pessimistic statements?

A pessimistic attitude focuses our executive mind on failure, encourages despondent feelings and saps enthusiasm for taking on a stress. Optimistic beliefs foster positive emotions, increase energy and make success possible.

Optimists expect that good fortune will last and bad times will pass. They tend to take credit for their successes. They believe they can succeed if they keep working at something. When optimists fail, they don't blame themselves unnecessarily, and they recognise the role circumstances played in the outcome. 'I gave it my best shot' and 'You can't win them all' are their typical responses to a setback.

On the other hand, pessimists believe that good luck is fleeting and bad times will persist. Pessimists undervalue their role in creating success; they thank luck for their wins. They might say, 'I was just in the right place at the right time'. Pessimists interpret setbacks and failures as proof that there's something wrong with them. They tend to blame themselves when things don't work out and think, 'I never get it right'.

A combination of lack of belief in ourselves, a pessimistic attitude and memories of past failures can prevent us from ever engaging with stress.

Stress Responses

For some folk, a noxious cocktail of beliefs about their stress responses blocks mental processing. These ideas generate despair, overwhelm the executive mind and encourage the deep mind to default to an avoidant coping strategy. Common beliefs of this kind include, 'I'm going mad', 'I'll never get well', 'There's something seriously wrong with me', 'My life is ruined', 'Things are only going to get worse' and, an old favourite, 'Real men don't cry'. By themselves, these attributions can impede our ability to deal with stress, but when a few combine, they can scuttle any prospect of a brighter future.

The work culture of some occupations encourages problem-creating beliefs, and police, military and emergency service personnel are most at risk. For example, police officers know that, in dangerous situations, the entire team's safety depends on every member carrying out their duties. Consequently, officers who believe that their stress reactions are a sign of weakness tend to keep their problems to themselves because they're afraid they'll lose their jobs if others find out. Sadly, many put off seeking help until their suffering becomes dire.

And yes, real men and real women do cry. And it's a good thing they do. Crying purges stress hormones from our bodies, clears the mind and leaves us feeling calmer and more emotionally balanced. Some of the bravest, toughest and most dedicated people I've met — clients who were members of elite military and police units — know that tears can help wash away suffering.

It's worth repeating that stress reactions, such as anxiety and posttraumatic stress, are not a sign of mental disorder or personal weakness. PTSD and other strategies for dealing with severe stress arise from healthy, protective psychic processes. Regardless of a person's training, background or strength of character, there's always a set of circumstances that can potentially induce them to avoid and not engage with stress.

The Need to Keep a Stress Reaction

Treatment can go awry if a therapist doesn't account for the context that gives a problem its meaning. When a psychologist forgets that a client lives in relationships, families and communities, their interventions may not help. It's rare, but a few people hold beliefs that explicitly prevent them from ever

ATTITUDES AND BELIEFS

engaging with their problematic stress response.

In his 2015 book, *The Body Keeps the Score*, Bessel van der Kolk described the following interaction with a Vietnam War veteran patient. '... I eagerly asked Tom how the medicines had worked. He told me he hadn't taken any of the pills. Trying to conceal my irritation, I asked him why. He replied, "I realized that if I take the pills and the nightmares go away, I will have abandoned my friends, and their deaths will have been in vain. I need to be a living memorial to my friends who died in Vietnam."'[2]

In a similar case, my client, "Richard", was the sole survivor of a motor vehicle accident in which his wife and two children died. When I talked to Richard about his intrusive memories and how he might relieve them, he was adamant. 'I don't want to do anything that might change my memories of the accident. They're the last time I was with my family. I won't let them go.' Richard never came back after that first consultation.

For my client and van der Kolk's patient, beliefs about their troubling memories forced them to rigidly avoid changing the way they thought about what had happened. Both men believed that their recollections were their only remaining connection with the departed. They both refused to let go of their suboptimal stress responses because to do so would be, in Tom's case, a dishonourable abandonment of fallen comrades and, in Richard's case, a final separation from lost family. For both men, if they were to change their stress responses, they'd have to work through a web of beliefs and assumptions about honour, grief, memories, dreams, their ongoing responsibilities to the deceased and much more.

Tom and Richard clearly stated their reasons for wanting to keep their traumatic memories unchanged, but it's more typical for clients to not be aware of, or have control over, why they can't let go of old stress responses. I'll give you a couple of examples.

"Jenny" requested hypnotherapy for weight loss. She did well for about a month, and Jenny was pleased with her progress, but then she put on weight again. We discussed what was happening and Jenny told me how her relationships with family members had destabilised when she dropped some kilos. Her son, who was used to his mother complying with his demands, became angry as Jenny lost weight and gained confidence. However, Jenny's biggest obstacle was her husband's reaction. He wasn't happy with his increasingly slimmer, fitter and more self-assured wife. Jenny's husband became jealous that other men might find her attractive, and his escalating anger ended his wife's attempts to lose weight.

"Felice" sought treatment for a long-standing phobia of storms. She wanted to overcome her old stress reaction, but nothing I did helped. Exploring more deeply, I found out why. Felice had met her husband when she was young and living in the English countryside. Since then, she hadn't enjoyed her life because her husband had, as she put it, 'dragged' her 'all around the world', and she'd had to attend many business functions that she didn't enjoy. Felice yearned for her lost village life and resented losing it. At the executive mind level, Felice was unprepared to take on issues concerning her marriage and why she resisted going to her husband's business functions. So her deep mind ran an avoidant strategy. Whenever Felice learnt of an upcoming event she didn't want to attend, without understanding her reactions, she'd become anxious and scan weather reports. If Felice found any indication of a possible coming storm, she'd have a panic attack that kept her at home.

With Jenny and Felice, I initially focussed on their presenting problems. In both cases, I failed to account for the purpose of their avoidance. Jenny's overeating and Felice's storm phobia were protecting them from threats that were not apparent to them, or at first, to me. In both cases, their relationships with other people blocked them from engaging with stress, so their deep minds opted to maintain their old avoidant response.

If Jenny was to lose weight, she would have to resolve issues concerning her relationships with her husband and son, as well as her self-image and sense of self-worth. Faced with that onerous task, her mind defaulted to the avoidant strategy of putting on weight and subordinating her desire for change to the needs of others. For Felice, if she was to give up her phobia response, she'd have to work through a lifetime of resentment, her relationship with her husband and her self-efficacy beliefs. Felice's executive mind was not ready to take this on, so her deep mind remained committed to her established phobia strategy.

I'm sharing these stories about unsuccessful therapy, Dear Reader, to alert you to the possibility that you might encounter issues that you don't yet know about. If this happens, before you retreat to your old way of coping, consider the costs and benefits of avoiding or taking on the new challenge.

Other People and the World

Much that defines us and our civilisation — our prosocial traits of cooperation, empathy and love, as well as our antisocial stereotyping, prejudice and inter-group aggression — evolved as responses to the challenge of living with others. Consequently, our executive and deep minds automatically look for cues that identify other people as friends or foes.

Our extraordinary abilities to work with, and care for, strangers come to the fore when our community confronts deadly threats like the COVID-19 pandemic and natural disasters such as floods and fires. At such times, if we sense that we're amongst like-minded, trustworthy people, we work together as if we're members of one tribe. Pre-existing social schisms based on race, politics or background mean little when the stress waves roll in big and fast. But during times of high stress and danger, if we feel that someone doesn't care about us or even means us harm, we can quickly see them as enemies, as if they're from a hostile tribe.

Socially corrosive beliefs about others are more likely to develop if we're isolated without support during times of severe stress. This process played out during the lengthy pandemic lockdowns and contributed to the subsequent polarisation of the community. Such experiences can lead us to conclude that most other people are dangerous, deceptive and untrustworthy. When we hold such beliefs, our executive mind remains on high alert, and our deep mind is primed to react if we detect any threat in another person's appearance or demeanour. This vigilance distorts our thinking, impairs our ability to process stress and messes with our relationships and connection to community.

Exposure to biased information can also block our mental processing of stress. If all we hear is bad news, it's natural to assume that only bad things are going on. Health professionals who work with victims of violence are especially vulnerable to such ideas. If they come to believe that the majority of people are uncaring and potentially dangerous, they're at risk of burnout and vicarious traumatisation. A similar process can affect police and other front-line responders.

Early in my career, many Vietnam War veterans shared with me their stories of being shamed, harassed and abandoned by the Australian public. Hearing these accounts triggered a strong emotional reaction in me, and over time, my sadness for their plight turned into anger at how unfairly they'd been treated. I felt as if most Australians didn't care about our veterans. I woke up to what was happening when a counsellor who attended a conference presentation I gave insisted that I must be a war veteran. She couldn't believe that I hadn't served because, as she explained, I had the 'distinctive look' of a returned soldier. That set me thinking.

I recognised that my anger stemmed from the disturbing stories of rejection I'd heard. Over time, I realised that only a minority of Australians were capable of the thoughtless disregard inflicted on our veterans, while the majority respected their service and sacrifice. With this insight, I could let go of my anger, regain emotional stability and continue helping my clients. I'll give you another example of how exposure to skewed information can powerfully affect our beliefs and prevent us from resolving stress.

"Rick", a child protection officer, sought treatment for anxiety and depression. He worked in an understaffed unit that was responsible for protecting children at high risk of violence. Rick described a harrowing workplace scene where, each morning, staff had to choose which few of the many serious reported cases they could attend to that day. After years of dealing with incidents of men's cruelty to women and children, Rick adopted the terrifying false belief that all men must be evil. In Rick's mind, it followed that he was also evil, which made him profoundly ashamed to be a man. As it was for me, when Rick understood the impact of his false belief, he was able to engage with his stress and begin his healing journey.

When you look for it, there's plenty of evidence that most people are cooperative and law-abiding. If we humans were inherently aggressive and unreliable, how could it be that millions of people travel safely to work each day, and a hundred thousand spectators can pack peacefully into a sports stadium to watch opposing teams compete?

Health and Healing

Some people shy away because they assume that the process of changing their stress responses will be painful. This belief goes back to Freud's day and still influences behavioural therapists who ask clients to relive stressful memories.

Nonetheless, we now know that learning new ways of responding to stress is best accomplished when we're calm, and mental processing can be gentle and rapid.

Physical Pain

To treat physical pain, standard medical practice used to enforce a rigid, four-hourly schedule for giving analgesics; the belief was that relieving pain 'on demand' could lead to dependence on pain-killing medications. Nowadays, doctors consider the experience of pain to be harmful in itself, so nurses tend to give medications pre-emptively to minimise discomfort.

Our next imaginal experiment explores how beliefs about pain can affect our response to the stress of physical suffering.

Ψ

1. Imagine that you've suffered an acute injury that causes a sharp pain in your lower back.
2. Now repeat a few times, 'I can't move with this pain. If this doesn't let up, I'll never be able to work again.'
3. Notice the emotions that come with these words.
4. Then rate your feelings on a scale where 0 represents no distress and 10 is very distressed.
5. Clear your mind when you've done that.
6. Now repeat a few times, 'That hurts a lot, but the pain will ease. I'll get over this'.
7. Notice the emotions these words engender and rate your feelings on the above 0–10 scale.

Ψ

Did you sense how expressing different beliefs affected the way you responded to the imagined pain?

Our suffering due to acute pain, injury or disability intensifies if we believe that the problem might persist for a long time or be permanent. Such beliefs need to be confronted and dealt with because they create despair, consume emotional energy and hinder our ability to ride the stress. But when an acute injury develops into a chronic disability, we need to address a different set of beliefs that come into play.

I'll use a personal account of a chronic medical problem to further illustrate the impact that our beliefs have on mental health and our ability to ride stress waves.

Chronic Illness and Disability

When I was in my mid-30s, an inner ear infection ruptured my eardrum. A doctor inappropriately prescribed antibiotic drops that were toxic to the auditory nerve and unsuitable for use when the eardrum is torn. This treatment left me with severe tinnitus in the form of a continuous, high-pitched hissing noise in my left ear. Another doctor I went to told me that my auditory nerve would never recover and the sound would worsen as I got older, which it has. It seemed there was nothing that I could do to make things better. Losing forever the sound of silence was sad enough, but finding out that the condition could be fatal — one doctor told me about a patient with tinnitus who shot himself — left me depressed.

Months later, I heard a psychologist on the radio say that tinnitus only becomes a problem if sufferers think that the noise in their head is a threat. I certainly did. He explained that this sense of threat triggers the fight-flight-freeze response, sets up a state of high alert and results in an obsessive focus on the sound. The psychologist's solution was to tell his tinnitus clients, 'A noise in the head can't hurt you; it's just the music of the brain' or something like that. I'll always have tinnitus. It's clear and loud as I write this, but I usually don't notice it, and it causes me no grief. The new perspective solved my problem; it changed my relationship to the stress of hearing the noise in my head. With this information, I was able to pay attention to other things, and I could accept my permanent disability.

Years later, when I told this story to a group of Vietnam War veterans, they were puzzled that I'd ever considered tinnitus to be a problem. They believed that the hearing damage and buzzing noises they all experienced were the inevitable consequence of being exposed to rifle and artillery fire. For them, the experience was common, so none believed it to be a big deal.

The pain and disability we experience does not create our suffering. It's how we think about these stresses that determines the way we respond.

Addictive Substances

Some occupations have cultural beliefs about the value of self-medicating with substances. At a stress-management session I ran for volunteer firefighters, one fellow announced, to applause, that they didn't need counselling because they had 'Dr Beer' to turn to. Dr Beer has his place but he won't keep us afloat when we're grappling with powerful stress waves.

The first time someone imbibes one of these substances, they feel less anxious, and this encourages further use of the drug. If this pattern of obtaining relief from a cigarette, drink, pill or shot is repeated often enough, the affected person can mistakenly conclude that they can't control their anxiety without the drug. I'll use the example of tobacco to illustrate how particular beliefs about addictive substances encourage dependence and undermine self-efficacy. A similar process plays out with other addictive substances such as alcohol, benzodiazepines and narcotics.

When the tobacco habit is seamlessly integrated into their lifestyle, it's almost impossible for a smoker to realise how the drug affects them. In non-smokers, a natural, nicotine-like substance in the brain helps to regulate nerve impulses. When a person becomes addicted, their brain's production of this chemical drops off, and their body becomes reliant on tobacco's artificial version of the substance. From then on, whenever the nicotine in a smoker's blood falls to a critical level, they feel tense, so they light up a cigarette to get the familiar anti-anxiety benefit. From that sequence of events, the smoker's executive mind can mistakenly believe that they need nicotine to cope with stress.

In reality, a smoker's use of tobacco weakens their body's natural ability to regulate anxiety. Most of the smokers I've worked with can't believe that they'll ever be able to relax if they give up tobacco. But once they sort out their mistaken beliefs about what's going on and stop smoking, they discover new, empowering things about their ability to deal with stress.

There's another important belief that undermines smokers'

ATTITUDES AND BELIEFS

ability to self-manage stress. When a client requests hypnotherapy to quit smoking, I ask if they've ever stopped smoking in the past. Almost all tell me that they've been able to quit a number of times, but after a while, they always returned to the habit. When they come upon a particular kind of stress, a pernicious belief undoes their good work. It might be after a minor car accident or late at night when they're at a party, but the common theme is that someone offers them a cigarette in unusual circumstances, and they think that one smoke won't matter. They're wrong to believe that; smoking the cigarette fires up their old urge, and they've taken up smoking yet again.

I counter this troublesome belief with a post-hypnotic suggestion. I ask them to imagine that they're feeling anxious and someone offers them a smoke. I then suggest that if they find themselves in a similar situation in the future, they'll stop and think. I tell them to imagine that the offered cigarette multiplies over and over — like Mickey Mouse's brooms in the *Sorcerer's Apprentice* — until they see a twisting line of thousands of cigarettes stretching years into the future. Hopefully, when this image pops into their mind, they'll say, 'No thank you'. For a reformed smoker, there is no 'just one more'.

The next chapter investigates the roles that our emotions play when we're riding stress waves.

Chapter 8

Emotions

> Human infirmity in moderating and checking the emotions
> I name bondage: for, when a man is prey to his emotions,
> he is not his own master, but lies at the mercy of fortune.
> *Baruch Spinoza (1632–1677)*

LIKE THE PHILOSOPHER BARUCH SPINOZA, many people assume that to be the master of our fate, our executive mind needs to moderate and check our emotions. But as we've seen, we're more than our conscious executive mind. As uncomfortable as it is, the deep-mind-generated fear and anxiety we sometimes feel when we're exposed to stress is designed to protect us. To ride stress waves, we need to understand how our emotions work and how to best use them.

As children, we learn that positive emotions, such as happiness, love and compassion, are good, and negative emotions, such as anxiety, anger and guilt, are bad. This encourages us to think that we should escape or suppress unpleasant feelings. But in times of stress, our anxiety, anger and other stress-related emotions serve positive functions; they let us know there's danger about and help us respond to the threat.

When we confront a big stress wave, all our emotions have a role to play in informing, protecting and motivating us.

Some emotions soothe, while others cause angst, even when functioning just as they should be. If we resist the impulse to escape and stay with the unpleasant feelings long enough, they can help us decide how to improve things. Heed the emotions that warn and protect you from danger, and work with those that motivate and energise you to take on the stress. When you've done that, you can safely let go of the anxiety and anger.

I'll concentrate on the emotions that you're most likely to meet when big stress waves come your way: anxiety, caring, anger, depression, guilt, courage, fear of death and grief.

Fear and Anxiety

> Just as courage imperils
> life; fear protects it.
> *Leonardo da Vinci (1452–1519)*

Do you think of anxiety as a friend or a foe? Should we welcome anxiety or wish it would go away? If we believe that anxiety is an enemy, our executive mind is at odds with the way Nature intended us to use the emotion. Fear and anxiety alert us to the presence of danger. If we avoid anxiety, we expose ourselves to potential threats, and by flicking the job of protecting us on to the deep mind, we can perpetuate and intensify our distress. But when we treat anxiety as a signal rather than a symptom, the question shifts from 'How do I get rid of this horrible feeling?' to 'What is it telling me?'

Health professionals who think that fear and anxiety are symptoms of mental dysfunction typically try to reduce their clients' distress without exploring the source and meaning of the danger signal. In effect, they extinguish the warning light without figuring out why it's flashing. Some doctors prescribe anti-anxiety medications with no investigation of the real-world threats that concern their patients. And too many psychologists treat anxiety as a learnt fear response, which they counter without considering the protective function it serves.

Of course, feeling anxious doesn't always mean we're at risk of imminent harm. Anxiety can signal a threat that comes from within or from outside of us. The jolt of fear when a fin breaks the surface at the beach signals an external danger and triggers a rapid exit from the surf. (Unless, as once happened to me, you promptly realise it's a dolphin's fin.) In contrast, the shiver of fear you get when you hear about a shark attack on the radio signals a threat from within. The anxiety might link to an empathetic imagining of what it would be like to be mauled, or it might come from a childhood memory of a gory story or a day at the beach when the shark alarm sounded. When we understand what our anxiety is telling us, we can decide how we're going to deal with the threat or challenge.

If we respect our anxiety, it becomes a link, a kind of trace, that we can follow back to the source of our stress. Insights come when we stay with the feeling and consider what it means. To assess any threat, we must resist the impulse to escape and give our executive and deep minds time to determine what's happening. Then we have to decide whether we'll ignore the stress or take it on. And for this task, the 'stress scan' is the ideal tool.

The Stress Scan

I'm encouraging you to respect your anxiety, but that doesn't mean that I want you to put up with discomfort any longer than you need to. Merely tolerating anxiety won't help; to maintain optimal mental health, we have to heed the emotion and respond appropriately.

Regular, at least daily, use of the stress scan ensures that you won't overlook issues that need attention. Good times for running a stress scan are when you wake in the morning and before you go to bed at night. But you can perform a scan any time you like. It's simple to run, and it doesn't take long.

Ψ
1. Find a quiet place and pay attention to your feelings.
2. Look for emotions associated with threat and danger. Specifically, scan your body and mind for any:
   - Sadness (grief, sorrow, despair, unhappiness, depression)
   - Anxiety (fear, concern, unease, dread, panic, nervousness)
   - Guilt (shame, regret, remorse, self-reproach)
   - Anger (irritation, outrage, resentment, hostility)

   The acronym SAGA is a good way to remember the emotions you need to scan for.
3. If you run the stress scan and all you detect are emotions associated with feeling safe, secure and well (joy, happiness, relief, delight, pride, acceptance, friendliness, trust, kindness, affection, love, wonder), then enjoy your day.
4. But if you find any traces of sadness, anxiety, guilt or anger (SAGA), rate the intensity of your emotion on a 0–10 scale where 0 is no distress and 10 is very distressed.
5. The next step is to determine whether the stress is transitory and unimportant or likely to persist and require attention. To do this, compare your ratings over a few days.
6. You can safely ignore the stress if the ratings decrease to near zero. If your ratings remain the same or increase over time, then you need to engage with the stress, learn from it and work out how you're going to resolve the threat and make the future safer.

Ψ

We often encounter events or information that provoke a stress reaction but don't warrant much thought or effort. If our stress scans indicate that our anxiety quickly dissipates, we can safely ignore the threat. But if our scans detect any sadness, anxiety, guilt or anger that persists for a few days or longer, we need to engage with the stress.

If we discover that the persisting stress is due to something we're responsible for and can affect, we need to process the threat

EMOTIONS

and resolve it. But if we find that the stress arises from something we have no power over or responsibility for, we have to change how we think about the problem.

The next tool helps us discriminate between those stresses we can affect and those we can't.

Rationing Emotional Energy

To ride stress waves, we need to balance our concerns with our capabilities. If we worry too much about things we can't change, we'll have less energy for the threats and challenges we need to deal with.

The next tool can help you decide where and how to focus your emotional energy. It's based on what Stephen Covey calls our 'circle of concern' and 'circle of influence'[1]

Ψ

1. Compile a list of all the things that concern you about yourself, other people and the world at large. Include every issue that has caused you to feel anxious or could cause you to feel anxious. Take your time; the list could be long.

2. Sort the items on your list into the following two categories:

   a) Things that you have some control over and can affect, versus

   b) Things that you have no control over or ability to change.

3. Now find a large sheet of paper — the old 'butcher's paper' is ideal — and draw two concentric circles, one inside the other. The outer perimeter represents the limits of your circle of concerns. The smaller interior circle represents the outer bounds of your circle of influence.

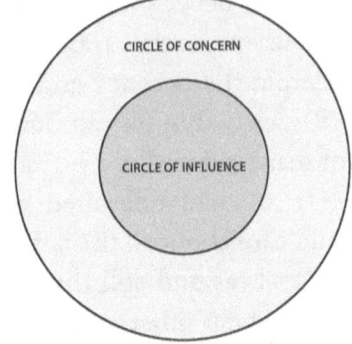

Circles of Concern and Influence

4. Take from your list all the things that you have the power to affect, then record them within your circle of influence. Put your most important concerns closer to the centre.
5. All the other issues that you have no responsibility for, or ability to affect, go in the space between the inner circle and the outer perimeter (your 'doughnut of concern').
6. Reflect on the concentric circles and what they contain.

Ψ

Sorting our list of stresses into those we can control and those we can't gives us new information about the things that create tension in our lives. Further, writing down our list and arranging the stresses visually on a chart facilitates an objective perspective for thinking about the threats and challenges that come our way. Keep your deepest concern and commitment for those people and things that you're most responsible for and have the greatest ability to help, and extend your caring to include yourself.

Stephen Covey also recommends that we think of ourselves as 'assets'.[1] An asset creates wealth or generates benefits. We care for material assets; why wouldn't we top up the oil in our car's engine? But it's not as easy to see that our minds and bodies also require care and maintenance. Covey posed a provocative question about the need for self-care: How much wood will you cut if you never sharpen your saw?

Our prosocial traits of cooperation, empathy and love underpin the decency and concern for others that characterise a civil society. But like all our emotions, if empathy and caring are not managed well, they can hamper how we deal with stress.

If we had unlimited mental and emotional resources, we could care about all the suffering in the world, take on the biggest stress waves and still thrive. But our resources are finite, and if we're to help others, we need to ration our feelings. Burning out is a costly solution to the problem posed by caring. When someone gives up and drops out, there's a cost to them and everyone else. You're important to all the people you care for and who care about you. Remember that anything you do to nourish and protect yourself contributes to the well-being of your family, friends and community.

Letting Go of Unnecessary Anxiety

When our stress scans indicate persisting anxiety, we need to work out what the emotion is telling us. When we resolve the threat, the feeling will ease. But sometimes, we can't wholly resolve a stress in the short to medium term. In such situations, we can often safely tone down the strength of the warning signal.

The following tool helps us decide how much of our anxiety we need to keep.

Ψ

1. Assess your current level of perceived danger (anxiety) using a scale where 0 is no danger and 10 represents extreme danger.
2. Now think rationally and objectively about the threat. Use your executive mind to rate the real-world extent of the threat on our 0-to-10 scale where 0 is no danger and 10 represents extreme danger.

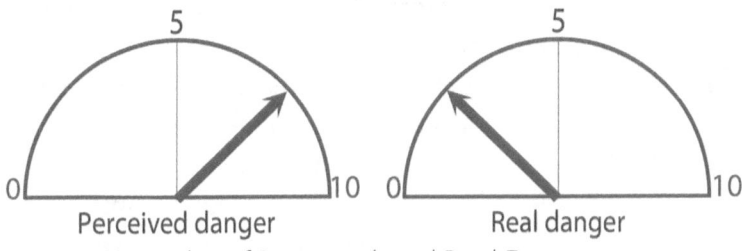

Scales of Perceived and Real Dangers

3. Compare the gap between the rating of your level of perceived and actual danger.
4. You can safely let go of the unnecessary feelings represented by the gap between your ratings of perceived and actual danger.

Ψ

When we feel anxious, visualising the dials of perceived and actual danger gives us an objective perspective on what's happening.

Another method for managing anxiety in the short term is to make a formal, fair-dinkum agreement with yourself that you'll engage with the challenge in the future. When you enter a date and time in your diary and commit yourself to getting back to the problem later on, your deep mind can safely lower the intensity of your anxiety. As with the dials tool we just discussed, this technique encourages an objective perspective on the stress and commits us to taking appropriate action.

Anger

> I have learnt through bitter experience the one supreme lesson to conserve my anger, and as heat conserved is transmuted into energy, even so our anger controlled can be transmuted into a power which can move the world.
> *Mahatma Gandhi (1869–1948)*

Anger is a natural response to stress that prepares us to fight off danger. Taking a sedative to soothe anger is akin to lowering our guard in a fight; the medication might relieve our angry feelings, at least in the short term, but it could weaken us when we need to act and be strong.

The emotion of anger worked well as our kind evolved. Anger's adrenaline spike, with its supercharged strength and devil-may-care disregard for personal well-being, is what's needed when a wild animal wanders into your cave. Anger still serves its ancient protective purpose, but the emotion is trickier to use in modern times. The ability to throttle a dangerous animal was once valued, but controlling anger is essential when we can't, or

Cranky Cow

shouldn't, get our hands on the people and things that threaten us.

Intense anger functions like a trance that restricts our awareness of what's happening around us. It interferes with our executive mind's ability to think things through and rules out considered action. If anger fails to fulfil its purpose of neutralising danger, the emotional energy can be redirected so it harms us or innocent bystanders. Turned outward, uncontrolled anger can fuel the abuse of family, friends and other people; rates of domestic abuse and other forms of violence increase during times of great stress. When anger is turned inward, it can morph into depression.

We can control anger, or anger can control us. When anger takes over, people can say and do uncharacteristic things they later regret. If you melt down, take responsibility for your actions as soon as your rage eases. If you've hurt others, apologise promptly and sincerely. Don't let avoidance, embarrassment or a self-serving rationalisation prevent you from making things right. It's important for you and the person who copped your rage to learn from the experience so you can make the future safer.

Just as it's best to repair a leaky roof when the sun's shining, work on your anger when you feel calm. To break anger's hold, think things through and draw on all your key mental processes. Ask questions such as 'What triggers my anger?' and 'Why do I lose control?' Explore the beliefs, memories and thoughts that feed your anger. Imagine how you might respond differently. Think about how you can channel this powerful emotion to help, rather than hinder, your mental processing of stress.

Depression

When we're living through the listless haze and mental fog that come with an episode of severe depression, it's difficult to see how feeling this way helps us ride stress waves. Nonetheless, our flattened emotions make it clear that the old ways of dealing with stress are no longer working and we need to change how we think and act. Depression is a natural response to stress that forces us to go to ground. Rumination (the repetitive thoughts that come when we're depressed) and our lack of energy and motivation can give us the break we need to work out how we're going to make things better.

A protracted episode of severe depression is one of those times when a psychoactive medication can sometimes help. When depression is severe and we can't think clearly, medications can provide temporary relief so we can mentally process stress. But it's important to remember that medications are tools for riding stress waves, not treatments for a so-called mental disorder. When we've thought through and resolved the stress, we need to discontinue the medications.

Next, we'll look at a vexing stress response that's particularly difficult to resolve.

Guilt and Shame

The emotion of guilt serves an important function; it lets us know we've done wrong or failed to do what's right. Guilt tells us how our actions measure up against the moral principles that matter to us and our community. When guilt is intense, it can take the form of shame, which makes us feel unworthy and cuts deep into our sense of self-worth. Guilt is especially challenging when others are harmed due to our actions or inaction.

If guilt motivates us to own up to our failings and do what we can to put things right, the emotion has done its job, and we can let go of the feeling. Acknowledging and rectifying our mistakes can lead to personal growth and learning. But unresolved guilt blocks mental processing because it induces us to avoid thinking about what happened.

When we're children, being rewarded for doing what's right and being punished for doing what's wrong can make us vulnerable to the false belief that we must be responsible for bad things that happen to us. For example, children can conclude that they caused a car accident involving their mother because they argued with her that morning, or because they didn't tell their mother that they loved her before she left, or for some other reason that seems irrational to an adult. Children are not the only ones susceptible to mistaken beliefs about punishment and reward.

For some adults, notions about why good and bad things happen spawn self-defeating beliefs that if something bad happens to them, they must deserve it. This idea encourages them to accept their suffering as punishment, which prevents them from thinking about their stress. And unresolved guilt can cause lifelong suffering.

War generates much stress and guilt. "Rob" was a 60-year-old veteran who'd been a professional soldier in Malaysia, Korea and Vietnam. He felt guilty about an incident that occurred while he was leading a patrol in the Vietnam jungle. Rob had left a young, wounded soldier behind, concealed until the patrol could come back for him. They returned to find that the enemy had tortured and killed the young man. Rob couldn't overcome his guilt until I guided him through a technique we'll work with later.

I asked Rob to close his eyes, recall what had happened and then give the memory a better ending. When Rob opened his eyes, he described how he had imagined himself ordering another soldier to stay with the wounded man. As soon as he did that, in his mind's eye, Rob watched as the soldier multiplied, over and over, until dozens of identical soldiers were standing there. Rob instantly realised this was what he would've had to do, but that was impossible; he couldn't have left enough men to save the wounded man's life. For Rob, imagining a new ending eased his guilt, but there are other ways to deal with this vexing emotion.

To resolve severe guilt, it can help if we take an impersonal 'legal' perspective. The law specifies penalties for every offence, and for serious crimes that attract a prison sentence, authorities release an offender when they've paid their debt to society.

Left unaddressed, long-term guilt resembles a self-imposed life sentence for a crime that never went to trial. Only the worst offences deserve such a penalty.

As a clinical psychologist, when I prepare pre-sentence reports for the courts, my job is to help the judge determine an appropriate penalty for an offender who has pleaded guilty to criminal charges. The judge wants a professional opinion about four things: the offender's insight into their actions, any remorse or sorrow they feel, what they've done to make amends or reduce the risk of further offending, and whether there are any mitigating circumstances.

The following tool incorporates features of a forensic assessment and provides a systematic way to work through troubling guilt. If at any stage you feel an intuitive resistance to the virtual day-in-court process, engage with the stress and work out why you feel that way. Some common issues revolve around forgiveness, retribution and the notion of 'original sin' (the Roman Catholic Church doctrine that holds we are all born sinners).

Ψ

1. If you feel guilty, you believe you've done something wrong. Continue when you're ready for your imaginal day in court.
2. A defendant must answer specific questions before a judge imposes a sentence. Proceed when you're ready for questioning.
3. Detail your offence in writing, as it might appear on a police charge sheet. Proceed when you've done that.
4. Explain why you did what you did. How do you now understand your offence? How do you feel about your actions? Proceed when you've done that.
5. Have you done anything to address what you did or the harm you caused? Is there anything that would prevent, or make less likely, your re-offending in a similar way in the future? Proceed when you've done that.
6. Outline any mitigating circumstances.

7. Do you deserve further punishment for your crime? Is there anything you need to do to make up for your offence or to pay off your debt to others? Can you forgive yourself and let go of the guilt you've held onto for so long?

9. Take your mental processing of the guilt from here.

Ψ

How the imaginal day-in-court plays out depends on a person's circumstances and the nature of the event that gave rise to their guilt. Entrenched beliefs about what they did or didn't do often shift before the process runs its course. The experience is always unique for clients who work with their guilt in this manner. I'll give you a few examples.

"Jan", who ran a soup kitchen, felt guilty because she couldn't care for the many others who needed her help. The procedure helped her realise that her resources were limited and that she needed to also care for herself.

"Carol" felt guilty because she couldn't reconcile her daughters' wish to visit their grandfather with her duty to protect them from her sexually abusive father. The virtual-day-in-court process triggered a sense of righteous indignation, which countered her guilt.

"James", a Vietnam war veteran, felt guilty because he hadn't followed through on a promise to take care of a dying mate's family when he returned home. For James, his virtual day-in-court led to him realising that it was too late for him to contact his deceased friend's family. So he repaid the debt he felt he owed through welfare work with other veterans.

Perhaps, like Rob, who left the young soldier in the jungle, imagining a new ending for your guilt-causing memory will yield a healing insight. Or perhaps, like Jan, Carol and James, having your day in imaginal court will help you determine what you can do to set things right.

Courage

> I learned that courage was not the absence of fear but the triumph over it. The brave man is not he who does not feel afraid but he who conquers that fear.
> *Nelson Mandela (1918–2013)*

Courage gives us the strength to face dangerous stress waves; it's the emotion that harnesses our fear, anxiety and anger in the most stressful times. Courage is not mere bravado. Rather, it's founded on a realistic appraisal of a threat and a principled determination to take it on and succeed. Courage complements the executive mind's decision to pursue a worthy goal, regardless of the personal cost.

Acts of courage stand out in our personal and social histories; it's the outstanding quality I see in my clients as they work through trauma and tribulation. There is little written about this stress-related emotion in the scientific literature, but I found practical insights in two literary genres: the wartime speeches of Sir Winston Churchill[2] and the novels of J.R.R. Tolkien.[3]

In his speeches, Churchill engaged with the existential threat posed by the seemingly unstoppable Nazi plans to invade England. He rejected the wishful thinking of appeasement, took the stress wave head on and told the truth about what lay ahead. In his maiden speech as Prime Minister, Churchill told the British people, 'We have before us an ordeal of the most grievous kind. We have before us many, many long months of struggle and of suffering ...' Those words offered no false comfort, and his audience knew straight away that their leader understood their fear and would not understate the danger. Churchill then let his audience know that they were part of a worthy cause greater than themselves: 'You ask, what is our policy? ... It is to wage war ... against a monstrous tyranny, never surpassed in the dark, lamentable catalogue of human crime'. And Churchill offered hope: 'I feel sure that our cause will not be suffered to fail among men. At this time, I feel entitled to claim the aid of all ...'[4]

EMOTIONS

J.R.R. Tolkien's epic fantasy novels were inspired by his time as a soldier in World War I and the impacts of industry on the English countryside. In Tolkien's *The Lord of the Rings*, Aragorn prepares his troops for battle and likely death by telling his men, '... I see in your eyes the same fear that would take the heart of me'. Aragorn's self-revealing statement established rapport with his troops and legitimised their fear and anxiety. He then acknowledges the severity of the threat and calls for action, by saying, 'A day may come when the courage of Men fails, when we forsake our friends, and break all bonds of fellowship, but it is not this day. An hour of wolves and shattered shields when the Age of Men comes crashing down, but it is not this day! This day we fight!'

"Tom", a husband and father of two young sons, faced a cruel task. I was helping Tom's wife, "Alicia", cope with terminal cancer. I felt so sad for Tom — a good man who had to lose both the wife he loved and the life they shared. Tom was afraid and troubled by visions of Alicia's funeral. I didn't know what I could say to help. There was no way to avoid or soften the prospect that Tom faced. But then, Aragorn's speech popped into my mind; my deep mind intervened when my executive mind floundered.

All I could think of was to say words along the lines, 'The day will come when you go to Alicia's funeral, but that's not today. The time will come when you will care for your sons by yourself, but that time is not now. For today, tomorrow and the following days, your job is to enjoy being with Alicia and the boys. Draw on your strength as a man to do what you have to do'.

To find courage when we're anxious, we must face the threat, acknowledge and respect our emotions and commit ourselves to doing what we need to do, regardless of how we feel. Courage serves us well, but we need more when terrifying stress waves break on us and we confront our fear of death or we have to grieve for precious people and things we've lost.

Fear of Death

> We are such stuff as dreams are made on,
> and our little life is rounded with a sleep.
> *William Shakespeare (1564–1616)*

It's getting harder to avoid thinking about our death, the demise of others and the destruction of living creatures and natural systems. Talk of lethal threats is now part and parcel of everyday life, and the old distractions don't work as well as they once did. Our minds generate anxiety to warn us of danger, and as the risks multiply, this protective emotion won't abate unless we find a way to deal with the stress waves that death generates. But this is a special threat. With good management and luck, we can avoid death for a while, but not forever — all living things die.

How are we to respond to our existential predicament? As with any stress, we can either avoid or confront the threat. We might find temporary relief by ignoring death and focussing on other matters. But that passes the job of protecting us to the deep mind, which, in this case, is likely to render us vigilant and reactive. And if we spend a lot of time worrying about death, we undercut our enjoyment of life.

Only we humans have to deal with this most ancient challenge; animals don't dwell on their mortality. Our species has grappled with this reality in myth, religion and philosophy since the beginning. Knowing that death is inevitable, how are we to live well and joyfully as we confront and do what we can about this implacable threat? It's a conversation that, I'm sure, doesn't sound like fun to you, but it needn't be too tough. We're in this together, so here we go. Let's talk about what we need to know about death and what it can teach us about life.

Thus far, I've not been so ill or injured that I've been near to dying, although a few times, only luck saved me. I've recently realised how much death has been a part of my life, and writing this book is responsible for that. To engage with the stress, I began by compiling a list of the personally significant deaths that came readily to mind. The result surprised and provoked me. I must have learnt much from death without knowing I was doing so. Perhaps you'll find that you've also been processing this stress without realising it.

During my three score and ten-plus years, I've grieved for the deaths of more than sixty family members, friends and close colleagues. The list blows out if I include deaths that affected me emotionally, even though I didn't know the deceased personally. These include the stories that clients shared with me. And, as it would also be for you, the toll runs to millions if I include the deaths that I learnt about during my education and from reading and the media. Compiling my list triggered some tears, but I wasn't as distressed as I thought I might be. And engaging with death brought on memories and insights about how life has shaped my attitude to death. I'll share some of what I learnt.

I recalled my childhood religious education and thought about why the story of Jesus's torture, execution and resurrection resonates through the ages; it deals with the brutal realities that many powerless people confront and offers hope that goes beyond death. My musings took me back to my university days, where I studied philosophy and psychology and experimented with psychedelics. This was a time when, for me and other men my age, conscription posed the very real prospect of a violent early death and a legally mandated duty to kill other people. Then I thought about my career as a clinical psychologist and what my war veteran clients taught me about state-sanctioned killing on an industrial scale. I realised that, no matter how difficult or protracted the transition, death frees the dying from suffering. I thought about family members, friends and clients who demonstrated courage and the strength of the human spirit as they confronted death.

Running from the stress of death can blight relationships with friends and family who are dealing with terminal illness. And the relief afforded by avoidance can cost us a lifetime of regret.

A now-deceased relative of mine told me how he travelled across the country to see his dying father, but when he got to the hospital room, he couldn't bring himself to go inside. He always regretted that he hadn't said goodbye to his father.

Our fear of death can also be hard on the dying. After doctors diagnosed "Tom", a high school friend, with terminal cancer, Susan and I would visit him whenever we passed by. Tom shared his bitter disappointment that a close mate wouldn't see him because the friend couldn't muster the courage to visit Tom in the hospital. It's better to face our fear of death and find a way to deal with it that allows us to do what we need to do. The best we can do for loved ones who are dying is to be there, comforting them when we can. As difficult as that can be, confronting the stress of impending death also prepares us for the later challenge of dealing with our grief.

From all this thinking about death, I came to understand the lasting benefits of mentally processing stress. For instance, I'm not anxious about climate change. The issue hasn't troubled me much since I was a young man working through stress waves generated by the threat of nuclear war, pollution, environmental degradation and the rest. I know what's at stake, I'm informed and I support environmental activism, but I've come to terms with what I can and can't do about such things. The anxiety and anger that I processed as a young man prepared me for what lay ahead.

I'll discuss some insights that have helped me and my clients work through the fear of death.

Liberation in Dark Times

Sometimes even to live is an act of courage.
Lucius Annaeus Seneca (c. 4 BC–AD 65)

The saddest entries on my list were the folk who took their own lives; most did so to escape intolerable suffering, and a few acted impulsively. But for some depressed folk at the end of their tether, contemplating suicide can free them to think about life-affirming change. When appropriate, I'll gently invite a suicidal client to talk about their self-destructive thoughts and impulses. When all goes well, their despair gradually settles as they work through what taking their own lives would mean for them and for others who know and care about them. I suggest that when ending our life is the last card we've got to play, then all other options in the game of life are on the table. I ask them, 'If you knew you were to die tomorrow, what would you be free to do today?' Disrupting their fixated, potentially deadly, avoidant train of thought sometimes opens them to hitherto unconsidered possibilities and new perspectives.

For some of my clients, mental processing of their intended suicide results in a renewed desire to live and see how a different course of action would work out. The literature on what's known as 'post-trauma growth' contains many accounts of depressed folk who fend off suicidal thoughts by radically changing their lives to pursue some long-forgotten passion or interest.[5] When all seems lost, there's nothing to stop us from thinking the unthinkable. We're liberated to imagine a life beyond the dire predicament that burdens us in the present.

Clients who gave up their suicidal intentions highlight a potent tool for dealing with our fear of death: the way we think about life, the universe and our place in it.

The Unity of All Things

> I do not fear death. I had been dead for billions and billions of years before I was born, and had not suffered the slightest inconvenience from it.
> Mark Twain (1835–1910)

For me, the Buddhist 'Yin-Yang' symbol represents the insight that life and death arise together as aspects of an underlying unity. Life and death cannot exist without each other, and they eternally transform one into the other. Just as there can be no light without the dark, no 'on' without an 'off', there is no life without death. The black-and-white dots in the Yin-Yang symbol remind us that death is inherent in life, and life is inherent in death.

Yin-Yang Symbol

All living things arise from the universe and act as independent entities until they die and return to wherever they were before they were born. As I remember how Alan Watts put it, the universe makes people like a tree makes leaves. Or, as Albert Einstein explained in a letter to a grieving father, we human beings are 'a part of the whole' known as the 'universe', and our feeling of being separate from the rest is a 'kind of optical delusion' of consciousness.[6]

The forms that life takes are temporary patterns. There's not one atom in our body that hasn't already been endlessly recycled through deep time. Our human form is like a whirlwind or an eddy in a creek that exists and moves about for a while before it settles, loses shape and dissolves back into the air or water from which it arose.

As I write this, looking out my window, I see cows, sheep and wallabies grazing around a giant fig tree. To me, the animals, the tree and the grass appear to be different things. But suppose I could watch through a time-lapse camera that condenses decades into seconds and ages into minutes. I'd see a continuous stream of animals being born, eating grass, living, dying and dissolving back into the ground to become nutrients for the trees, and so on. From this long-term perspective, it's apparent that the animals, grass and tree are not separate things but are, in reality, interdependent, interacting components of the over-arching system we call life.

Life is a game the Universe plays with itself. The unbreakable rule of this game is that all things must pass. For us, life's great challenge is figuring out what we'll do with the time between when we arrive and when we leave. To my mind, the most sensible approach is to accept the rules and play the game of life as well as we can. Living our lives worrying about things we can't change makes no good sense. We'll deal with death when we need to, but until then, life is for living. Our day to die will come, but in the meantime, our job is to enjoy life as we work to make our world better for our being in it.

But it takes more than intellectually understanding the unity of all things to assuage our fear of death.

On Acceptance

> Above all, I have been a sentient being, a thinking animal, on this beautiful planet, and that in itself has been an enormous privilege and adventure.
> *Oliver Sacks (1933–2015)*

A story I heard long ago has stayed with me. A teacher holds up a fine crystal glass and tells a student that 'this glass is already broken'. The lesson I took from this is that the glass's inevitable fate makes it even more precious and enjoyable while it's still intact. This idea is also linked to my memory of a stone relief on a Javanese Buddhist temple. The image was of a meditating 'bodhisattva' (one who seeks awakening) sitting atop a pile of skulls. He holds a lotus in one hand while his other hand is raised, palm forward with a couple of fingers pointing upwards to signify the warding off of evil. Despite his grizzly throne, the bodhisattva's countenance was reassuring, as if to say 'fear not'.

Look far enough into the future and we can see that everything will end. About five billion years from now, the Sun will consume the Earth. Like every other creature that has ever lived, we and everything we love on this planet will eventually assume different forms. But if we can accept the existential bottom line — there is no life without death — we can let go of our anxiety about mortality, appreciate what we have and do what we can to improve the world we live in.

Deep in the drought that culminated in the 2019–20 firestorms, our creek stopped running for only the second time in the more than 40 years we've lived here. Our paddocks had no green grass and, on the ridges, mature trees were dying from thirst and heat stress. It seemed that Nature had forgotten how to rain. One day, as I looked at our parched forests, I despaired that they could be dying. Realising that no matter how much I cared or how hard I worked, I couldn't protect the forests, I felt grateful and at peace with what was happening. If worse came to worst, I would at least have the profound privilege of bearing witness to the death of these forests that I care for. When we can't change the world around us, our only option is to change ourselves and how we relate to reality. This attitude stayed with me, and the experience changed how I think and feel about the coming stress waves that'll wash over us and our farm.

I wish I could offer you advice about achieving a state of acceptance, but I can't. The relief I felt by accepting that our forests could be dying was the latter stage of a process that had been going on in me for a long time. To find peace through acceptance, we have to come to terms with the big issues of life and death, who we are and what we can and can't achieve.

In my region, the 2019–20 fires inflicted a devastating, irreplaceable loss of globally significant forests in one fierce season. As terrible as this stress was, Susan and I had to grieve for what we lost and then find a way to protect and celebrate what we still have. What the bushfires burnt makes what's left even more precious. There's no point in worrying about death — not ours, Mother Nature's or the planet's. Accepting that our forests and everything else will ultimately disappear has freed me from worrying about how all this will turn out. I no longer feel anxious about the possibility of further droughts and fires, and I'm optimistic about the future.

But before we can accept a stress like death that we can't avoid or do anything about, we have to properly work through any unresolved grief we harbour.

Grief

The loss of someone we love cuts deep, as does the death of a beloved pet or the destruction of treasured natural places, plants and animals. There's no easy way through the sense of loss, and we have to deal with each day as it comes. And there's much that can interfere with our riding the stress wave of grief.

My great-aunt never overcame her husband's death because the benzodiazepine sedative her doctor prescribed on the day of the funeral set up a life-long avoidant stress response. From then on, my great aunt broke down whenever her deceased husband was mentioned, and she took the sedative daily to prevent her anxiety from spiralling into panic.

The belief that 'enough time' has passed and we need to 'get on with life' also blocks the mental processing of grief. There's no set period for working through this emotion. It doesn't matter whether weeks, months or years have passed since the death of a loved one; grief can remain unresolved until we find a way back to emotional balance.

Buddhism recognises that suffering arises from attachment. It seems reasonable to believe that if we weren't attached to others, we wouldn't mourn their passing. Similarly, if we weren't attached to being alive, I suppose we wouldn't fear death. But what are we to do with this insight? Do we, like the solitary yogi meditating in a cave, avoid anguish by severing our attachments to others? Or do we accept the suffering that comes with caring and loving and get on with the challenges and delights of life?

The Importance of Ceremony

Sudden, unexpected death often leaves unfinished emotional business. Ideally, an appropriate ceremony or a funeral is held to ease grief. The sharing of memories and talking with friends and family connects the deceased's passing to the broader story of their lives and what their life meant to others. This gives us a potent tool for working through the stress of grief. Some of my adult clients suffered unresolved sorrow because, as children, they were deemed too young to attend a funeral, and they never got to say goodbye to a lost parent or loved one. A few were not even told that their parent had died.

My sister Kerri's funeral was the best it could have been, given the tragic circumstances. It was 1986, and I was in town to meet my then 23-year-old sister, who'd been at a retreat where a visiting Tibetan Buddhist monk was teaching. After we met, Kerri left town to return to her retreat, but she died on the way when her car rolled. As the eldest sibling and the only family member in the area, I had to arrange Kerri's funeral. Strange to say, not long before her death, Kerri and I had talked about what she'd want if she died while we were travelling together to attend our grandmother's funeral. I knew Kerri wanted her ceremony to honour her Buddhist religion and my parents' Christian faith.

I was fortunate to find Bill, a Uniting Church minister, who offered to coordinate the ceremony with Kerri's Buddhist teacher. My memory of each man blessing my sister's grave is clear to this day. And for the rest of her life, my mother was comforted by her memories of Kerri's funeral. Not long before her passing, Mum smiled as she recalled speaking with Kerri's Tibetan teacher; he held her arm and, with a radiant smile, through an interpreter, reassured my mother that Kerri was already well on her way to being reborn.

My memories of Kerri's funeral are linked to a neighbour's ceremony that took place years later. At "Harry's" funeral, "Reverend Judy" delivered an inspired sermon celebrating Harry's love of the bush. She reassured his family that Harry was at peace as he had returned to Mother Nature and was now one with the natural world he loved and protected. This comforted me, and I think fondly of Harry when I drive past the forest he cared for. It feels as if Harry lives on in the trees. For me, Kerri's Tibetan Buddhist teachers, Reverend Bill and Reverend Judy, embody compassion, true religion and the commitment to relieving the suffering of others by acknowledging death and its place in the order of things.

Unfortunately, working through grief after natural disasters is complicated by the lack of formal places to mourn and perform ceremonies to mark the loss of beloved animals and places. Scientists with the World Wildlife Fund estimated that nearly three billion animals died in the 2019–20 bushfires.[7] I was sad to see two senior conservation scientists — men about my age — sobbing as they addressed a NSW parliamentary committee on the destruction of koala colonies that they'd studied for years. This was no funeral, nor was it an appropriate ceremony to alleviate the grief felt by these men and the audience. When a documentary-maker mate of mine went to interview a coral reef scientist, he found a depressed man living in the rainforest. The scientist couldn't resolve his grief over the plight of the Great Barrier Reef, and he'd given up on humanity.

I hope these folk found a way to resolve their grief and again enjoy their lives. More than ever, the world needs capable, dedicated people with the skills to protect and heal Nature. When someone who cares gives up and backs away from big stress waves, we're all worse off.

Resolving Grief

We work through our grief during the day, and the mental processing goes on at night while we sleep and dream. I couldn't sleep much for weeks after my father's death. I kept flashing back to scenes of him dying in my arms while I was caring for him through the night. But then I had the extraordinary experience of my first 'lucid dream' (a dream in which the dreamer knows they're dreaming and stays asleep).

In the dream, my father was alive, and as I looked at his face, I became lucid. That is to say, I knew Dad was dead, and at the same time, I knew that I was dreaming. It felt real when I touched my father's arm. I was elated, aware and sound asleep. When I told

Dad he'd died, he looked at me, and we set off on a series of adventures. At one point, up ahead, I could see what looked like a brightly lit hospital room. I turned to Dad and said, 'We know what that's about; we don't need to go there', and then I woke up. That ended my grieving. Of course, I knew it was just a dream and that my father was dead, but realising that I could think about Dad without getting lost in his death scene reassured me. I put up a photo of my father and knew he'd always be a part of my life. Now, when I think of Dad, only good times come to mind.

Versions of our next technique have helped my clients resolve their grief. If you suffer sorrow over someone's death, perhaps it can help you.

Ψ

1. Setting up

    Before you move from one step to the next, check with your intuition that you've completed the stage you're working on. Think through and resolve any issues that arise before you continue with the procedure.

2. Make contact with the deceased

    Remember how the deceased looked when they were well and happy. Imagine that they're standing in front of you, in good health and calmly listening to what you've got to say. It's time to begin an important conversation.

3. Talk with the deceased

    In the privacy of your mind, tell the deceased how sad you are that they died. Let them know what they mean to you and how important they are. Take all the time you need to tell them everything you never got to say to them. Thank them for all they did for you. Settle any unfinished business. Only proceed when you've done all that.

4. Update the deceased

    Tell them about what's happened since they passed away. Let the deceased know how their death affected you and others. Include news about significant life events that involve people they knew. Proceed when you've done that.

5. Request advice

   Ask the deceased what they want you to do with your life. Find out how they'd like you to respond to their passing. How can you best honour their life? Only proceed when you've asked all you need to ask.

6. Say goodbye, for now

   Ask the deceased if you can call on them again in your memories, imagination and dreams. They were, still are and always will be an important part of your life. You now know you can draw on their wisdom and guidance whenever you need to. Thank them for being with you and say your goodbyes.

7. Reorient to your surrounds

   After you've done that, let them gently fade away, knowing you can call on them again anytime you want. When the time is right, open your eyes, bringing all that you've learnt with you.

Ψ

If we try to avoid grief, we leave unresolved one of the most potent stresses we'll ever encounter. It's difficult to confront death. But in time, we can accept our losses, welcome the deceased back into our lives and refocus our attention on life and the living.

This concludes our discussion of tools, tips and techniques for working with the emotions most often associated with stress. Next, we examine how we can use the key mental process of language to ride stress waves.

Chapter 9

Language

> The people of that age were phrase slaves ... There was a magic in words greater than the conjurer's art. So befuddled and chaotic were their minds that the utterance of a single word could negate the generalizations of a lifetime of serious research and thought.
> *Jack London (1876-1916)*

AS EPHEMERAL SPOKEN WORDS that dissipate with our breath or as written ideas preserved for generations to come, language changes minds, societies and history. With words, we learn from and communicate with other people. And talking to ourselves helps us think. Words have defined meanings, but like music, they also have rhyme and rhythm and come packed with implicit meanings, emotions, images and memories. When we string words into sequences, we hope their explicit meanings and subtle associations mesh to communicate what we want to say.

Words can attract, heal and strengthen. A psychotherapist practices their healing art through language. But words can also repel, harm and weaken; they're the weapons advertisers and propagandists wield to persuade and deceive.

Depending on how we use them, certain words and phrases can block or bolster our ability to ride stress waves. We'll begin with classes of words that reliably distort thinking.

Troublesome Words

Through implication, association and unconscious suggestion, troublesome words exaggerate problems and prospects, raise doubts about our character, generate guilt and cause unnecessary stress.

Generalisations

> Always and never are two words you
> should always remember never to use.
> *Wendell Johnson (1906–1965)*

Words that generalise, such as 'always,' 'every,' 'never,' 'nothing,' 'all,' 'none,' 'everybody' and 'nobody' can undermine our confidence, magnify the scale and seriousness of difficulties and amplify the power of opponents. For example, if a person panics during a stressful event and subsequently fears that they'll 'always' panic in similar situations, then that's what's likely to happen. On the other hand, trying to bolster confidence with exaggerations such as 'Nothing bothers me' or 'I always come out on top' renders the speaker potentially vulnerable to just a single, undeniable setback.

Hope and Try

The next thought experiment explores the implications embedded in the word 'try'.

Ψ

1. Repeat the phrase, 'I'll try to do better'.
2. Notice any feelings that come with saying the word 'try'.
3. Now rate how confident you feel that you'll actually do better using a 0–10 scale, where 0 is no confidence and 10 is very confident.
4. Next, repeat the phrase, 'I will do better'.
5. Notice any emotion that comes with that sentence.
6. Now rate how confident you feel that you'll actually do better using the above 0–10 scale.

7. Compare your ratings and the feelings that each statement engendered.

Ψ

Could you sense a different emotional, and perhaps motivational, effect when you said the two sentences?

For many, when they use the word 'try', it carries a subtle implication that failure is possible, perhaps even likely. If you were distressed, would you prefer someone to say, 'Try to relax', or would a simple reassurance such as 'You're okay' be better? If a tradie tells you they'll try to finish a job on time, how confident would that make you feel? And 'try' is not the only word that automatically generates doubt.

Hope is a wonderful emotion in dire times. As Desmond Tutu put it, 'Hope is being able to see that there is light despite all of the darkness'. But when it's used as a verb, 'hope' can foster doubt. Would someone saying 'I hope so' reassure or concern you?

Must and Should

The psychologist Albert Ellis claimed that 'must' and 'should' are two of the most energy-sapping words in the English language.[1] He coined the cheeky term musturbation for the too-frequent use of the word 'must'. When we're under pressure, the words 'must' and 'should' deliver an emotional punch and conjure up negative feelings that muddy our thinking.

We'll explore this effect with the next two thought experiments. You'll need to pay close attention because the sentences we'll work with are mundane and unemotional.

Ψ

1. Say a few times the sentence, 'I must buy some milk'.
2. Notice any emotion that comes with saying that.
3. Then rate the feeling on a scale where 0 is no emotion and 10 is very strong emotion.

4. Now repeat the sentence, 'I want to buy some milk'.
5. Notice any feeling that comes with that statement.
6. Rate the emotion on the same scale where 0 is no emotion and 10 is very strong emotion.

Ψ

Did you sense any difference when you switched from saying 'must' to 'want'? If you noticed a change, can you identify the feeling engendered by the word 'must'? Is there somewhere in or on your body where you feel this?

Many people report that using the word 'must' makes them feel pressured, and they most often locate the impact in their stomach or chest.

Given that such a trivial statement about milk can induce any negative feeling at all, it's no wonder self-talk peppered with statements such as 'I must get over this' or 'I must get back to work' can hinder healing and the mental processing of stress.

Let's look at another pressure word that induces a different unpleasant emotion.

Ψ

1. Please say a few times, 'I should do more to help'.
2. Notice any feeling that comes when you say that. Can you describe the feeling?
3. Then rate the feeling on a scale where 0 is no emotion and 10 is very strong emotion.
4. Now say, 'I would like to do more to help'.
5. Notice how that feels. Can you describe the feeling?
6. Then rate the emotion using the same 0–10 scale.

Ψ

The effect of the word 'should' is subtle, but for people who use it frequently, the word can foster a sense of obligation. In our thought experiment, the word 'should' can make us feel guilty because it implies we'd be negligent if we didn't do more to help. For someone who's depressed, using the word 'should' can be immobilising. And when we direct a 'should' statement to other people, as in 'They should do this', the word encourages a critical, judgmental attitude that may or may not be appropriate.

If you find yourself overusing generalisations or the words 'try', 'hope', 'must' or 'should', notice when you use them and work out how to better express what you want. For instance, you might substitute 'could' for 'should'. For my client, "Rhonda", her depression lifted when she changed her habitual use of the word 'must'. Rhonda didn't limit herself to saying 'I must clean the house' and 'I must do the shopping'; she even made demands on the weather by saying, 'We must get some rain'. How could she not feel pressured? Rhonda felt better when she learnt to use alternative sentences such as 'It would be good if we get some rain' and 'I'd like to do the shopping'.

Next, we look at language that directs our attention to what we don't want to think about.

Negative Language

What happens when you read, 'Don't think of a black horse'? Of course, you think of a black horse. Could you do otherwise? So why did you do what I asked you not to do?

When I read that sentence, it's as if I have to think about the black horse before I apply the 'do not' instruction. 'Do not' statements force us to think about what we want to avoid, and this undermines our motivation to improve things. And when we use negation to communicate with others, they have to think about what it is we don't want them to do or think about.

Our next thought experiment explores the effects of negative language.

Ψ

1. Imagine that you're about to give a speech when someone comes up to you and says, 'Don't be nervous.'
2. Notice how this advice makes you feel. Identify the emotion.
3. Now rate how confident you feel about giving the speech on a scale where 0 is no confidence at all and 10 is very confident.

4. Again, imagine you're about to give a speech, but this time somebody says to you, 'You'll be great.'
5. Notice the feelings that come with this statement, and rate your confidence about giving the speech using the above 0–10 scale.
6. Compare your emotional response and the confidence ratings for each statement.

Ψ

Could you sense the effect of the negation? Did it induce you to think about feeling nervous, even though that's the last thing you'd want to do at such a time?

"Terry" sought my advice about difficulties he was having with self-hypnosis. He'd read a book on the subject and had inadvertently scripted all his self-hypnotic suggestions in the negative, along the lines, 'I don't feel hungry', 'I will not eat fatty foods', 'I won't smoke tobacco'. Terry couldn't understand why he was still hungry and smoking more. Terry's executive mind knew what he wanted to achieve, but he kept giving himself confusing messages that unintentionally focussed his attention on the things he didn't like. Terry was back on track when he began to talk to himself about what he wanted, not what he didn't want.

When I was a teenager learning to ride a trail bike down mountain tracks, a friend taught me to fix my eyes where I wanted the front wheel to go. He said, 'If you look at the ruts, you'll be in them'. My friend's advice was sound. Saying such things as 'Don't be nervous' and 'Don't look at the ruts' makes the thing you want to avoid more likely to occur. Another mate, who's been a top-class cricketer, was advised by a test-team player, 'When you're batting, only look at the gaps between fielders; never look at the fielders'.

Our next thought experiment examines the differing impacts of two alternate versions of self-talk that deal with similar concerns.

Ψ

Compare the effects of running the following two versions of self-talk in your mind.

Script 1: 'I must try to go to the gym today because I don't want to end up dying from a heart attack. I should go every day, but I always find an excuse for not wanting to go. I hope I don't back out today.'

Script 2: 'I want to go to the gym today to keep up with the grandchildren. Sometimes I find excuses not to go — and that's okay — but today I am up for the exercise because I want to be fit and healthy!'

Ψ

Keep your eyes and mind on where you want to go and what you want to achieve. Avoid negations and express what you say to yourself and others in positive terms.

We next examine the impact of positive and negative language when we motivate ourselves.

Motivation Style

> In the long run you hit only what you aim at.
> Therefore, though you should fail immediately,
> you had better aim at something high.
> *Henry David Thoreau (1817–1862)*

I smoked tobacco when I was a young man. Back then, television quit-smoking ads warned of illness and death as they showed tar being wrung from lung-shaped sponges. As intended, these ads made me anxious. So like other smokers, when I saw them, I reached for a cigarette. I justified my avoidant response with the thought: 'If I've damaged my lungs, one more smoke won't make much difference'. Thankfully, a medico friend undid that nonsense for me. He told me to forget all that 'stuff about lung cancer'. He said the best reason for quitting tobacco is that your lungs will heal, you'll get your wind back and, in a few years, you'll be as fit as ever. This information transformed the way I motivated myself. I was no longer trying to avoid the harm.

Now I wanted the health benefits that quitting cigarettes would bring. And when the nicotine withdrawal bit, I concentrated on the positive reasons why I was giving up. I've been a non-smoker ever since.

The problem with negative quit-smoking campaigns is that they trigger the very anxiety that people smoke tobacco to avoid. You can try to frighten yourself out of smoking, but it's easier to stick with a new routine when you focus on the good things — the health, fitness and extra cash — that come with being a non-smoker. Here's one more example of positive motivation.

When I help clients prepare for surgery, I encourage them to think about the benefits that the operation will bring. With their executive mind enjoying positive images of the future, their deep mind can take care of all they have to do before, during and after the surgery to realise their goal of attaining good health.

Mental processing is easier when your executive mind looks ahead rather than back. Set your sights on the change you want to achieve and work out how you'll get there. Head towards what you want, not away from what you don't want. And be patient with yourself when the old negative thinking reappears, as it inevitably will for a while.

Names and Labels

In Shakespeare's romantic tragedy, *Romeo and Juliet*, Juliet questions the significance of her lover's family name: 'Tis but thy name that is my enemy; thou art thyself ... O, be some other name! What's in a name? That which we call a rose by any other name would smell as sweet ...' (Act 2, Scene 2).[2]

Was Juliet right? If we called roses 'skunk weed' or 'bog flower' would they smell as sweet?

Names matter. People tend to see males with ever-popular Biblical names such as Matthew, Mark, Luke and John as more credible. I read that using the middle initial in your name increases positive evaluations of a person's intellectual capacities and achievements. What do you think? Do I sound smarter as 'Dr Wayne Somerville' or 'Dr Wayne R. Somerville'? But the power of names goes beyond affecting our impressions of things, other people and ourselves.

Names can powerfully affect how we think about and react to environmental stress waves. Susan was a member of a government-appointed working group that needed a name for the then-newly-identified dieback ravaging native forests along Australia's eastern seaboard. The committee knew that wherever you found dying trees, there were plague numbers of the noisy, native bell miner bird, so it seemed appropriate to name the problem 'bell miner associated dieback' (BMAD). Our next thought experiment explores the implicit power of this name to affect how we think about and respond to stress.

Ψ

1. Say the phrase 'bell miner associated dieback' a few times.
2. Then rate your feelings about the bell miner bird on a scale where 0 is very negative and 10 is very positive.
3. Now repeat the statement, 'To solve the dieback problem, we need to do something about bell miners'.
4. Rate how much you agree with this statement using a scale where 0 is strongly disagree and 10 is strongly agree.

Ψ

Did associating the name bell miner with dieback induce a somewhat negative feeling about the bird? Were you inclined to agree with the claim that, to treat the dieback, we need to do something about bell miners? If you did, you're not alone.

On the strength of these name-generated ideas, thousands of native birds were shot or mist-netted and euthanised for no worthwhile result. Bell miner associated dieback is a poor name for the problem. The moniker obscures the true nature of the threat, misleads thinking and blocks an appropriate response to the stress. As I'll explain later, the invasive weed lantana is the true villain. You cure the dieback by removing the lantana, not the native bird.

If you re-run the above thought experiment, replacing each mention of 'bell miner associated dieback' with 'lantana associated dieback,' you'll see why I think the latter would be a better name for the problem. But it's too late for that now.

Our next imaginal exercise investigates the effect that the names we use for one of the greatest environmental threats of our age, the destabilised climate, have on how we react to this stress.

Ψ

1. Say the word 'change' a few times.
2. Notice the emotion that comes with the word. Rate the feeling on a scale where 0 is very negative and 10 is very positive.
3. Now repeat the phrase 'climate change' a few times.
4. Notice any emotion that the phrase evokes. Rate the feeling on a scale of 0 to 10, where 0 is very negative and 10 is very positive.
5. Finally, say 'global warming' a few times.
6. Notice any emotion associated with the phrase. Rate the feeling on our 0–10 scale.

Ψ

Did you associate any positive or negative emotions with the word 'change'? For me, the word elicits neutral feelings. After all, change can be good or bad. It's an opportunity to make things better or worse.

When you rated your emotional reactions to the labels 'climate change' and 'global warming', did either phrase feel more or less favourable than the other?

The fossil fuel industry sought to derail the debate about human impacts on climate by attacking the global warming label. They argued that record-breaking blizzards prove that the build-up of atmospheric greenhouse gases can't be making the planet warmer. Unfortunately, in response to this dodgy argument, climate scientists changed the name and made matters worse.

Could there be a more innocuous and inaccurate label for what's happening to global weather systems than to call it 'climate change'? Imagine the fossil fuel industry spiel: 'Who knows? We might get more rain, even if somewhere else becomes drier. If the Arctic melts, the Northwest Passage will open, and we can drill for more oil and gas. Humans are adaptable. Let's leverage climate change to our advantage.'

The problem is not that the climate is changing. The threat we face in the Anthropocene (the epoch in which human activity changes Earth's geology and ecosystems) arises not from a changing climate per se but from the radical destabilisation of the Earth's weather systems. Agriculture and the growth of civilisations have only been possible in the stable climate that humans have enjoyed during the 12,000 years since the last Ice Age. But now, escalating atmospheric levels of carbon and trapped solar energy push climate systems towards tipping points.

Global warming is a more accurate label than climate change, but it doesn't properly describe the threat. The name connotes a gentle, tactile image of warmth, which doesn't sound so bad. A better label for the problem would be 'climate crisis', 'climate disaster' or 'climate destabilisation'. These words more accurately represent the news we hear about the constant resetting of records for land and ocean temperatures; unprecedented storms, droughts and floods; rising levels of atmospheric methane and carbon dioxide; the retreat of glaciers and polar ice, and the rest.

Beyond the destabilised climate, names and labels feature in political debates and obstruct rational thinking. I've heard politicians slander citizens who oppose damaging developments as 'green ideologues', 'extremists', 'lunatics', 'radicals' and 'eco-fascists'. But by definition, 'conservative' describes people who want to conserve ways of life that have worked in the past. Conserving water, air and soil used to be an uncontroversial traditional value, at least for country people, but it's been usurped by the goal of 'conserving profits'. Conversely, 'radical' and 'extreme' are appropriate descriptors for those who would force harmful, irreversible changes onto communities and natural systems.

Subtle phrase changes also affect the way we think about ourselves, other people and the kind of society we live in. Worse still, these words can impede the ability of trauma survivors to resolve their stress. If we think of folk who are poor, displaced or doing it tough as 'down on their luck', the phrase fosters compassion and a desire to help. By contrast, if we describe those not well off as 'losers' or 'leaners', these words encourage a hard-hearted, uncharitable attitude. Similarly, using such terms when we think about ourselves can block us from processing stress.

Our next thought experiment explores a word used widely by advertisers to sell products and, in political discourse, to block deeper thinking about environmental threats.

Ψ

1. Say the word 'natural' a few times.
2. Notice any emotion that comes with this word. Rate the feeling on a scale where 0 is very negative and 10 is very positive.
3. Now say the word 'gas' a few times.
4. Notice any emotion that comes with the word. Rate the feeling on a scale where 0 is very negative and 10 is very positive.
5. Finally, repeat the phrase 'natural gas' a few times.
6. Notice any associated emotion and rate the feeling on our 0–10 scale.

Ψ

What feeling did the word 'natural' by itself induce? For me, it conjures mainly positive associations because it suggests Nature and is the opposite of artificial.

How did you rate the emotions associated with the word 'gas'? For me, 'gas' conjures mostly neutral feelings.

With the combined words 'natural gas', could you sense positive feelings engendered by the word 'natural' transfer to the word 'gas'? Did you rate 'natural gas' more positively than you rated 'gas' by itself?

'Natural' gets attached to many words, such as natural foods and natural lifestyle, to cite two examples from thousands. Early on, the gas industry rebranded coal seam gas as natural gas. Pro-industry advertisements featured the words paired with pictures of paddocks, horses and actors acting like happy farmers, with ne'er a gas well in sight. They wanted to link their product to the positive feelings associated with such images and the word 'natural'. The gas industry's advertising eased the anxiety of threatened communities for a while, but only by preventing people from thinking about the negative impacts of the proposed development. The natural-gas word spell was easily countered.

Methane is indeed natural: it exists in Nature. However, the industrialisation and pollution caused by coal and shale seam gas mining are made by man. Counter-slogans readily came to mind: 'Coal seam gas: it's natural, like arsenic, cancer and death'.

Talking About Stress

Talking with a trusted person is a valuable tool for working through stress. Converting ideas into spoken language forces us to order our thoughts and make them explicit; this helps us work out what we truly know and think. Expressing a thought out loud can instantly reveal flaws in our reasoning and whether we're using any of the troublesome words and language patterns that impede mental processing. Discussing matters with someone else also gives us new information and a different perspective. But to safely use the tool of talking with others, there are some ground rules to follow.

We and our conversation partner need to agree that the dialogue will continue until the stress is properly addressed; the discussion shouldn't be a one-off event. Working through a tangled issue takes time and a willingness to go down dead-end detours, and both participants have to be free to change their minds. Real harm can be done if we only talk about stress once and do so in public.

Describing a distressing experience to a group of people was a core component of a counselling technique known as 'critical incident stress debriefing' (CISD).[3] During the 1980s and '90s, when I debriefed police officers, bank staff, train drivers and others exposed to trauma, the then-standard procedure was to have people talk in a group about how they felt during the incident. We now know that, during post-trauma debriefing, participants should not be asked to relive or recount what happened or how they felt.

In the U.S., the health of people who described their feelings during group counselling soon after the 9/11 attacks on the World Trade Center was monitored for two years.[4] It turned out that those who chose not to speak did better than those who talked. Nowadays, television reporters sometimes interview survivors during the immediate aftermath of a catastrophe and ask how they felt during the event. Such questioning can seriously compromise mental health. But why would discussing what happened during a severe stress cause harm?

During the traumas in my life, things sometimes seemed unreal, as if I was in a dream. Our nocturnal dreams are dense with meaning and detail, but we usually don't remember them. Dreams arise in visual and intuitive areas of the mind. Have you ever woken from a vivid dream you thought you'd never forget, only to lose it a few minutes later? Unless we describe the dream out loud or write it down as soon as we wake, it isn't available to our daytime consciousness. Perhaps something similar happens when someone talks about what happened during a distressing incident; their dreamlike fragments of impression, feeling and meaning get consolidated into an indelible memory. And for some unfortunate folk, telling their story on national television transforms personal tragedy into public history.

Writing About Stress

To translate memories of stress events into writing, we have to take an objective perspective and reconstruct the experience in a linear sequence, from beginning to end. Since James Pennebaker's research in the 1980s and 90s, we've known that a few days of brief sessions of writing can help relieve problematic stress responses.[5]

In a 2024 interview, Pennebaker attributed the therapeutic effect of 'expressive writing' to engagement with, and cognitive processing of, the stress.[6] He observed that while we're writing, we have to think about the incident, which sets us 'pondering' and perhaps talking to other people. And according to Pennebaker, constructing self-contained, individual sentences to express an idea, and then arranging these sentences into sequential order, 'forces' us to restructure how we think about the stress.

I've never asked a client to write briefly about stress, but two of my clients have written books, and both benefitted from doing so. For one client, a member of an elite police unit, the task of writing a book about his career helped him process traumas that he'd never discussed. The protracted exercise of writing, editing and publishing his book changed how he dealt with his stress reactions. For my other client, writing a book assisted him to resolve longstanding traumas as he recovered from a medical crisis.

When I conceived the idea of writing this book a few years ago, I knew that if I followed through, the experience would change me, and it has. I recommend writing as a great way to figure out what you know about something. It's not easy for me to arrange my thoughts into a coherent story, but doing so has taught me much.

You might like to experiment with the tool of writing about your stress in the form of poetry, a short story or even a book.

We now shift from language to tools, tips, and techniques for using our key mental processes of thought and reason to ride stress waves.

Chapter 10

Thinking and Reasoning

Change your thoughts if you wish to change your circumstances. Since you alone are responsible for your thoughts, only you can change them…Therefore, start now to think only those thoughts that will bring you health and happiness.
Paramahansa Yogananda (1893–1952)

IN THIS CHAPTER, WE'LL discuss forms of thinking and reasoning that affect mental processing. We'll also work with tools and techniques that utilise rational thought to ride stress waves.

Thinking Styles

Psychologists distinguish between 'field-dependent' and 'field-independent' thinking. Someone who employs field-dependent thought focusses primarily on cues from the external environment. They're especially influenced by others and the world around them. In contrast, someone who uses field-independent thinking looks inward for guidance. They base their thinking and reasoning on their ideas and beliefs rather than on the perceived opinions and reactions of others.

Too much reliance on thinking at either extreme of the dependent–independent dimension can block our mental processing of stress. If we adopt a field-dependent orientation, we're prone to overlook or downplay our own needs and interests.

Conversely, relying on field-independent thinking can lead to our not taking into account the opinions and needs of others. When riding a stress wave, use both thinking styles. Consider both your and other people's feelings and perspective.

A related cognitive style contrasts 'principle-based' and 'emotion-focussed' thinking. When a person's thinking is based on principles, they act according to their understanding of what's appropriate, even if that entails personal distress. In contrast, when a person's thinking is focussed on how they feel, they're more likely to avoid taking on stress if doing so would require effort or make them uncomfortable.

When we're dealing with severe stress, a reliance on avoidant coping strategies, combined with field-dependent and emotion-focussed thinking, greatly diminishes our prospects of success. Thinking this way would have us look only to others for direction, and we'd be unlikely to effectively resolve the threat.

Again, when dealing with stress, it's best to use a judicious balance of principles-based and emotion-focused thinking styles.

The Fallacy of Hindsight and the 'What Ifs'

Asking 'what if' questions about the past, present or future is productive when we're considering how we'll handle a stress wave. But there are times when this otherwise useful tool can get in our way.

Catastrophic thinking begins with 'what if' questions such as 'What if I'd been in the car accident?' or 'What if the bushfire destroys our house?' Asking too many 'what if' questions distracts our attention from what's actually happening and interferes with our ability to learn from setbacks and near misses. No good comes from dwelling on unpleasant things that have already occurred or from worrying unproductively about what yet might take place.

In a related pattern of thinking known as the 'fallacy of hindsight', our executive mind focusses on things that happened in the past which, from our current perspective, appear obviously ill-advised. Questioning why we did or didn't do something can help us learn from the past, but merely ruminating and going over and over what happened restricts our attention and blocks mental processing.

To counter what-if thinking and the fallacy of hindsight, understand that back then, when the initial stress event occurred, you didn't know what you know now. When what-if thinking traps you in the past or the future, ask whether the answer to your question can teach you anything of value now, in the present. If so, explore and learn from what you've done and think through what you might do. But if there's not much left to learn, drop the what-ifs and switch to more productive thinking.

Flawed Reasoning

If we fall prey to 'polarised thinking' — also known as 'black-or-white' or 'all-or-nothing' logic — we frame ideas and experiences in rigid, absolute terms so there's no nuance or middle ground. A situation is good or bad. We either succeed or we fail. But the world doesn't work like that; things are rarely all good or all bad, and no one always succeeds or always fails. With polarised thinking, there's a risk we'll interpret minor setbacks as complete failures and give up on our goal of achieving optimal mental health.

A person who uses the cognitive operation known as 'filtering', draws conclusions from just one part of an event. After a severe stress, their thinking gets stuck on an aspect of what happened, and they ignore, or 'filter out', everything else. For instance, a trauma survivor might only think about something they regret doing and ignore the times when they acted in a way they could be proud of.

'Personalisation' is a form of filtering that leads to the conclusion that we or others are to blame for a distressing event when, in fact, external factors were more important in determining the outcome. 'Discounting the positive' is another version of filtered reasoning that doesn't just ignore positive information; it explicitly rejects it. For example, someone might think, 'Judy said I looked nice today, but she was just being kind, and I look awful'. People with pessimistic beliefs use this logic when they attribute their success solely to luck. Pessimistic beliefs also encourage 'magnification', the thought pattern that automatically exaggerates our shortcomings and discounts our desirable qualities.

When people indulge in 'mind reading' or 'fortune telling', they assume, with no good reason or real evidence, that they know what someone is thinking or how they'll react. For example, if someone believes they'll never be able to control their emotions, they're fortune-telling. If they take it for granted that a frowning person must be angry with them, they're mind-reading. Habitual fortune telling and mind reading cut the user off from the real world around them and limits their ability to think realistically.

When we want to identify and rejig problematic thought patterns, reason gives us some ideal tools for the job.

Reasoned Thought

> I know you won't believe me, but the highest form of Human Excellence is to question oneself and others.
> Socrates (469–399 B.C.E.)

Our ability to reason makes it possible for us to see distorted thinking patterns for what they are: unnecessary, avoidable and correctable errors of logic. To free ourselves from such negative, limiting beliefs, we have to notice when they hijack our thinking and work out where the truth lies. We can thank the ancient Greek philosopher Socrates for giving us the mental processing tool of 'Socratic questioning'.

The Socratic method has us ask a series of targeted questions to critically evaluate how we're thinking. With this tool, we actively challenge our thoughts to pare away false assumptions and illogical thinking to reveal deeper truths and insights. This new information becomes grist for further mental processing. Socratic questioning helps us to clarify issues, investigate the impact of beliefs and thoughts, and find new, better ways of thinking and behaving. With practice, you can apply the technique to any issue, emotion or thought you encounter as you ride stress waves.

In the next exercise, I'll use a common negative self-belief to illustrate how you might employ Socratic questioning to overcome obstacles to your mental processing.

Ψ

1. Your task

    Assume that you think you're a failure who always gets things wrong. Imagine how you might respond to the following questions that challenge your beliefs.

2. Clarify the issue

    Could you explain why you think that? Can you give examples of what you mean? How do you feel when you think that? What's the main issue for you here?

3. Look for exceptions

    Have you ever done something well? Can you give an example of when you succeeded or got things right? What was different on those occasions?

4. Explore history

    Has anyone ever said such things to you? When you say them to yourself, can you hear anyone else voicing similar things? Have you always felt this way? How old were you when you first had that thought?

5. Challenge assumptions

    What assumptions are you making here? Is it possible to take a different point of view? Do you think that you can change these beliefs?

6. Check evidence and reasoning

    What evidence do you have for believing that about yourself? How reliable is that evidence? Do you have all the information you need to understand why you think those things? Is there any evidence that contradicts your statements?

7. Seek alternative viewpoints

Can you argue against your negative beliefs? Is there another way of looking at things? If someone close to you thought that about themselves, what would you say to them? Do you need to keep this old way of thinking about yourself? Could you think differently?

8. Evaluate implications and consequences

How does thinking like this affect you? If other people you know thought like that, how would it affect them? What are the long-term implications of these beliefs? What's the worst thing about thinking like this? What's the best thing about believing these things? How would you feel if you didn't think this way?

Ψ

Holistic Thinking

The advent of the digital computer transformed psychology and inspired new ways of thinking about ourselves and the environment. The new perspective was holistic, and the focus shifted from causal connections between isolated, elementary parts to appreciating how entire systems operate. From the mid-1960s, cognitive psychologists created models of attention, perception, imagery, memory, beliefs and all our other mental processes. In biology, scientists began to think about our world and all it contains as a complex, interacting system.

It was the late 1980s, and "Andrew", a family therapist, was briefing me for a session at a community health unit. I was to watch through a one-way mirror while another psychologist worked with a disturbed family in the next room. Andrew had a task for me. He showed me the intake notes and asked for seven hypotheses (possible explanations) about why this family was troubled. This was our warm-up: a flexing of mental muscles to get us ready for the creative effort of finding a way to resolve this family's stress. As our colleague in the next room interviewed family members, we tossed around ideas about what could be going wrong.

Andrew was an expert in what's known as 'systemic family therapy': an approach that assumes that problems serve a positive function in a disturbed family. Andrew taught me to think of the family as a system in which each member plays a role. The family system was stuck in a way that was creating distress. Our job was to inject new information, which might change the way members thought and interacted. We hoped that this would shift the family towards better mental health. Years later, I remembered this training when Susan and I confronted a huge stress wave that threatened the native forests on our property. Dear Reader, please indulge me as I give you some background context before I return to our discussion of holistic thinking.

When we arrived in the Northern Rivers region of New South Wales in the 1970s, the local forests were accessible; we could walk or ride horses pretty much where we wanted. We assumed that our heavily logged forests would regenerate if we stopped cutting them down and kept cattle out until the bush recovered: we practised a kind of 'passive silviculture'. By the early 1990s, we knew we had it wrong. Our forests were in deep trouble, and we didn't know what to do about it.

Everywhere that logging had disturbed the canopy, the invasive weed lantana (*Lantana camara*) now grew as tall as a house. The weed formed an impenetrable barrier. We couldn't hack into the forest with a machete, let alone ride a horse there. Once-abundant koalas, gliders, possums and other native animals that needed to move along the ground had disappeared. In 1999, we looked across the valley and saw that the natural blue-green tinge of the eucalypt forests was turning an unhealthy-looking brown and spreading in a front. This was our first contact with the ecological catastrophe known as bell miner associated dieback, which you heard about earlier when we discussed the power of names.

We faced stress waves on two fronts. We had no practicable way to control the lantana in our steep, rugged country, and we didn't know why the trees were dying or if there was anything we could do about it. Grieving for what we'd lost and depressed about our ailing forests, we thought about leaving. But then, a series of events transformed how we responded to the stress. In 2005, a national dieback forum produced a review of the scientific literature, but offered no practical solution to the problem.[1] Then I remembered my family therapy training.

I was thinking about the relationship between trees, insects, birds and lantana when I realised that a forest is like a big family. From a family therapist's perspective, the task was to figure out what was disturbing the forest's equilibrium and how we might trigger natural healing. Susan and I compared healthy and dieback-affected forests, and there were clear differences. Dieback-free areas had little to no lantana, diverse bird life, healthy lower and mid-storey plants and an intact canopy. The sick forest was just lantana, with dead and dying trees and abundant bell miners. Thinking of the forest as a system, I drew up the following model of a pathogenic feedback cycle that could drive the dieback.

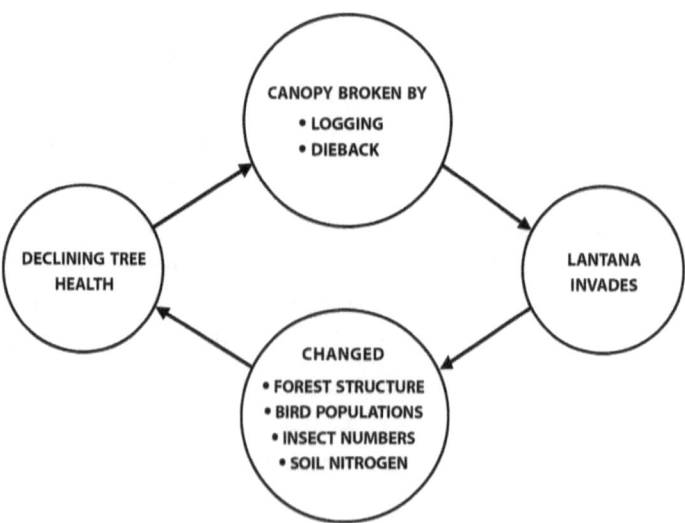

A Systems Model of Forest Dieback

When logging breaks the canopy, lantana invades, replacing the native ground cover and forest mid-storey. The weed increases nitrogen and phosphorus in the soil and in the leaves of trees, which attracts sap-sucking insects known as 'psyllids'. Meanwhile, the lantana protects bell miner nests from currawongs, goannas and other egg predators. With this breeding advantage, bell miner populations increase, and this aggressive, territorial species chases away other birds that usually eat the insects. The psyllid insects form 'lerps' (sugary coatings) over themselves, which birds like to eat. However, due to a quirk of nature, when the bell miners eat the lerps, their beaks do not remove the underlying insects. Consequently, the psyllid forms another sugary coating, and insect numbers explode. Trees repeatedly defoliate in a futile attempt to throw off the insects. Seed production fails, trees die and the forest ecosystem collapses.[2]

Looking at our model, we asked where we might break the vicious cycle of forest decline. Even if we could change soil chemistry, kill all the bell miners or inject trees with insecticides, we'd still have a landscape covered in lantana. Psyllid insects and bell miners are native to the Australian bush; logging and lantana are the only out-of-place factors. That led us to a cure for dieback: remove the lantana and keep it out until the canopy recovers and the forest heals itself.[2] As with family therapy, we needed to identify and change a key factor causing the trouble so that the forest system could return to health.

Systems thinking was also crucial for the development of sustainable agriculture and grazing practices.[3] In the mid-1950s, scientist Allan Savory worked on the problem of desertification in what is now Zimbabwe. Earlier in his career, Savory accepted the mainstream belief that overgrazing degrades grasslands. The solution seemed obvious, and some 40,000 elephants were slaughtered to no good effect. This tragic failure forced Savory and others to change the way they thought about the problem.

They wondered how the original native grasslands of Africa and North America had maintained fertility and supported grazing herds for millennia. This led them to thinking about natural grassland as a system.[3]

Savory's 'holistic management' and other contemporary regenerative farming practices are based on the realisation that, in natural grasslands, predators don't allow herbivores to graze for long in one place. Big cats, wolves and other hunters keep the herds confined and moving so the grass never gets eaten to the ground. The animals' hooves and manure aerate and fertilise the soil but don't pulverise or overload it with nutrients. Beneath the ground, the length of chewed-down grass is matched by an equivalent dying back of roots, which adds carbon to the soil. But boundary fencing and hunting prevented herds from travelling far and reduced the number of predators. Savory's revolutionary solution was to mimic the natural system by having farmers frequently move their stock from one confined area to the next.

If we only think about the cause-and-effect relationships between isolated factors, we're blocked from seeing the blooming, buzzing complexity of the real world. Focus too narrowly, and we miss crucial information that we need to ride stress waves. A healthy system — be it a forest, a person or a society — can respond to a threat and successfully regain its equilibrium. When working with a stress wave that affects an entire system, look for where the natural cycle might be compromised. Compare it to other examples that are working well, identify anything you don't find in a healthy system and ask how this might be causing stress. From this, you can get clues to where you might intervene.

For me, systems thinking has been an invaluable tool; it helped me with some of the biggest stress waves in my life. Comparing the psychological functioning of people who, after a trauma, did or didn't develop a posttraumatic stress reaction alerted me to the role played by intrusive thoughts and memories, and these became the targets of my therapeutic interventions.

THINKING AND REASONING

Comparing healthy and unhealthy forests led to our identifying lantana, not a native bird, as the key problem-causing factor in forest dieback. Perhaps you'll be able to apply holistic thinking to some of the stress waves that come your way.

From thought and reasoning, our focus now shifts to the key mental process of attention itself.

Chapter 11

Attention and Awareness

> No problem can withstand the
> assault of sustained thinking.
> *Voltaire (1694–1778)*

OUR PHENOMENAL CONSCIOUSNESS (the rich reality of our subjective experience) is constrained by whatever we pay attention to. This key mental process enables us to concentrate on a threat or challenge long enough to work out what we'll do about it. When we know how to use them, meditation, contemplation and 'metacognition' are valuable tools for practising the art of riding stress waves.

Meditation

Meditation practices expand our ability to sustain and focus awareness; meditation strengthens our 'mental muscle' of attention.

During meditation, the executive mind focusses on an object (e.g., a mandala, flame or flower), an idea or feeling (e.g., compassion or loving kindness) or an activity (e.g., breathing, praying with rosary beads or reciting a mantra) as we allow distracting thoughts and self-talk to come and go without our engaging with them.

There are many meditation techniques. In 'concentrative meditation', attention is fixed on one particular object, a sensation or an area on the body. Practitioners of 'mindfulness meditation' aim to maintain a non-judgemental awareness of everything in their perceptual field at that moment; they cultivate mindfulness as their attention drifts around their body or the external environment.

My preferred mediation practice is to sit quietly for half an hour or so as I focus on my breathing, allowing thoughts and perceptions to come and go.

Contemplation

When we practice contemplation, we focus our executive mind on some phenomenon, experience, concept or situation. But unlike most meditative practices, during contemplation, we look for insights. To this end, we deliberately engage with, investigate and think deeply about what we're attending to.

Some traditional forms of meditation incorporate contemplation by encouraging practitioners to concentrate on such matters as life and death, 'karma' (the sum of a person's actions in this and previous incarnations that decide their fate in future lives), spiritual 'liberation' (the recognition that all things are essentially variants of an underlying unity), the vastness of the universe and the nature of the human condition.

Metacognition

Metacognition is our ability to be aware of, understand and work with our thought processes; it's thinking about thinking. We practice metacognition when we seek to understand and change how we think and do things. This awareness tool allows us to take a perspective that's 'above' and outside our usual thinking. A more objective point of view can help us learn from our experiences and apply the new knowledge when we're dealing with stress.

Chapter 12

Perception

> If the doors of perception were cleansed everything would appear to man as it is, Infinite. For man has closed himself up, till he sees all things thro' narrow chinks of his cavern.
> *William Blake (1757–1827)*

THE KEY MENTAL PROCESS OF perception generates our world of subjective experience. At the boundary where our bodies end and the external world begins, our seven senses of sight, hearing, touch, taste, smell, proprioception (our sense of bodily position, location, orientation and movement) and interoception (our sense of the internal state of our bodies) let us know what's happening in and around us.

It seems simple enough. Our visual sense works like a camera; what we see is accurate, and things are pretty much as we perceive them to be. We interact effectively with our environment, so reality must be orderly and predictable. But things are not as straightforward as they seem at first.

When photons (massless elementary particles that make up electromagnetic radiation) vibrate with a frequency human eyes can detect, they pass through the lens and fall in an upside-down pattern onto the back of our eyes. The photons land on the retina, a flat sheet of light-sensitive cells, and the optic nerve registers them as a hit. This is the physical interface between us and the world around us. When we're awake, our subjective reality is generated from this two-dimensional pattern of photons striking the back of our eyeballs.

It's a similar process for all our senses. The mind builds what we hear from two-dimensional patterns of vibrating air particles that hit our eardrums. A sensitive arrangement of tiny bones behind the eardrum transmits the impact to the auditory nerve. Sensations of taste and smell arise from cells in the nose and tongue that register contact with substances.

We can never know what another human or animal is experiencing. Perceptions of reality differ from person to person, and a fly, a bird and a horse see the world differently from us and from each other. Each being experiences reality through internally generated perceptions that function like the instruments on a car's dashboard. Information about speed, location, outside temperature, fuel, oil pressure and other metrics allow us to monitor what's happening in and outside our vehicle, but this information is only a representation of what's really going on; it's a 'map' and is not the 'territory' itself. By analogy, our perceptions tell us about what's happening inside and around us. But like the car's dashboard, this represents what's in us and out there and is not the underlying reality itself.

Our perceptions serve us well. Even though the world we know differs radically from that perceived by, say, a bird, our and the bird's senses accurately and reliably identify objects that need to be avoided. If our eyes are open, neither we nor the bird are likely to collide with a tree. But it's when our senses deceive us with perceptual illusions that we can gain a deeper insight into how our minds create reality.

Consider the following optical illusions.

In the next graphic, the logs across the road are the same length. Knowing this, can you make the logs look the same? I can only see the further log as longer than the nearer one.

Logs on Road Illusion

For me, this illusion says something about how context distorts the way we judge the scale of obstacles.

Can you see the old woman in the following drawing?

Woman Illusion

Can you also make out the elegant young woman?

It's easy to see each woman in turn, but not simultaneously.

In the next illusion, created by Edward Adelson, the squares on the chequerboard marked A and B are the same shade and colour.

Chequerboard Illusion

Don't take my word for it. Cover the other squares with your fingers or cut holes in a piece of paper so you see only the two labelled squares.

It doesn't matter how hard you try; you can't make the logs in the first graphic appear equal in length, you can't see the old and the young woman simultaneously, and you can't make the chequerboard squares look the same. These are not tricks. There's no deception or sleight of hand involved. So where are these illusions created? It can't be in the figures themselves. Nor can the perceptual errors occur in the space between us and the graphics. We have to conclude that the illusion somehow arises in our minds and is projected outwards, so it appears to be out there.

Determining the colour of things has been essential for human survival, and our perceptual system evolved to detect differences in a forested world with lots of shadows. In the chequerboard illusion, the task for our mind is to determine the colour of the squares, but that decision can't be based solely on the actual light reflected off the chequerboard. In the real world, shadows vary the intensity of light, and our mind has evolved strategies to identify and compensate for this effect. That accounts for the chequerboard illusion. Our mind expects a regular arrangement of squares, considers the shadow and decides what the pattern of photons means. What we perceive is our mind's best guess at what's actually there.

Optical illusions teach us that powerful parts of our mind, over which we have no conscious control, determine even such fundamental things as how we see the world. The old woman/young woman illusion shows us that perception tends to be an all-or-nothing affair; an effect studied by 'gestalt' (German for 'unified whole') psychologists in the early 20th century.

Like seeing a glass as half empty or half full, what seems evident to our senses can reflect our beliefs and how we use our mental abilities. Some see nothing but bad news and portents of disaster, while others, with the same information, see grounds for hope and green shoots of promise everywhere.

Chapter 13

Memory and Imagination

> Some people go on remembering all the suffering they passed through, and how terrible the pain was, from an operation that took place 20 years ago! Over and over again they relive the consciousness of that sickness. Why repeat such experiences?
> *Paramahansa Yogananda (1893–1952)*

WITH OUR MEMORY, WE can reconstruct and learn from the past. In our imagination, we can create scenarios, envisage possible futures and work out how to improve things.

Memory is not like a library of pictures, videos and stories that accurately record what happened. Memories are never factual replays of the past; our recollections are always reconstructions.[1] This core feature of our memory accounts for hallucinations and false memories, but it also makes it possible for us to resolve past stress events, learn from them and work out what we could do differently in the future.

If we allow our memory and imagination to run on auto-pilot, with no executive-mind supervision, we're likely to experience high levels of anxiety when we recall or imagine distressing things. For traumatised people, the less control they have over the vividness and content of their imagery, the greater their distress.[2] This effect powerfully influences the way they interact with stress.

The mental health impacts of undisciplined memory and imagination arise from what psychologists call the 'functional equivalence' of perception and visual imagery.[3] This equivalence also accounts for why psychological therapies work. I'll elaborate.

When we remember or imagine something, our mind draws on mental and physiological processes similar to those activated when we experience such an event in the real world. If you vividly remember or imagine something frightening, you will feel frightened; this is genuine fear, not imaginary fear. The emotion affects your mind and body as if the threat was in front of you. That's why the flashbacks and memories associated with posttraumatic stress reactions are so damaging. It's not the trauma itself that causes the most harm. It's reliving the stress in memory and imagination that undermines health. This also explains why a problematic avoidant response can develop when someone has not directly experienced a stressful event.

For my client, "Mitch", his intrusive, distressing thoughts and memories were not of any actual trauma that he'd been exposed to during his career as a senior police officer. Rather, his recollections of 'near misses' fired up vivid, catastrophic elaborations of tragedies that never occurred.

Some of my train-driver clients suffered similarly; it was the near miss, not actual accidents, that fuelled their severe stress responses. They described incidents in which they watched, powerless, as a car accelerated when the driver decided to beat the train to an upcoming level crossing. A bridge on the North Coast rail line haunts many drivers; it's where local kids 'play chicken' with oncoming trains by delaying, to the last moment, their leap into the creek below. And sometimes, severe emotional reactions are delayed until long after the stress event passes.

A psychologist friend told me about a woman client who arrived home not long after a man burglarised her apartment. The woman had processed her stress and was doing well until, many months later, she learnt that the intruder had been apprehended and charged with murder. Her reaction was delayed but dramatic. She suffered what's known as a 'delayed-onset' posttraumatic stress reaction that was driven by her imagining what could have occurred if she'd arrived home while the burglar was still there.

In this chapter, you'll find tools, tips and techniques for using your memory and imagination to ride stress waves. I'll show you how to master your imagery and introduce you to methods for resolving stress, learning from good memories and planning what you'll do in the future.

When you practice these tools and techniques, set yourself up to succeed. Find a suitable workplace, and adjust your attitude and physical surroundings so you feel comfortable and secure and are unlikely to be interrupted. Cultivate a relaxed, open frame of mind. Explain to your partner, friends or family what you're doing and ask them to field phone calls and other interruptions.

Work at your natural pace, and please be patient with yourself. If you feel rushed or your heart isn't in it, remember that you have all the time you need and take a break.

As we've been doing, I'll sometimes ask you to rate your feelings on a scale. The first number that pops into your mind is fine. Begin and end sessions gently. A gradual return from imagery work strengthens the connections between inner experiences and our normal day-to-day consciousness.

Controlling the Emotional Impact of Imagery

> Sooner or later you need to confront what
> has happened to you, but only after you feel
> safe and will not be retraumatised by it.
> *Bessel van der Kolk (1943–)*[4]

In this exercise, we'll use a low-stress training memory to practice techniques for controlling the emotional impact of imagery. With what you learn here, you can change the sensory quality of your stress memories and reduce their emotional impact.

Ψ

1. Find a training memory

    Look for a suitable memory of someone saying something to you that made you feel a bit angry. A rude person in a shop or an irritating politician on TV — that kind of minor stress — would be fine. If you can't find such a memory, it doesn't matter. You can benefit from this exercise by just thinking about what you read.

2. Training memory criteria

    The training memory needs to satisfy all of the following conditions. It should:

    a. Involve only a mild degree of anger, say about 3 or 4 on a 0–10 point scale where 0 is no anger and 10 is extreme anger

    b. Not be a recollection of a very distressing incident or trauma or a situation that's currently causing you stress

    c. Not be especially meaningful to you

    d. Not involve family members or anyone you should respect

    Continue when you've found a training memory that meets all four criteria.

3. Check that your memory is suitable.

    You're in complete control and can open your eyes whenever you like. But for now, close your eyes and recall what happened in this training memory. Let the old feelings return and rate the emotion on a 0–10 scale where 0 is no anger and 10 is extreme anger. Proceed if you rated the angry emotion as 4 or less. If you rated it higher than that, please find another memory and check it against the suitability criteria.

4. Engage with your training memory

    With eyes closed, focus on the memory from the perspective of actually being there. Notice how that feels. Now, I'll ask you to make a series of changes to your memory. I want you to notice the feelings associated with each change and rate the accompanying emotion on our 0–10 anger scale.

MEMORY AND IMAGINATION

5. Take a third-person perspective

   Imagine that you're drawing yourself out of the scene, pulling back so you're looking on from a distance. Watch yourself and the other person over there. Notice how that feels. Rate the emotion on the 0–10 anger scale. Now switch the perspective back to how they looked when you were there. Proceed when you've done that.

6. Adjust brightness

   Make the memory much brighter, as if it's lit up. Notice how you feel and record your rating on the 0–10 anger scale. Now make the scene dull and indistinct, as if you've turned the brightness and contrast right down. Notice how that feels and rate the emotion on the 0–10 anger scale. Return the scene to its original brightness. Then proceed.

7. Compare colour versus black and white.

   Add lots of colour to the scene. Make it vibrant. Notice the feeling and rate it on the 0–10 anger scale. Return the colour to how it was in the beginning. Then proceed. Now drain the colour away so it becomes a black-and-white scene. Notice how you feel and rate the emotion on the 0–10 anger scale. Return the colour to how it was in the beginning. Then proceed.

8. Vary distance

   Bring the other person in the memory up close, so they're right in your face, saying the same provocative things to you. Notice how you feel and rate the emotion on the 0–10 anger scale. Now push the person away so they're way over there. Notice how you feel and rate the emotion on the 0–10 scale. Adjust the distance between you and the other person so it's about the same as it was in the beginning. Then proceed.

9. Change size

   Imagine that the other person is growing bigger and bigger until they're towering over you. Notice how that feels and rate the emotion on the 0–10 anger scale. Now shrink the person down until they're tiny, standing before you. Watch them carry on as before, but now they're very short. Notice how you feel and rate the emotion on the 0–10 anger scale. Return the person to their normal size. Then proceed.

10. Adjust volume

Imagine that you're turning the volume up very loud so it sounds as if the other person is shouting at you. Notice how you feel and rate the emotion on the 0–10 anger scale. Now turn the volume down so the other person is whispering. You can see their lips moving, but you must pay close attention to hear what they're saying. Notice how that feels and rate the emotion on the 0–10 anger scale. Return the volume to how it was in the beginning. Then proceed.

11. Add another person

Imagine that you're adding a supportive person to the scene, perhaps a good friend or someone strong and trustworthy. You might choose someone you know or a character from movies or television. Notice how you feel and rate the emotion on the 0–10 anger scale. Thank the person for being there and then imagine them leaving the scene. Proceed after you've done that.

12. Add a circus monkey

Imagine a circus monkey standing behind the other person. You can see the monkey, but they can't. Watch the monkey imitate everything the irritating person is saying and doing. Notice how that feels and rate the emotion on the 0–10 anger scale. Let the monkey fade away. Then proceed.

13. Substitute a cartoon voice

Give the person a cartoon voice that you think would suit them. Donald Duck, Homer Simpson, Eric Cartman, the choice is yours. When you've heard them speaking with the cartoon voice, notice how you feel and rate the emotion on the 0–10 anger scale. Return the other person's voice to normal. Listen to them saying the old things with their usual voice. Then proceed.

14. Compare negative and positive self-statements

As you interact with the other person in your memory, repeatedly say to yourself, 'I can't cope; they make me so angry'. Notice how that feels and rate the emotion on the 0–10 anger scale. Now, as you're listening to the other person, say, 'I can handle this, they can't affect me'. Notice how you feel and rate the emotion on the 0–10 anger scale. Then proceed.

15. Enhance the memory

To wrap up this exercise, I want you to adjust your memory so it has the least possible unpleasant emotional impact on you. Tweak the sensory nature of the scene to diminish the other person's impact on you. You can use any combination of the interventions we've worked with. Notice how you feel and rate the emotion on the 0–10 anger scale. After you've done that, take a deep breath and let the memory fade away.

16. Return to your surrounds

Taking all the time you need, when you're ready, gently open your eyes and bring the good feelings with you; they're worth keeping.

Ψ

I first used a version of this 'cognitive control training' exercise with "Bill", a 67-year-old veteran of World War II and the Korean War. Bill arrived agitated, panicky and gasping for breath due to emphysema. He stood in the doorway to my office, said he was only there because his doctor insisted and emphatically declared that he'd be off if I mentioned the war. If I was to help Bill, I had to do something credible which didn't involve talking about his stress memories. The idea came to me to adapt a procedure that Richard Bandler described in 1985.[5]

I asked Bill if anything had upset him lately. I was looking for an irritation, not the aggravating insult he came up with. 'Bloody young copper. I was at the club bar, and he knocked my beer over with his elbow, but he didn't apologise. If I was younger, I'd have him. I think about the mongrel all the time. I can see his face, his stupid smirk. Every time I see a police car or go past the police station, I want to punch him.' In his mind's eye, Bill could see the police officer as if he was with us in the office.

'Would it be all right to use your imagination to muck around with the police officer who knocked your beer over?' I asked. Bill agreed, and he cruised through the imagery transformations. He didn't like it when he imagined the police officer up close, but he enjoyed making him sound like Elmer Fudd.

Bill did come back to see me. At our next meeting, he said he now smiled whenever he thought about the police officer or walked past the club and the police station. But Bill had changed more than his memory of the spilt beer. He used the technique with other stress memories. Bill's self-help therapy enabled him to share with me the traumatic history that he'd been holding on to for so long.

During World War II, Bill served with Australian forces who demilitarised the Hiroshima Guard not long after the U.S. dropped the atomic bombs. Bill subsequently served with the Australian Army in Korea, and during the severe winter of 1951, Bill's battalion lived in open trenches with the enemy nearby. Every day since then, in memories and nightmares, Bill relived what had happened in Japan and Korea. His most stressful memory was of an event in Korea after the day's battle died down. In the frozen trenches, Bill had to deal with his dead mate's eviscerated body. Bill was keen to tell me what he'd done with this memory during the week since we'd first met. When he woke from his nightmare about Korea, Bill looked at it from a distance, converted it into a black-and-white scene, turned the volume down and reassured the 'younger Bill' in the memory that he did survive. Bill continued with therapy, processed his stress experiences — some he shared with me, others he kept to himself — and achieved much relief from his old reactions. I'm privileged to have known Bill as a client and a friend.

In research for my Doctor of Psychology degree, I used a variation of the training procedure you've just completed with long-term PTSD sufferers.[6] After a couple of hours of training, over subsequent months away from the clinic, many subjects updated their old stress reactions so they no longer met the criteria for PTSD. Where it's relevant, I'll let you know how these subjects responded to the exercise so you can compare your experience with theirs. For brevity, I'll put up with the regal tone and hereafter refer to them as 'my subjects'.

Changing Perspective

> The best way to dissociate yourself from your difficulty is to be mentally detached, as if you were merely a spectator, while at the same time seeking a remedy.
> *Paramahansa Yogananda (1893–1952)*

The first transformation was to change the perspective in your training memory. Did you notice an effect when you switched from the first to the third-person viewpoint?

For my subjects, changing the perspective of an anger-inducing training memory moderately reduced their distress rating. When I interviewed them a month later, 39 percent of subjects rated changing to a third-person perspective as strongly useful for processing their actual traumas. But for five subjects, the switch to an observer's perspective had the opposite effect; it increased their anxiety. As one woman explained, she looked back on herself and realised how unfairly she'd been treated as a child.

We can recall the past and imagine the future from two viewpoints.[7] When we imagine or remember something from a first-person perspective, it's as if we're there again. If we view imagery from a third-person perspective, it's like we're looking on as an observer. Remembering an event from a first-person viewpoint brings back physiological, behavioural and emotional responses similar to those experienced during the original event. Taking a third-person perspective fosters a more detached, dispassionate attitude. Consequently, when we change the perspective in a memory from a first to a third-person viewpoint, the emotional intensity usually decreases. This helps us to think rationally and maintain our attention on the stress event.

Most people naturally remember life events from the first-person perspective. Researchers find that no one has trouble switching to a third-person perspective and back again, and each point of view is as easy to maintain as the other.[8] Before their training, about 90 percent of my subjects naturally remembered their traumas from a first-person perspective. A month after training, their viewpoint had switched, and 80 percent reported that they now took a third-person perspective when they recalled stress memories.

Taking the observer point of view in memories and imagery is akin to 'observational learning', the process by which we gain information and learn skills by watching others do things.[9] Sports psychologists use the third-person perspective to help their clients objectively analyse their own sporting performances. Clinical psychologists employ the third-person perspective to reduce distress during work with trauma memories.

In one variant of these kinds of techniques, clients simultaneously watch the stress event on one side of a split screen while, on the other side, they can see an image of a place in which they feel safe.[10] In an even more elaborate version, clients imagine that they're sitting in a movie theatre, looking at an image of themselves on the screen just before the start of the stress event. They then visualise themselves floating out of their body up to the projection booth, where they watch a black-and-white replay of the event. This method culminates with the client taking a first-person perspective to feel what it was like to survive. They then run the memory backwards in colour.[11]

The third-person perspective can reduce the emotional impact of the memories you're working with and help you to think objectively. Use the first-person perspective to understand how the thing you're imagining would feel if it was real.

Adjusting Brightness and Colour

Did you notice any change in feeling when you adjusted your training memory from bright to dark? What about when you switched from colour to a black-and-white image?

For most of my subjects, these transformations made little difference to the emotionality of their training memory. One Vietnam War veteran reported that it felt better when he changed an actual memory of battle from colour to black-and-white.

But for two other combat veterans, the switch from colour to black-and-white increased their anxiety because it reminded them of watching war reports on black-and-white television.

The more vivid a memory image is, the closer it resembles an actual perception. The vividness of an image is determined by its clarity and liveliness; that is, the brightness of its colours, the sharpness of its outline and how dynamic the image appears. The percept-like quality of a vivid image can give us the feeling of being in the imagined situation.[12] Interestingly, the vividness and emotionality of a recalled stress memory can be diminished by pairing the memory with various tasks which consume some of our executive mind's working memory capacity.[13] We'll discuss this effect later when we're examining psychological treatments for anxiety and traumatic stress.

Varying Distance

Did you notice an emotional effect when you varied the distance between yourself and the person in your training memory?

You might have found that drawing the antagonistic person closer intensified your discomfort while pushing them away felt better. Many people's feelings change as they vary the space between themselves and a person in their memory. For my subjects, as they imagined the person getting closer, their anger increased, and as they pushed the person away, their anger decreased. A month after the study, nearly a third of my subjects rated increasing the distance as strongly helpful when working with their actual trauma memories. But that's not how it always works. As with all the transformations we're working with, it's your reaction that matters.

If an antagonistic person comes too close for comfort, they invade our personal space, which can trigger the fight-flight-freeze response. A psychologist friend likened this critical zone to the length of our arm held out with a clenched fist. But if the person we're thinking about is family, a friend or a lover, drawing them closer can enhance positive feelings.

As in real life, so it is in our imagination; similar rules apply. When we remember or imagine something, the distance we maintain between ourselves and the people and events in the scene affects our emotional experience. Anxious folk often recall their tormentors and horrors up close. This intensifies their distress and enhances the perpetrator's perceived power. It feels much better when we take control of our imagery, push hurtful people away to a comfortable distance and draw helpful people closer.

Altering Size

Did the size of your imagined provocateur matter to you?

When my subjects made the irritating person larger, most felt more threatened and angry. Conversely, they were more relaxed and in control when they shrank the person down. A month after working with their training memory, 37 percent of my subjects reported that making the person smaller in their stress memories was strongly helpful.

Adjusting Volume

How about changing the volume of the aggravating person's voice? Did it make a difference for you?

For my subjects, adjusting their memory from loud to quiet reduced their level of distress, on average, from 8 to 2 on a 0–10 anger scale.

Some sounds, such as a favourite piece of music, are better turned up. Pleasant-sounding auditory images warrant adjusting to make them richer and more resonant. But if you're mentally processing events that involve distressing sounds, such as a crash, shouting or explosions, turning the volume down and muffling the noise can prevent you from being startled and help you focus your attention where it's needed.

Adding Support

Did adding a friend or ally to the training memory change your feelings? Did you feel an enhanced sense of support?

Nearly half of my subjects rated this transformation as strongly useful for managing their trauma memories.

Children don't have the physical strength or maturity to defend themselves against hostile adults. Consequently, adult survivors of childhood abuse often feel powerless when they recall what happened to them as a child. Enduring severe stress alone amplifies suffering, but knowing that others care counteracts despair. Children can survive even appalling circumstances if they know that someone loves them. When we mentally process a stress response, if we feel alone and unsupported, it's more difficult to imagine what we might do differently. At such times, remembering the people who like and love us, and even incorporating them into what we're imagining, can help us tap into the strength that comes with fellowship and connection to others.

Using Humour

Did humour make a difference to your training memory?

For my subjects, adding a circus monkey reduced the aggravating person's impact by an average of about four points on a 0–10 distress scale. I think all subjects smiled when they first imagined the monkey. A month after training, 26 percent of subjects rated adding the monkey as strongly useful for managing their actual trauma memories. But only 15 percent of subjects rated giving the person a cartoon character's voice as strongly useful. For one of the good folk who reviewed an early version of this book, the image of the circus monkey made her sad and angry because it reminded her of the cruel treatment of circus animals.

Humour can relieve stress. Even though it might seem callous to outsiders, emergency, medical and police service personnel sometimes share black humour to help them cope with horrific events. However, humour can also function as a form of avoidance. If we routinely make light of serious things, we're less likely to learn what we need to learn from the experience. So please use the tool of humour carefully when you're working with your stress waves.

Positive and Negative Self-Statements

Did the positive and negative self-statements affect your emotional reaction to the training memory?

More than half of my subjects rated positive self-talk as strongly to very strongly useful when working with their actual trauma memories. This finding highlighted the powerful blocking and facilitating potential that negative and positive self-statements have on our mental processing of stress.

If during the training, the negative self-statement felt more natural for you to voice, explore whether you hold any beliefs about yourself that could hinder your work. Do you have a fixed, negative mindset about yourself, other people or the world?

Enhancing the Memory

When you adjusted your training memory so it had minimal emotional impact, what specific changes did you choose? What transformations were the most helpful? You might use this information as you mentally process your real-life stress memories.

You now have the tools to control the emotional intensity of your memories and imagery. With these techniques, you can keep distracting emotions in check as you ride stress waves. Next, we'll work with some imagination-based tools for learning from the past and resolving problem-causing stress reactions.

Resolving Stress Memories

We'll work with three tools for mentally processing stress

memories. These techniques all encourage you to take the third-person perspective and engage with stress memories as the adult you are now.

A particular technique might work well with all your recollections, or perhaps you'll use a different method for each memory. Modify the procedures to suit your needs and preferences. As you process stress, you'll probably be able to remember the details of what happened, but not necessarily. These tools can help even if you can't recall the original event.

Transferring Adult Resources

We'll begin with a procedure that reviews a stress memory from the third-person perspective and then encourages the transfer of adult resources to a 'younger you' in the memory. Heed your intuition as you work with this tool. Remember that whenever you want to, you can modify the intensity of your feelings by changing the sensory qualities of the imagery. You're in control, and at all times, you can draw upon your adult knowledge, experience and strength. Pace yourself as seems right. The processing might go quickly, but sometimes, a particular stage could take a while for you to work through. Complete each step before you proceed to the next. You can converse with the younger you silently, in the privacy of your mind. After you've read the instructions, begin the exercise with your eyes closed. Of course, you can open your eyes any time you want to.

Ψ

1. Locate a relevant memory

    Close your eyes and locate the first memory related to the stress reaction you're working on. Proceed if a memory comes to mind. If you recall nothing or feel a sense of resistance, explore why you feel that way and why nothing comes to mind. Take your mental processing from there.

2. Review the stress event

    Imagine that you're in a movie theatre looking at a

blank screen in front of you. Watch the memory play out on the screen. Then, as an adult observer looking on from a distance, watch and listen to everything that happened to you in the past. Remember your adult strength as you let the younger you go through the event, from beginning to end, up on the screen. Remind yourself that you're safe. Proceed to the next stage when you sense that you've seen and heard everything you need to know about the experience.

3. Transfer adult resources

Now give all your adult wisdom, understanding and support to the younger you in the memory. You might imagine hugging them. Reassure them that they'll never have to go through that again. In the privacy of your own mind, talk to them about what happened. Tell them that, no matter how tough it was back then, they did survive. Proceed when you sense that you've said all you need to say to them. Explore any resistance you feel.

4. Check your readiness to give up old reactions

Check that the younger you is comforted. Perhaps you can see that they're more relaxed? Proceed when you sense that the younger you is reassured and ready to relinquish the old emotions. If the younger you is not prepared to let go of the old stress response, engage with this part of your psyche, explore why you feel this way and address these issues. Perhaps the old response is still required for protection?

5. Let go of out-of-date reactions

In your own way, help the younger you let go of all the old, out-of-date feelings. Reassure them that, as an adult, you'll protect them from now on. You might imagine yourself comforting them so they become one with you again. Proceed when you sense that the younger you has let go of the old emotions. Explore any resistance you feel.

6. Confirm the release of old emotions

Check how you feel. If that younger part of you has let go of the old tensions, you'll feel good inside, perhaps better than you've felt for a long time. If you do indeed feel good, proceed to the next stage. If not, investigate why you feel as you do and work out what you can do about it.

7. Look for other problem memories

    Check with your intuition whether any other memories are still creating uncomfortable feelings. If you sense there is, recycle the entire procedure for the next memory. If you feel that you've done all you need to do with your stress memories, you can be pleased with your work.

8. Reorient to your surrounds

    As always, end your session gently. Let the imagery fade as you open your eyes and attend to your surroundings. Bring with you all the good feelings that are worth keeping.

Ψ

The method of transferring adult resources incorporates features from therapies that, over the years, have gone by such names as 'analytic'[14] and 'ideodynamic hypnotherapy'[15], 'ego state therapy'[16], 'inner child work'[17], 'neurolinguistic programming' (NLP)[18] and 'imagery rescripting'[19]. In variations of this technique when it's used to process traumatic childhood memories, therapists have asked clients to visualise that they're taking the younger self to a safe place or that their adult self intervenes to rescue their younger self by driving the perpetrator away.

My subjects ranked this as one of the two most helpful techniques for processing their trauma memories. Perhaps you'll also find it useful.

The next tool also encourages a review of stress events from a third-person perspective, but it differs in that it asks you to give the memory a new storyline and a more favourable ending.

Rescripting Memories

Severe stress can fracture the sequence of autobiographical memories that underpin our sense of who we are. This leaves us with an interrupted account of our life that's stuck at an unpleasant time in the past. The procedure you're about to work with can repair our life narrative so that a severe stress event no longer seems like an ending but becomes just another chapter in our ongoing story.

Ψ

1. Access and review the memory

    Close your eyes and relax. At all times, remember your adult strength. You can open your eyes whenever you want. Look for a memory related to the stress you're working on. When you've located one, imagine that you're looking at a large, blank screen in front of you, as if you're in a movie theatre. As an observer looking on from a distance, watch and listen as the memory plays, scene by scene, from beginning to end. When you've seen the old movie all the way through, allow the screen to go blank again, and proceed to the next step.

2. Make a new movie

    Imagine that you're a movie director. Up on the screen, re-make the old movie to give it a new storyline and a better, more satisfying ending. Take all the time you need to do this. You can direct yourself and the other actors on the screen to behave as you wish. You're in charge. If you see something you don't like, stop the action, rewind the movie, make the changes you want and start again. You can add extra elements to the movie and change it in any way you want. You might make the action realistic, or you can creatively craft a new story. When the movie looks and sounds good, proceed to the next step.

3. Review the new movie

    It's time to try out the new movie to see if it's better than the old one. From a first-person perspective, run the new movie through as if you're actually in it. When you've done that, if the new movie still looks and feels alright, proceed to the next stage. If the new movie doesn't work or has unexpected negative effects, reflect on what you've learnt and then remake the movie on the screen. Proceed when you've confirmed that the new movie looks and feels okay.

4. Reorient to your surrounds

    End your session gently. Let the imagery fade away as you open your eyes. Bring with you what you've learnt and all the good feelings you've earnt.

Ψ

In my doctoral study, when they gave their practice memory a new ending, my subjects' average distress rating fell by more than four units on a 0–10 scale. A month later, 43 percent of subjects rated the tool of changing a memory's content and ending as strongly useful for managing their trauma memories.

In some treatments, clients change their trauma memories so they feel more powerful and in charge. The therapeutic effects of such interventions — and the process that you've just worked with — stem partly from the experience of controlling imagery. And when we change a memory that's frozen in time, we open ourselves to new ways of thinking about what happened.

A memory of an event is a re-created story that seems complete, but the ending — the last scene we remember — is an arbitrary point in our life's timeline. No matter how terrible or wonderful the event was, our lives continued from that moment on without interruption. After even the most dreadful experiences, life went on, and we can draw on everything that happened after that time to change how we think about the past.

The movie metaphor also suggests a possible reason why changing a memory can resolve stress.

Movie genres have distinct structures and rules. Traumatic memories follow a horror movie trajectory. These stories typically end at the worst possible time and place, with terrible events like the hero's death or the return of zombies. In drama and adventure genres, while it's sometimes acceptable for a hero to die at the movie's climax, it's more usual for them to survive.

In terms of the cinematic analogy, when we change a trauma memory, we switch the genre from horror to a drama or, even better, to a hero's story in which the protagonist takes on challenges, endures hardships and ultimately succeeds. Suffering is no longer the central theme and the movie ends with hope for the future.

The usefulness of changing memories for the better goes beyond treating traumatic stress. The method can also help us learn from past events, whether positive or negative. When we make a new movie, we tap into the executive mind's ability to direct our thoughts and the deep mind's creativity and store of knowledge. Running the new movie from a first-person perspective re-engages our emotions to see how the imagined improvement stacks up against reality.

Next, we practice a technique that draws on good memories to bolster confidence, self-esteem and resilience.

Working with Good Memories

Webs of related memories underpin who we are and how we think about ourselves and the world. Since the pioneering days of Pierre Janet, Sigmund Freud and Carl Jung, clinical psychologists have mostly worked with the unpleasant events in people's lives. Dealing with these memories is but one thing we can do to update our stress reactions. You've met methods that help you learn from stress memories. Now, we'll explore a tool for tapping into your recollections of success, support, love and other positive experiences.

Ψ

1. Find a good memory

    Close your eyes, relax and look for a memory of a particularly happy time when you felt confident, comfortable and safe; a time with a worthwhile experience or lesson that's relevant to you now. When you recall a memory, proceed to the next step. If no memory comes to mind, explore why this would be so. A suitable memory might appear as you do this.

2. Review the memory

    Explore this good memory from a first-person perspective, as if you're there again. Let the pleasant feelings come back as you remember everything that happened. Take all the time you need to learn from this experience. When you've seen and heard it all, proceed to the next step.

3. Adjust the memory for best effect

    Adjust this memory so it has the strongest positive

emotional impact on you. You might play with the brightness, colour, distance or anything else to enhance the positive feelings. If there's sound, make it richer. Perhaps add some sparkle. Proceed when you've done that.

4. Reorient to your surroundings

When you've learnt all you need to learn, gently drift back to your surroundings. Bring the good feelings with you. When you open your eyes, you can be relaxed and comfortable. Enjoy what you've remembered.

Ψ

Next, we work with a tool that uses imagination to create new possibilities for the future.

Crafting the Future

This technique begins with an image of a desired future and then works backwards through time to end at the present. This is one way to think through how you'll respond to future stress waves. Adapt this technique to suit youself and the stresses you're working on.

Ψ

1. Create an image of a desired future

Imagine there's a blank screen in front of you. Create a static image on the screen representing a desired future in which you've resolved a threat or achieved an important goal. Proceed when you have a clear image of success or achievement.

2. Work backwards through time

Up on the screen, beginning with your image of the future, work backwards through time to create a series of scenes that depict each major step you'll need to take to achieve your goal. When you've created scenes that connect the future to where you are now, proceed to the next stage.

3. Test your work

You now have the scenes for a mental movie. To try out what you've created, take a first-person perspective and imagine that you're in the new movie. Run it forward from the beginning until you arrive at your future destination. If you encounter problems, return to the third-person perspective and re-work your initial version of the movie. Then test your work again. When your movie looks and sounds how you want it to, proceed to the next step.

4. Polishing the plan

Begin fine-grained editing of your movie by imagining how you'll realise each scene. When you've done that, reorient to your surroundings. Gently open your eyes and bring with you all that you've learnt.

Ψ

A journey is a popular metaphor for the process of getting to where we want to be. One step follows another until we arrive at our destination. However, the journey metaphor is incomplete unless we also have a map to guide us. If we've got the wrong map or don't have a destination in mind, it doesn't matter how long or hard we work at it, we won't end up where we need or want to be. In this ever-quickening age, it's easy to get caught up in the day-to-day busyness of life, so we never lift our heads, take stock and think about where we're headed. The danger is that we can work hard only to find, years down the track, that we're no closer to where we really want to be.

If we imagine what success would look like, it becomes easier to work out how we'll get there. When we use the mental processing tool of imagining our ultimate destination, we 'begin with the end in mind'.[20] Improve and refine your mental maps as you work towards long-term goals. Think of where you want to end up, and getting there will be easier.

Guided Imagery

Our next imaginal experience uses a guided imagery script based on the work of Harry Stanton[21] and others. The script gives you a sample of the kinds of imagery that you can use to promote relaxation, encourage exploration of issues and foster problem solving. Use or adapt this script to your needs and taste.

Ψ

1. The pond

    Imagine that you're strolling in a beautiful garden. Enjoy the light as it plays off the plants, trees and flowers. Somewhere in the corner of this garden, there's a pond. Imagine that you're standing quietly at the edge of this tranquil pool of water. It's shaded, glassy and deep. On the other side of the pond, there's a blossoming fruit tree with a branch full of flowers that reaches out over the water. As you stand there, looking at the pool, imagine that a rustle of wind sets loose a few petals. Watch them drift and spiral down until they touch the still water and create concentric circles of ripples that spread outwards, making delicate patterns on the glassy surface. As you relax further into the comfort, let yourself become absorbed in that scene.

2. Disposing of unwanted things

    When the time's right, leave the pond and continue your walk through the garden until you come to a clearing where a small campfire is burning. You can dispose of the things you'd like to be rid of in this fire. Imagine that you're holding a piece of writing paper in one hand and, with a pen in the other hand, write down a list of all the old habits, fears, doubts, worries, bad memories, regrets, guilt and anything else that you want to let go. When you've done this, throw the list into the fire and watch as the smoke from the burning paper spirals away.

3. Removing barriers

    When you're ready, leave the fire and continue down the garden path until you reach a barrier blocking your way. It might be a branch, a fence, a gate or something else. The barrier can represent anything that gets in your way. Imagine yourself, once and for all, removing the barrier so you can continue your walk through the garden.

4. Re-orient to your surrounds

    When you're ready, drift back to your surroundings. When you open your eyes, you can be awake, relaxed and refreshed.

Ψ

We'll wrap up our work with memory and imagination by examining the impacts of one of our contemporary world's greatest sources of stress-provoking imagery: the media.

Media Stress

When my generation sat in front of the first televisions and watched the evening news, the pictures were black-and-white, with little graphic portrayal of suffering. Over the years, the daily dose of distressing information that the media streams into households has increased incrementally. There was a time when you would never see a trauma broadcast as it occurred. Those days have gone.

Today, we live with media that peddles tragedy and violence to a passively receptive audience that's becoming desensitised to what they see and hear. If you want jaded people to notice an advertisement, you need to arouse them, and sex is not the only way to do that. Every evening, the television news cuts from disturbing images and stories to pitch products. All the while, the entertainment industry churns out ever more violent movies and video games.

For parents, the mental health impacts of modern media and the internet are of great concern. A friend told me that he feels powerless to protect his son and daughter from the traumatic stress they're exposed to on their phones and computers. Online bullying has been with us for some time, but the live broadcast of suicides that so worried my friend is a new threat that could cause devastating harm to vulnerable young people.

Many years ago, I ran a *Lara Croft* game on my computer. The goal was to keep Lara alive by having her dodge, jump and weave until she inevitably met her end; I rarely got Lara over a pit of spikes. I'd then reboot, and off she'd go to another grizzly death. A few times, Lara advanced far enough to drown. We know that practising an action in imagination improves the actual performance of that behaviour and even affects what we dream about.

So, how could it be a good idea to encourage children and young people to enjoy vivid imagery of a woman's violent death? Most of us can distinguish fantasy from reality, but what about alienated adolescent males who live with poverty and bleak futures? What worthwhile life skills or attitudes do they pick up as they practice killing scantily clad women?

In a radio interview, I heard a commentator with military expertise express surprise that a murderous U.S. high school student got off half a dozen lethal headshots as teachers and fellow students ran for their lives. Such accuracy is usually associated with the armed forces. The commentator didn't appreciate that shooter games are military-grade, virtual training exercises that desensitise soldiers to death and teach them to kill efficiently.[22]

24-year-old "Charles" came to see me after the 9/11 attacks on New York's World Trade Center. He hadn't slept for days as he trawled the media for videos of people jumping from the imploding infernos. Charles was not alone in his obsession with the violent imagery; endless replays seared the event into memories around the world. For months after 9/11, parents across the U.S. reported symptoms of anxiety and post-traumatic stress in their children. Researchers found that kids who watched more television after the attacks experienced higher levels of distress.[23] The effect was international; during the first six months after the attacks, schoolchildren in England — who had only seen the incident on television — also experienced intrusive imagery and moderate-to-severe post-traumatic stress reactions.[24]

Like a half-heard song, unfinished, stressful stories can draw us into compulsive, repetitive thinking about what happened, and the media is chock full of horror stories with no endings. Television news punches out emotionally charged fragments of imagery and events that usually end abruptly when things are at their worst, with no resolution in sight. We witness the carnage of a car crash, explosion or earthquake but never find out how things turn out for the people involved. Instead, the scene switches to an advertisement to reassure us that buying this or that will solve some problem or satisfy a desire we have.

For many of my war veteran clients, giving up the nightly TV news rapidly reduces their anxiety. For people who want to reboot old stress reactions, my media prescription is simple: don't watch the television news, avoid violent video content and stay away from social media echo chambers.

I'm not suggesting that you give up news media. Rather, I recommend being mindful of what information and imagery you let into your wonderfully sensitive and receptive mind. To keep abreast of things, read newspapers or listen to the radio but, as we'll discuss later, not just before you retire to bed. Printed media can keep you informed without exposing you to inflammatory visual imagery.

But sometimes, we can't look away. There are stress waves that, if we take them on, will expose us to disturbing stories and imagery. At such times, we need to get anything of value from such information, but we'll soon reach a point of diminishing returns. When we know all we need to know about an issue, it's time to focus on how we'll resolve the threat and make the future safer. There's no need to immerse yourself in horrifying stories unless you can learn something new and useful from them. Pay attention to news that informs you about things you're responsible for and which you can affect, and let the rest go by.

We've finished reviewing tools, tips, and techniques for working with memory and imagination while we're awake. But new learning and mental processing of stress continue during daydreams, when we sleep and while we dream at night. We're off now to the fantastic realms of reverie and dreams, where we ride stress waves even as we nap and sleep.

Chapter 14

Sleep, Dreams and Daydreams

> We sleep, but the loom of life never stops, and the
> pattern which was weaving when the sun went down
> is weaving when it comes up in the morning.
> *Henry Ward Beecher (1813–1887)*

AN ANCIENT BIOLOGICAL RHYTHM determines how our executive and deep minds operate throughout the day and night. Superimposed on the daily tide of consciousness that washes over us as we pass from wakefulness to sleep and back again, a never-ending set of smaller waves, known as the 'basic rest-activity cycle', pulse through our bodies and minds every 90 to 120 minutes of our lives.[1] Culture and climate shape local variations such as the siesta, but human societies universally structure their daily waking routines around these waves of consciousness.

On a working day that begins at 9 a.m., our energy levels are up, and concentration comes easily, for about 90 minutes. But by mid-morning, our mental activity shifts as we enter what's known as the 'natural trance' or the 'ultradian break'.[2] This is when we take our morning tea break. About 20 minutes later, we attribute our feeling refreshed to the partaking of stimulants and socialising rather than the passing of the trough in this wave of consciousness. Work comes easy for about 90 minutes until the next trough arrives, and then it's time for lunch.

So goes our daily life. The ebb and flow of the basic rest-activity cycle continues throughout the day and on through the night.

When we're awake, our eyes dart around, and the electrical activity pulsing through our brains is fast and chaotic. During this time, we mostly think about things, but sometimes we have dreamlike experiences. Then as we relax in bed at night, attention drifts, our eyes roll slowly in their sockets, the brain's electrical activity synchronises and rhythmical 'alpha waves' (cycles of 8 to 13 hertz) pulse through our brains. If we're asked what's going on in our minds, we usually say we're thinking or relaxing. Then sleep arrives.

A barrier of amnesia separates our waking and sleeping lives. When we're awake, we usually don't remember what we experienced as we slept through the night. But if you gently rouse a sleeper at any time and ask them what's going through their minds, they'll tell you that they're either thinking or dreaming; they're always doing something.

Just as we fall asleep, at that point where we can't keep our eyes open, our brains return to an electrical pattern that's similar to when we're awake, and our consciousness changes dramatically. Reports of thinking become rarer as we enter what's known as the 'hypnagogic' period of vivid, uncontrollable, hallucinatory visions.

After a few minutes of 'hypnagogia', the imagery disappears as abruptly as it arrived, and for about the next 30 minutes, our mind returns to prosaic thinking as we drift deeper into sleep. The brain's electrical activity slows as we descend towards deep sleep, where we remain for about 20 to 30 minutes while our bodies produce human growth hormone to assist physical healing. Then off we go again, cycling back up through the sleep stages until we arrive at what's known as 'rapid eye movement', or REM, sleep, and we have our first fully-fledged dream of the night.

The first REM dream lasts about 10 minutes before we descend back to deep sleep. This cycle repeats five to seven times every night. As the evening progresses, our dreams become longer, more vivid, sexier and more aggressive. Then as we wake up, we spend a few minutes absorbed in vivid 'hypnopompic' imagery that resembles the hypnagogia of sleep onset.

What goes on when we're awake affects what we think and dream about when we're asleep, and we take the legacy of the night into the next day. The concerns might be similar, but our executive and deep minds handle them differently when we're asleep and when we're awake. During sleep, and especially as we dream, our minds work on unfinished emotional things and other stresses that we didn't, or couldn't, attend to and process during the day; Freud called them the 'day's residue'.[3] And if we pay attention to emotional things before we go to bed, we can inadvertently set the agenda for the entire night. That's why you shouldn't watch violent movies or the television news or read vexing emails before you retire. Make it a routine to finish your day with positive thoughts and experiences. Desiderius Erasmus' advice from four centuries ago is still sound: 'Before you sleep, read something that is exquisite, and worth remembering'.

Respect your sleeping and dreaming mind. Prime it properly, and it'll work creatively through the night, rewarding you with ideas, insights and solutions in the morning. And sometimes, the payoff for our mind's work comes as dreams that, under certain circumstances, we remember.

But before we get to the tools and techniques for working with dreams, I have a few tips about sleeping for you.

Sleeping Well

Sound sleep rejuvenates our mind and body, builds resilience and supports our nocturnal processing of stress.

We're rarely aware of things that disrupt our sleep — mainly because we're asleep at the time — but there are clues that let us

Good Sleep

know when we need to change things.

Temperature and Noise

Some people like to burrow under a pile of blankets, but if they sleep too hot, they'll unknowingly spend less time in deep sleep where our physical body repairs itself. Sleeping too hot is associated with immune system dysfunction and increased rates of illness and other health problems.

If you wake feeling sweaty around your neck and head, or your pillow is damp, over a week or two, gradually reduce the number of blankets on your bed. When you do this, it might seem too cold when you first get into bed, but you'll soon get used to the new weight and warmth, and your sleep will improve.

Sleeping with too much ambient noise also reduces the time we spend in restorative deep sleep. Wearing soft earplugs can reduce the impact of noise on your sleep cycle. If you find wearing these plugs uncomfortable, try softer versions; the health benefits are worth the trouble.

But speaking from personal experience, there's nothing more important during sleep than breathing.

Sleep Apnoea

'Apnoea' means 'without breath'. In a condition known as 'obstructive sleep apnoea', a person's breathing is repeatedly blocked when relaxing throat muscles cut off their airway.

Sleep apnoea is a shared joy. Bleary-eyed partners spend long nights on alert, waiting for their afflicted others to gasp for air and prove that they're still alive. When the disorder is severe, breathing can stall hundreds of times in a night. This plays havoc with sleep cycles and harms health as oxygen levels fall and blood becomes acidic. Sleep apnoea is underdiagnosed, even in older men who are most at risk, and this is a potential problem for both sexes of any age. Children nowadays rarely undergo tonsillectomies and adenoidectomies, and this has led to an increase in rates of undiagnosed sleep apnoea related to respiratory tract infections. We don't know to what extent this breathing disorder contributes to problematic stress reactions in children.

Sufferers are unlikely to know that they have sleep apnoea. This ignorance encourages mistaken beliefs about why they can't concentrate and always feel tired. I didn't believe it when the sleep clinic doctor told me that I was waking up hundreds of times every night. I was certain I was sleeping soundly when, in fact, I was repeatedly waking up, although never for long enough to form a memory of being awake.

It's worth a medical follow-up if you're tired throughout the day or you have great difficulty staying awake while watching movies or travelling as a car passenger. A telling diagnostic question is, 'Does your partner say you stop breathing and gasp for air while you're asleep?'

If you suspect you might have sleep apnoea, get a referral from your doctor for an assessment at a sleep clinic. I can recommend using a positive airway pressure unit to manage the condition. When you're riding stress waves, there's nothing better than getting a good night's sleep.

Insomnia

When I first set up my 1976 university study of the experiences we have at sleep onset, none of my subjects would fall asleep.[4] It didn't matter how late it was, how tired they were or how long I left them lying in the dark; they just wouldn't nod off. I eventually realised that my mentioning sleep was the problem because this put them on alert, watching for sleep to arrive.

Insomnia

When I changed my instructions and simply asked them to lie in the dark, every subject fell asleep within minutes.

We can't force ourselves to fall asleep. The more we try, the less likely slumber becomes. If getting to sleep is a problem for you, take the pressure off. Remind yourself that missing some sleep is no big deal. Staying awake for periods of time is only an issue if you think it is. Insomnia becomes a problem when you give it a name and believe that it's a threat to your well-being. Before then, it's just a change of routine.

If you've been awake for a while, don't lie in bed worrying or thinking about things. Rather, get out of bed and do something useful. Sit somewhere that's not very comfortable; a chair designed for work is good. After a while, you'll yawn and stretch. That's the signal to go back to bed, slip under the covers and imagine something repetitive and pleasant. If you're still awake 10 minutes later, get up and return to work. Then try the bed again when you next feel drowsy.

The invention of electric lighting changed the nature of human sleep. A few generations back, our sleep cycles were linked to the natural transitions of day and night. There's only so much you could or would want to do by candle or firelight. Medieval Europeans typically retired to bed not long after sunset for what they knew as their 'first sleep'.[5] They would then wake around midnight, and when they felt drowsy again — an hour or so later — they went back to bed for their 'second sleep'. Such was the routine in less brightly lit times.

If you find yourself wide awake in the middle of the night, it doesn't mean you're suffering from insomnia. Do what your ancestors did: get out of bed until it's time for your second sleep.

Keep your bed for sleeping, dreaming and making love. Never work or check emails in bed. If you use it for worry or work, your mind will associate your mattress with being awake and active. Your bed will become what's known as a 'conditioned stimulus', and the sight of your bed, or even just thinking about going to bed, will bring on the 'conditioned response' of being awake and alert. That's why you need to get up if you're not sleepy. There's a proper place for every activity.

We'll now discuss tools and techniques for processing stress during the phases of the basic rest-activity cycle when our executive mind is dreaming or in reverie and our deep mind runs the show.

The Natural Trance

If you've ever tried to interest an audience or hold children's attention around lunchtime, you know what glazed eyes and drooping heads look like. During this down phase of the wave in the basic rest-activity cycle, you'd do better to declare a break and get back to teaching about 20 minutes later when the fatigue lifts. Listen to your body's needs and give up trying to ignore them.

It matters what name you give the breaks you take during these episodes of natural trance. Some call them 'nanna naps', and in our hyperkinetic age, taking time off from work can seem indulgent. However, the business world knows these times as 'power naps', and some corporations encourage employees to use them. No one has a problem taking breaks for lunch or morning and afternoon tea, so what could be wrong with having 20 minutes off to recharge your energy and resolve stress?

A psychology professor at a conference I attended explained that the troughs in the basic rest-activity cycle are times of heightened stress; they're the peak periods for such things as accidents, cigarette smoking and incidents of domestic violence. The professor reckoned that taking breaks during these times is a powerful way to reduce fatigue and relieve stress.

External demands, coffee and other stimulants can mask the subtle indicators of an approaching natural trance. Still, you can tell that a trough in the cycle is coming when you notice the tell-tale signs of stretching, yawning, tiredness, hunger, poor concentration, doodling and staring vacantly into space. These regular troughs of drowsiness are ideal times for relaxation, creative problem-solving and processing stress.

It doesn't matter how you go about it when you notice the onset of the natural trance. You might think about something pleasant, like sitting beside a creek, walking in a garden or being at the beach. Or perhaps you'll just enjoy the comfort. When your mind and body are ready, and your executive mind is distracted, your deep mind will take you into reverie.

During the natural trance, it feels as if we're in a daydream. We don't lose control or pass out; if we need to, we can open our eyes and deal with the external world. If you're a bit sleep-deprived, when you first use the natural trance, you might fall asleep and wake feeling groggy. But as you keep practising, your sessions will become lighter, and after about 20 minutes, you'll stretch, open your eyes and enjoy the day with renewed energy and inspiration.

To use the natural trance when you're under time pressure, give up the idea of relaxing or meditating. Just attend to your breathing for a while. Notice how it feels to breathe in and to breathe out. Close your eyes and count each breath: '1' for the first in-breath, '2' for the out-breath, and so on until you reach 100. This will only take minutes, and there's no pressure on you to relax because all you're doing is counting each of your breaths. Nonetheless, you might be surprised by what happens when

Taking a Break

you're not paying attention.

In university, I discovered that I could study more effectively if, when I felt drowsy, I paused my thinking, closed my eyes and let my mind drift. After a while, I'd come back to my surroundings, always feeling relaxed and sometimes with fresh insights that came with no conscious effort on my part. The method works as well for me now as it did 50 years ago. To use this state of consciousness to process a specific stress, focus on the issue that concerns you as the natural trance comes on.

We're off now to the amazing states of consciousness we experience every time we fall asleep.

The Magic Theatre of Hypnagogia

Accounts of altered states of consciousness when falling asleep have appeared in Western literature for 2,500 years — and even longer in Eastern writings. In 1848, Alfred Maury coined the term 'hypnagogic imagery' for these vivid, hallucinatory visions. Hypnagogic images have inspired scientific breakthroughs, such as August Kekule's discovery of the structure of the benzene atom, and literary creations, including Enid Blyton's *Noddy* books. The hypnotic state that I and other psychologists work with is an induced form of hypnagogia.

As research for my honours degree, I studied what goes through our conscious executive minds as we fall asleep.[6] After I attached electrodes to their scalps to record brainwaves and to their faces to monitor eye movements, my subjects lay on a bed in a dark university laboratory. In an adjacent room, I watched their brain wave patterns on an electroencephalogram (EEG). As they drifted off, I interviewed each subject over an intercom, and then I left them alone until they fell asleep again. Over two nights, each subject gave eight reports of sleep-onset experiences.

The hynagogic theatre begins with a bizarre slideshow. The following were typical early sleep-onset answers to the question, 'What's going through your mind?'

'Buccaneer ships ... and a child listening to a tape recorder ... all superimposed ... there were several things in quick succession ... I think the last thing was a newspaper ... sort of held open ... before that was sort of an animal's head ... like a cross between a lizard and a crocodile ... it had a bonnet on it of some sort.'

After about a minute, the slideshow settles into a brief dream, like the following examples.

'I was in a ... Mexican police station ... and the captain was asking a policeman to read a chart ... and the word he had to read was "si", you know, the Mexican "yes".'

'There was a rabbit in a field ... just about to jump onto this disk that was spinning around ... the rabbit was trying to get to a person ... it had to jump over this disk ... it was just about to jump on it and get spun off.'

The closest most of us come to catching hypnagogia is feeling like we're falling or hearing someone call our name as we drift off. But for some folk, not knowing that hypnagogia is a normal experience can cause severe stress. For my client, "Michael", his hypnagogic imagery took on a sinister significance. Michael felt anxious and couldn't sleep. He'd become aware of his hypnagogic images and, not understanding what they were, feared that he was going insane.

You don't need fancy equipment if you want to explore or work with your hypnagogic visions. When you feel sleepy, prime yourself by thinking about an issue. Let your partner know what you're up to, and when they see your eyes closing or your head nodding as you drift off, have them ask gently, 'What's going through your mind?' As with all dreams and fleeting dreamlike imagery, as soon as possible, write down what you experience or describe it aloud so you can remember it.

Once the hypnagogic period passes and we're fully asleep, the next dreams we encounter are the familiar nightly dramas known as rapid eye movement dreams.

Rapid Eye Movement Dreams

> Even a soul submerged in sleep is hard at work
> and helps make something of the world.
> *Heraclitus (540–c.480 BC)*

Everyone dreams. People who claim they don't dream just don't remember their nightly adventures. When we're dreaming, the brain's electrical activity looks similar to when we're awake, and our brain consumes more energy than it does during the daytime.

Have you noticed the eyes of a sleeping partner or child dart around under their closed eyelids? These are the eye movements that give REM sleep its name. If there wasn't a switch to disconnect our bodies from our dreaming minds, we'd fall out of bed as we acted out our dreams. But the switch only partially paralyses us. When a sleeping dog or cat growls or meows and flexes its paws, it's probably dreaming of chasing a ball or a mouse. Like our pets, as we dream, the minute jerky movements in our muscles and our eyes track the action in our dreams.

Sweet Dreams

The classic tale of horror, *Frankenstein: or the modern Prometheus*, came to Mary Shelley in a dream. Over dinner, Mary, Lord Byron and her future husband, Percy Shelley, decided to compete to see who could write the best horror story. During the conversation, Mary heard stories of electrical currents making frogs' legs twitch.

That night, she dreamt about a scientist who created life and unleashed horror. But dreams do more than inspire creativity; they can also resolve long-standing, problematic stress reactions.

For my 60-year-old client, "Wendy", a spontaneous dream triggered insights that helped her resolve a lifelong pattern of avoidance. Wendy rarely argued with anyone and she always looked for others to solve her problems. But that all changed after she woke one morning from a particularly vivid dream.

In her dream, Wendy was holding onto a ledge on the side of a tall building. She was facing outwards, with her hands above her head and her feet dangling high above the ground. Wendy said she didn't panic during the dream; she felt 'quizzical' rather than anxious. Wendy recounted how, in the dream, she thought to herself, 'This isn't ideal', and when a bird landed on her feet, she thought 'That's interesting. I don't mind giving the bird a place to perch'. The dreaming Wendy wondered, 'How will I get out of this? I could be here until my arms give out'. No one was inside the building, so Wendy just hung there, waiting for someone to rescue her. After a while, she realised no one was coming to her aid, so Wendy decided 'out of curiosity' to try to save herself. She looked down, let go of the building with one hand, and twisted around to face the wall. From that position, she swung her leg up and scrambled onto the ledge. The dreaming Wendy was surprised at how easy it was to rescue herself.

Like most of us, Wendy rarely remembers her dreams, but she says she'll never forget this one. Her deep mind gifted her an undeniable lesson: Wendy could solve a big problem herself. When I last saw her, Wendy continued to attribute beneficial changes in how she manages stress to this dream.

We have about six REM dreams every night, so with a mean life expectancy of 82 years, the average Australian will have close to 180,000 dreams in their lifetime. Humans — and the many other creatures who dream — must have this ability for a reason, yet we spontaneously recall few dreams. It's likely that if there was an evolutionary advantage to remembering dreams, we would do so. This suggests that, for effective learning and problem-solving to take place, our awake executive mind does not need to know what happens in our dreams. It appears that our deep mind can resolve stress in a dream, even when we can't remember the experience. Nonetheless, there are times when remembering a dream can help us process stress.

When my clients ask their deep mind for a dream to address a specific issue, their subsequent experiences are always useful. I agree with Sigmund Freud that 'Dreams are never concerned with trivia'.[7] The process is much the same if you're requesting a daydream, a hypnagogic vision or REM dream. As you prepare for sleep or a daytime break, think about what you want to achieve. To request a dream, as you retire to bed, respectfully ask your deep mind for an experience that's relevant to your goals. For instance, you might want a dream that helps you resolve stress, tells you about a problem or advises you what to do next. Keep a notepad and pen by your bed. If you wake up during the night, go over the dream and write it down so you'll remember it. Record all dreams, no matter how brief or bizarre. When you've requested a dream, anything you remember will be relevant.

When you have your dream reports, it's time to decode them. I prefer the following method, based on Carl Jung's dream analysis, for working with dreams.

Ψ

1. Reflect on the dream

    Retell the dream story from a third-person perspective, as in 'the dreamer did this, then that happened'. Ask yourself how the dreamer was feeling and think about the general mood of the dream. Contemplate how this story might relate to your waking life.

2. Objectively define dream elements

    Give a dictionary definition for everything in your dream. For example, if there was a car, you might define a car as a vehicle, a means of transport that moves people from place to place. The question to ask is, 'What is a car?' rather than 'What's a car mean to me?' Continue until you've given an objective definition for every dream element. Reflecting on the dictionary definition of dream images can draw out salient features for the next step in the interpretation process: finding your subjective associations to the dream imagery.

3. Uncover your subjective associations

For each element, read your definition and think about what this could represent in your life. Does it remind you of anything? Is there anything else like this? What does it mean to you? With our example of dreaming of a car, your subjective association could be 'my body'. Look for the first impression that comes to mind.

4. Retell the dream story to incorporate new information

Go back over the dream from the beginning, but this time, add your subjective associations for each element. For example, you might say, 'The dreamer drove in a car, which she associated with her body,' and so on. As you do this, the meaning of the dream will emerge.

5. Put the dream message to work

What do you think the dream is telling you? You can apply the insights you've gained to the task that motivated you to request the dream in the first place. Or you might use what you've learnt to put a follow-up question to your dreaming self on another night.

Ψ

Sometimes, when our mental processing of stress is stalled, our dreams can get stuck in a repeating nightmare that wakes us up before our deep mind resolves the drama. To wrap up this chapter on dreams, we'll look at a tool for ending repetitive nightmares.

To End a Recurring Nightmare

Some treatments for trauma-related nightmares ask clients to intentionally alter the content of their disturbing dreams. Giving the nightmare a better ending can work well, and the therapeutic effect can be as strong when the imagined new ending is bizarre or even unfavourable.[8] The new dream ending just has to be different from what it was.

The following exercise gives you a tool for easing recurring nightmares by creating new endings for them.

Ψ

1. When you wake from a nightmare, don't reinforce the old dream story by going over it again in your mind. Instead, draw on what you've learnt in this book to create a new ending for the dream you've just had.
2. For a couple of weeks, run the new dream story through in your imagination for about five minutes before you go to bed at night. Use the skills that you've practised to make the new imagery vivid and emotionally potent.

Ψ

In the next chapter, we examine tools and techniques for using the key mental process of intuition to communicate with our deep mind and mentally process stress.

Chapter 15

Intuition

> Our gut feelings signal what is safe, life sustaining,
> or threatening, even if we cannot quite explain why
> we feel a particular way... Gut feelings also help
> us to evaluate what is going on around us.
> Bessel van der Kolk (1943–)[1]

WHEN I FIRST LEARNT HYPNOTHERAPY, my teachers recognised the importance of what they called 'the unconscious', but they treated the deep mind as if it was less intelligent than the executive mind. Their hypnotic suggestions were delivered as orders, such as 'Your eyelids will become heavy', 'You are going deeper into trance' or 'You will feel stronger with each day'. Suggestions were repeated — at least three times consecutively, one teacher recommended — to ensure that the unconscious got the message. This is not how we're going to work with the deep mind. We'll respect this powerful, protective part of our psyche as we use our intuition to ride stress waves.

Our deep mind is intelligent and knows more about us than we'll ever understand at the conscious level of our executive mind. The deep mind knows what's happening inside and around us and can access a vast store of memories and knowledge. When we understand how to communicate with it, and show respect, the deep mind can be reasonable, cooperative and caring.

Setting Up Signals

Our intuition does not typically express itself through words, so we need nonverbal signals that the deep mind can use to communicate with us. If we were working together in person, I'd ask your intuition to indicate 'yes' and 'no' with involuntary movements of your fingers or head. Known as 'ideomotor signals', these slight, automatic movements naturally occur when we think 'yes' or 'no', and psychologists use them to get feedback from a client's deep mind. But here, you'll be acting as your own therapist, so we'll use 'ideosensory signalling' as well.

I'll get you to interpret certain feelings or sensations as 'yes' and 'no' signals, but you'll probably also notice a physical movement or twitch associated with the signals you feel. This process can sound mysterious, but we're really just talking about the common experience of paying attention to your gut feeling and body language. Let's identify the sensations or feelings that you can use as signals.

Make yourself comfortable, then compare the changes in feeling, posture and expression when you say 'yes' and then say 'no.' For me, 'yes' feels a bit lighter, my voice lifts slightly and I want to open my hands, while saying 'no' comes with a heavier feeling, a more subdued tone of voice and downturned hands. Repeat the process, and when you can readily distinguish 'yes' from 'no', your signals are set up. Before we get to working with the deep mind, I'll tell you about another signalling method that might interest you.

In the 18th century, Anton Chevreul invented a means for converting minuscule ideomotor finger movements into the more easily observed sweep of a pendulum. When it's swung from a string that's held between thumb and forefinger, 'Chevreul's pendulum' settles into one of four possible movements: a clockwise circle, a counter-clockwise circle, a straight line from right to left, or a line towards and away from you. To set up the signals, you hold the string and think 'yes ... yes ... yes' until the pendulum settles into one of the four movements you can take to represent 'yes'. Repeat the process to set up signals for 'no', 'don't know' and 'don't want to answer'. When you've set up your ideosensory, ideomotor or pendulum signals, you're ready to work with your deep mind.

The Technique of Respectful Communication

Find a quiet place where you can notice subtle feelings without being disturbed or distracted. Begin by asking if your deep mind is willing to cooperate with you. That shouldn't sound strange, given that you're still reading this book. The question establishes an appropriate tone for your work. As the executive mind 'you', you're acknowledging the potency and worth of your deep mind. You're making it clear that this is a collaborative undertaking and that you respect all aspects of your psyche. But remember that your deep mind's primary job is to protect you, so be prepared for unexpected answers. If you get a 'no' response to your opening question — indicating that the deep mind is unwilling to cooperate — please don't feel disappointed or rejected. Cultivate gratitude for your inner wisdom. Your deep mind might have good reasons for not agreeing to your request at this time.

A guiding principle for using the technique of respectful communication is that there is no failure, only further information that you can feed back into your mental processing. A 'no' signal when you want and expect a 'yes' does not mean that anything has gone wrong or that you've failed. Rather, such unexpected responses indicate that you need to do more. Thank your deep mind and take things from there. Ask for more information and consider why your intuition might have a contrary take on your needs.

Once your deep mind agrees to cooperate, think about what you want help with and, with your goal in mind, construct your questions and requests.

If you're looking for specific information, use 'closed' questions that can only be answered 'yes' or 'no', as in a game of '20 questions'. For example, if you wanted to know more about some early stress in your life, you might frame questions along the lines of 'Is it alright for me to know about the first experience that has anything to do with my fear of heights?', 'Did this event occur at the age of five years?', 'Did the experience involve sadness, hurt, anger or guilt?' and so on.

To get your deep mind to carry out a specific task, ask for whatever it is you want it to do. It's that straightforward. Examples of this type of request are: 'Please bring the memory to the conscious level so I can hear, see and feel everything that happened', 'Locate the first memory that has anything to do with my stress', 'Let me know everything I need to know about the event', 'Find a good memory' and 'Help me become more confident'. With practice, you can use the tool of respectful communication to request help with whatever skill, knowledge or outcome you're after.

To get underway, figure out what you want your deep mind to help you with, write down appropriate questions and requests, and take this work where you will. Sometimes, our deep mind can decide that it's not in our best interests to know certain things, but it still agrees to help. If this happens, you can still work with your deep mind even though you'll be unaware of all that's happening.

Mental Processing Without Conscious Awareness

In the 1980s, "David" sought treatment for phobias of heights and medical procedures. He was depressed and couldn't face much-needed surgery. David was Jewish, and he told me about traumatic events that began when he was living in Germany as a seven-year-old child. David vividly recalled his sister telling him not to return home because Nazi soldiers were waiting there for him. His sister and parents were killed in Auschwitz, and for four years, David hid in the attic of a farmhouse. When the Nazis abducted neighbours and shot the house owner, David was shunted from location to location until the liberation. In the immediate post-war years, David suffered an intense fear of dying, but this eased over time. At 20 years of age, he enjoyed the flight to Australia on a small plane. The first time David feared heights was when, six years later, a workmate removed the ladder while he was working on a building frame. For the next 30 years, until his therapy, David's phobic fear of heights never let up.

When we first met, David was visibly anxious. His ideomotor signals were inconsistent and difficult to interpret. At the conscious level, David wanted help with his stress responses, but his deep mind seemed reluctant to cooperate. During our first session, David's signals indicated two problem-related memories, but we didn't get far that day. When David opened his eyes, he said that whenever I asked for a relevant memory, he 'dropped into a void' and visualised nothing.

At our next meeting, David was agitated, but this time, his ideomotor signals were clear and consistent; I took this to indicate a shift in the willingness of David's deep mind to work with me. David signalled that it was inappropriate for him to be consciously aware of a particular event. Still, the signalling confirmed that I could work with the memory, provided it was kept outside of David's conscious awareness. Respecting this feedback, I did not ask for details about what happened. During the rest of the session, when I asked David's deep mind to locate a relevant memory, he fell asleep and snored. David's signalling remained clear, so I continued the therapeutic work. When David opened his eyes, he smiled and said that he enjoyed the session. He couldn't recall anything about what we'd done, but he reported feeling a sense of 'satisfaction' when I asked him to support his younger self in the memory.

When we met again, David asked if the therapy might already be working. He said that, during the past week, on a regular delivery job, he had to pass by a large window on the 12th floor of a building. He usually managed this by looking away and squeezing up against the opposite wall. But this time, David stood quietly looking at the view before he realised what he was doing. When I last contacted David, six months after therapy, he rated his fear of heights as 'mild' and his avoidance as 'rare'. He wrote, 'Looking down from a great height, I noticed the absence of panic feelings. There was just a little fear, but no panic, not even deep down ... I was a little surprised at the total lack of panic feeling'. David was but one of my clients who successfully reformulated stress memories with no conscious awareness of what they were dealing with.

When "Sylvia" first came to see me, she was anxious, depressed and contemplating suicide. I steered away from exploring Sylvia's dreams because they suggested to me that she might have been sexually abused as a child. Sylvia seemed unaware of any such trauma, and I didn't want to breach what could be a protective amnesia. Over a half-dozen consultations, we addressed the thoughts that triggered Sylvia's despair, but her depression didn't lift until I worked with her deep mind. With Sylvia comfortably hypnotised and her executive mind distracted with the tasks (imagining this, that and the other) that I'd given her, the conversation began.

'Is the deep mind willing to talk with me?' A tremulous movement of Sylvia's right index finger and a slight nod of her head signalled 'yes'. I then explored the history of Sylvia's problems.

'Is there anything in the past still creating uncomfortable feelings or tensions?' 'Yes.' 'Did these events occur after the age of five years?' 'No.' 'Did they occur at five years of age?' 'No.' 'Did they occur at four years of age?' 'Yes.' 'Did they involve feelings of sadness, hurt, anger or guilt?' 'Yes.' 'Would it be all right to discuss these experiences with me?' 'No.' 'Would it be all right for Sylvia to know what happened back then?' 'No, no', the signal kept repeating.

Therapy continued after Sylvia signalled 'yes' in response to my question, 'Would it be all right for the deep mind to work with this memory while Sylvia is unaware of what happened in the past?' Sylvia's ideomotor signals guided me as we worked with memories related to her childhood stresses. When Sylvia opened her eyes, she felt relaxed, but there was no sign that she was aware of our work. I didn't know what happened to Sylvia when she was four years old; neither, apparently, did she. At subsequent meetings, Sylvia felt better, and I discontinued therapy when it was clear that her depression had lifted. But the story doesn't end there. Years later, Sylvia again sought my help.

When I next saw her, Sylvia said that her depression hadn't returned, but something else now troubled her. Sylvia told me she'd volunteered to be a subject for a demonstration in a counselling training course. When the lecturer asked Sylvia to focus on a feeling of tension in her body, in front of the class, Sylvia relived a memory of being sexually assaulted as a child. I don't know if Sylvia's volunteering was her deep mind's way of guiding her towards a resolution of her traumatic stress or whether unexpected circumstances inadvertently led to her becoming aware of what had happened. Either way, Sylvia was now ready to deal with her long-suppressed memory of this event.

My experiences with David, Sylvia and other clients reinforced the insight that our psyche goes way beyond our executive mind and our usual notions of who we are. These cases also demonstrate that, with the cooperation of our executive and deep minds, we can successfully resolve stress reactions outside of conscious awareness.

It's important to remember that we can use our tools and techniques even when we're unaware of what's going on. At such times, trust your ideosensory signals to let you know when your deep mind has completed each stage of the process. I have also benefitted from working with stress memories that I can't recall.

You'll hear more about this in *Part 3* of this book.

In the next chapter, we explore popular psychological therapies for the quintessential, deep-mind-driven avoidant stress response known as posttraumatic stress disorder.

Chapter 16

Therapies for Traumatic Stress

> Between stimulus and response there is a space.
> In that space is our power to choose our response.
> In our response lies our growth and our freedom.
> *Viktor E. Frankl (1905–1997)*

TREATMENTS FOR SEVERE STRESS reactions blossomed after post-traumatic stress disorder (PTSD) first appeared as a psychiatric diagnosis in 1980. Nowadays, even experienced clinicians are likely to be familiar with only one or two applicable therapies, and prospective clients confront a bewildering array of choices.

I'm reviewing influential psychological therapies so that, should you, Dear Reader, wish to consult a psychologist in person, you can make informed decisions about the treatments you'll be offered. But beyond that, as you learn about these techniques, I encourage you to look for ideas and processes that you can apply to your own work with stress.

Psychology lacks a paradigm or unifying theory, and psychologists tend to practise within isolated schools of therapy that they promote as unique. But in reality, most practitioners do similar things to help clients.

Shared Processes in Therapy

Psychological therapies for severe stress reactions are complex, multi-stage procedures that are marketed with distinctive brand names. But despite the fancy labels and confusing acronyms, all effective treatments share some common features.

Every therapy offers a safe, confidential setting where clients can discuss even terrible things with a professional who imparts knowledge, teaches skills and offers hope. All therapists deliberately or inadvertently help their clients to identify and change beliefs, attitudes and behaviours that impede their mental processing of stress. They also give a credible explanation of why their client feels distressed and offer a motivating rationale for the recommended course of treatment. All therapies encourage clients to engage with problem-related thoughts, feelings and memories.

A client's many experiences during multiple consultations conducted over weeks or months, along with all that goes on in their mind between meetings, are potential sources of new, beneficial information that can affect their processing of stress.

Any time a client recalls a memory in the presence of a therapist, they're also simultaneously paying attention to what's going on within and around them. This creates a state of 'dual attention' that reduces the vividness of imagery and consequently lessens the emotional impact of stress-related imagery and memories.[1,2] Psychologists also typically further divide a client's attention by having them recall stress memories while simultaneously doing such things as making positive self-statements, imagining scenes, feeling relaxed, tapping acupuncture points, watching a moving finger or listening to the therapist's voice.

By matter-of-factly asking a client to recall and rate an aspect of their stress-related experience on a scale, the therapist counters the client's previously habitual impulse to avoid such thoughts, feelings and memories. In 1996, Martina Reynolds and Nicholas Tarrier asked six patients with diagnosed posttraumatic stress disorder to rate just one symptom — their intrusive trauma memories — four times each day for two months.[3] That's all they did. Three months after they finished monitoring symptoms, four patients no longer had diagnosable PTSD, one had some residual symptoms and one still suffered a diagnosable disorder. The researchers speculated that the therapeutic effect of this simplest of interventions was due to their patients learning that they could voluntarily recall and assess their previously uncontrollable and intrusive stress memories. It's also likely that having the client repeatedly rate their stress responses on a scale contributed to the positive outcome.

Psychologists use a client's ratings of distress to track progress; the number tells the therapist if a treatment is working, helps them decide how long a session should be and determines when treatment can be wrapped up. These ratings also provide clients with therapeutic experiences. As you know, when we rate a feeling or emotion on a scale, we have to adopt a more detached, objective state of mind. In effect, any request to deliberately halt or change the flow of their experience to rate symptoms or to discuss what's happening exposes the client to new information about their ability to control their stress reactions.

We'll review a selection of established 'evidence-based' treatments for PTSD and other severe stress reactions. I'll discuss what each therapy asks of clients, what practitioners believe is going on when the therapy works, and the potential of each approach to cause high levels of stress.

We'll begin with the widespread use of medications to treat mental health problems.

Medications

In the *Introduction*, I argued against the use of psychoactive medications as a front-line treatment for anxiety and stress. Nonetheless, if we're so anxious, distressed and fatigued that we can't concentrate or think straight, the relief provided by a short-term course of medication can help us mentally process our stress. Medications have their place in the art of riding stress waves provided that they're used appropriately. We don't want the medication to undermine our resolve to self-manage stress or to result in addiction. This also applies to the judicious use of psychedelics and recreational drugs such as ecstasy (MDMA), alcohol and cannabis.

There are substantial risks and potential downsides, but a dose of a benzodiazepine that counters paralysing anxiety, or a drink of alcohol that gives a measure of 'Dutch courage', can be helpful if it enables a person to take on a threat and process stress that they would otherwise avoid. But what about psychedelics? We hear reports that ingesting a mind-manifesting substance such as LSD-25, magic mushrooms, peyote, ayahuasca or MDMA can cure PTSD, depression, alcoholism and other problematic stress responses. Locally, a trial of cognitive therapy combined with ingestion of MDMA to treat flood-related stress is underway. But is it the substance or the trip, the chemical or the experience, that transforms stress responses?

It's not likely that giving a psychedelic to an anaesthetised person would relieve PTSD or depression. The therapeutic effect of psychedelics is not so much determined by the type and dose of a chemical, as it reflects the interaction of set (the expectations, knowledge and motivation of the 'psychonaut'), the setting (the personal, social and environmental context of the trip) and the nature of the encounter with expanded consciousness. Psychedelic trips can heal because they propel us into profound new insights. Dissolution of our usual sense of self, a loss of the fear of death, immersion in the universal mind and an awareness of the unity of all things are hard-to-ignore experiences that give us new perspectives and insights to transform how we think about and respond to stress.

Hypnotherapy

Clinical hypnotherapy provides tools and techniques for working with hypnotic trance, which is an induced form of hypnagogia. The hypnotic state can be relaxing and informative, but by itself, it's not an effective treatment for anxiety and stress. Instead, hypnotherapy is usually considered an adjunctive therapy that enhances other interventions.

Hypnotherapists practise one of two broad styles of therapy. The so-called traditional, authoritarian approach uses direct suggestions to induce trance and encourage new ways of thinking and acting. This works best with folk who are good at following instructions and, consequently, is unsuitable for many. The alternative approach, known as 'naturalistic' or Ericksonian hypnotherapy, considers hypnosis to be a natural state of consciousness, similar to daydreams and the natural trance. These practitioners use more permissive suggestions that encourage the client to draw on the resources of their deep mind as they work towards creative solutions to their problems.

Systematic Desensitisation & Exposure Therapy

When the PTSD diagnosis first appeared, behavioural therapies that asked clients to re-live stress memories became the most widely researched and applied treatments for traumatic stress reactions.

In Systematic Desensitisation (SD), clients remember a trauma-related scene from a first-person perspective while simultaneously maintaining a relaxed state.[4] If the client signals an increase in anxiety, their attention is diverted from the memory, perhaps to a relaxing scene. After a short while, they're again asked to attend to the distressing memory while relaxing.

The process is repeated until the client can remain relaxed while recalling their trauma. Practitioners attribute improvements to a process they dub 'reciprocal inhibition' (the countering of anxiety by an incompatible feeling or behaviour). But the most popular behavioural therapy for severe stress reactions is 'exposure therapy'.

In exposure therapy, a client confronts the feared thing or situation, either in reality or in imagination. In exposure therapy for PTSD, clients relive trauma memories during multiple, lengthy sessions. Behaviourists consider anxiety to be a learnt fear response that has to be unlearnt, and avoiding the stress memory is seen as reinforcing the old fear response. So the thinking goes, if a client relives their trauma memory for long enough, their anxiety should subside. In effect, exposure therapy attempts to wear out a client's stress reaction.

Exposure Therapy for Fear of Heights, Spiders, Storms and Snakes

For distressed people, the sessions of re-living traumatic memories are a tough assignment. "Carl", a Vietnam veteran client, told me about an exposure therapy program that he attended in the early 1990s. Carl said the treating psychiatrist told veterans, 'I'll take you back and bring you out' and the doctor would 'keep you overnight ... there's speakers in the walls and they play machine gun fire, helicopter sounds, guys yelling out, "I'm hit, I'm hit, help me ... incoming" and all that sort of hoo-ha'. Carl declined the offer to continue the program and told his referring doctor, 'I'm not subjecting myself to all that. I've been trying to forget that sort of stuff.'

Exposure therapists claim that, for treatment to work, nothing should distract the client from their first-person reliving of the stress memory. Nonetheless, this claim is belied by their actual practice. As in other treatments, in exposure therapy, it's standard procedure to give clients information about their presenting problems and a rationale for the treatment. Exposure therapists also get clients to challenge beliefs that block mental processing, and they work with the client's thoughts and imagery. And during every exposure session, to check progress, the therapist regularly — sometimes as often as every two minutes — directs the client's attention away from the stress memory by asking them to rate their anxiety on a scale. To manage excessive stress, exposure therapists also routinely 'titrate' (that's their term) a client's anxiety by doing such things as reminding them of where they are, asking them to imagine their 'safe place', using a relaxation exercise, getting them to take a third-person perspective and asking them to open their eyes.

Exposure therapy sounds scientific, but that doesn't mean it's a good way to treat stress reactions. The treatment comes with caveats and risks. A significant number of clients drop out of treatment, some don't benefit at all and others are left with worsened stress reactions. The clinical literature cautions that exposure therapy is unsuitable for clients who suffer from psychosis, substance abuse, cognitive deficits, severe personality pathology or poor physical health. Exposure therapy is also not recommended for rape victims whose memories involve mental defeat or a feeling of alienation or permanent change. Nor is the therapy suitable for trauma victims whose memories generate strong emotions of guilt, shame or anger, or when their memories involve being a perpetrator.

Some folk might come out better for the exposure experience, but is that due to their fears being extinguished, or do they inadvertently mentally process and update their old avoidant coping response?

I'll finish this section with an account of how one of my clients resolved his traumatic stress reaction in a dentist's chair. As you read this case, think about whether my client's success was due to exposure and habituation. Can you identify other processes that might have been involved?

"Barry", a 46-year-old Vietnam War veteran, was in his dentist's chair, inhaling nitrous oxide and listening to the pulsing air conditioner. When he looked into the bright light through closed eyelids, Barry relived a wartime memory that he knew well. He was back in an intense firefight in a rubber plantation that continued into the night when a helicopter made a daring landing. Sitting in the dentist's chair, in his mind's eye, Barry watched the helicopter's spotlight turn on as it dropped through heavy fire and soldiers kicked boxes of ammunition out the doors. Barry lay behind a narrow tree as the helicopter touched down to pick up wounded men. Shrapnel shredded the canopy above him — Barry could again feel the leaves on his arms — as he waited for the bullet that would surely kill him. Barry opened his eyes in the dentist's chair, 'came half out of it' and realised where he was. He reassured himself that he had survived this battle, and there was no way the dentist was going to let him die now. Barry steeled himself to 'go back in' and 'see out' his memory. He did, and that ended the nightmare that had plagued him for years.

Cognitive Therapy & Cognitive Behaviour Therapy

Cognitive therapists assume that what goes on in our mind determines how we respond to stress. When faced with big stress waves, some people take on distorted beliefs and ways of thinking that impede their mental processing and encourage avoidant strategies. To root out these problematic cognitions, therapists ask their clients to keep a diary. When clients notice a change in their emotional state, they record any images, self-talk, thoughts or feelings that come to their mind. Then, working with the client, the cognitive therapist uses this information to root out and challenge blocks to mental processing.

Cognitive therapy (CT) also typically incorporates training in anxiety management, relaxation, problem-solving and other skills. As is the case with all psychological therapies for severe stress, in cognitive therapy, clients repeatedly rate their levels of distress on a scale. Therapists also employ techniques, such as taking the third-person perspective, to control emotion during work with stress memories.

Variants of cognitive-behavioural therapy (CBT) combine interventions based on reason and thinking with the reliving of the stress memory either in imagination or by writing down a detailed account of the event. As you know, translating subjective experience into writing facilitates a more objective perspective, which reduces stress and assists mental processing.

Some cognitive therapists take a different tack. Instead of challenging stress-related thoughts, they teach their clients meditation and mindfulness practices and encourage them to attend to their ongoing experiences in a dispassionate, nonjudgmental way. Acceptance and mindfulness-based approaches, such as 'acceptance and commitment therapy' (ACT)[5], 'mindfulness-based cognitive therapy' (MBCT)[6] and 'dialectical behaviour therapy' (DBT)[7] counter a client's avoidant coping strategies by encouraging them to accept their problem-related thoughts, beliefs and feelings.

Imagery Rescripting Therapy

Over the years, the elements of imagery rescripting therapy have been rediscovered, revised and relabelled several times. You'll be familiar with this therapy's core process of asking clients to change the phenomenal qualities of their stress memories and imagery.

By the 1980s, psychologists were asking clients to alter the contents of phobia-related memories and give them better endings. In 1992, my colleague, Jim Jupp, and I reported the successful treatment of phobias using a brief, low-stress therapy that had clients locate, review and work with their stress-related memories.[8] The method, which we called ideodynamic hypnotherapy, included viewing the memory from a third-person perspective and transferring adult resources to a younger self.

More recently, imagery rescripting therapists have prompted clients who were sexually assaulted as children to change their stress memories by giving them better endings and by adding new, imagined scenes to alter the meaning and emotional impact of the incident.[9,10] These interventions include asking clients to reassure the child, take the child to a safe place, and, as adults, enter the recalled abuse scene to drive the perpetrator away. Clients have also changed their stress memories by creating a more neutral setting, altering the assailant's appearance, tying up the attacker, creating a protective shield, using a one-way mirror and locking their assailant behind bars. Less specifically, therapists also get clients to take a third-person perspective and alter the physical characteristics of the scene. Sometimes, survivors of extreme stress and trauma spontaneously create their own version of imagery rescripting.

A colleague who treats traumatised children told me about a 'sand play' session she had with one of her young clients, a boy, who had survived a shockingly violent, fatal domestic incident. The boy never spoke a word, but during therapy, he spontaneously put a toy house in the sand tray and surrounded it with many toy soldiers whose guns all faced outwards to protect the home. He had found a way to work objectively with the rescripted imagery he created in his mind. In the sand tray, the boy could arrange and change memory elements to process his experience and explore what it would take for him to protect himself from similar dangers in the future.

The next therapy incorporates ideas and practices from traditional Eastern medicine.

Emotional Freedom Techniques

In the 1990s, Gary Craig developed what he called 'emotional freedom techniques' (EFT).[11] The therapy is now one in a field known as 'energy psychology'. Emotional freedom techniques and related approaches such as 'thought field therapy' (TFT)[12] combine methods common to all other treatments but with a distinctive feature. The therapist asks the client to pay attention to some feeling, thought or memory related to their 'core issue' (their problematic stress reaction) as they simultaneously voice verbal affirmations and tap a sequence of acupressure points with their fingertip.

EFT practitioners believe that negative emotions are due to a disruption in the body's 'energy system'. They're not referring to 'libido', which in Freud's theory, powers the psyche and can get stuck in a disturbing memory. Rather, the energy referred to in EFT is the Chinese 'Chi' or 'Qi', a universal force that's said to flow in our bodies along 'meridians' (pathways) and through 'chakras' (centres of energy). The idea is that free-flowing Chi is healthy, while blocked or out-of-balance Chi creates disease and emotional suffering.

A typical EFT session begins with a 'setup procedure', which purportedly readies the client's energy system for change by countering any pre-existing self-defeating beliefs. In the setup, the client repeats an affirmation out loud three times, while solidly tapping the 'karate chop point', which is located at the centre of the fleshy part of the outside of one hand. The affirmation identifies the stress to be worked on and takes the general form of, 'Even though I have this (insert problem description here), I deeply and completely accept myself'.

The EFT therapist then asks the client to think about their stress reaction and estimate their discomfort on a scale. Progress is assessed by comparing this initial pre-tapping scale score to later ratings. Tapping then proceeds, with affirmations, through a series of acupressure points; you'll find a description of the process online. After one or two rounds of tapping, the client gives another rating. If the number is zero, the therapist deems the problem solved, and the tapping stops. If the rating indicates persisting discomfort, therapy continues through further rounds of the 'basic recipe', using a modified affirmation, 'Even though I still have some of this (insert problem description here), I deeply and completely accept myself'. Therapists recycle the procedure until the client gives a zero distress rating. EFT therapists also do the familiar things to reduce distress during processing of stress memories.

The next treatment we'll review utilises eye movements, rather than acupuncture points, to alleviate stress reactions.

Eye Movement Desensitisation & Reprocessing

In the 1980s, American psychologist Francine Shapiro developed 'eye movement desensitisation and reprocessing' (EMDR) after she noticed that her disturbing thoughts eased when she moved her eyes back and forth. From this fortuitous observation, Shapiro created a treatment for traumatic stress that's still influential. When it first appeared, EMDR generated much interest among psychologists because it offered a relatively brief treatment for traumatic stress that was less demanding than exposure therapy.

When a client attends an EMDR session, the therapist asks them to describe a stress-related memory and to rate the associated emotion on a scale. The client is then directed to focus their attention on a visual image, a negative self-statement or an emotion that's associated with the memory. At the same time, they watch the therapist's index finger move rapidly back and forth in a horizontal plane in front of their eyes. After a while, they're instructed to 'blank it out, and take a deep breath', recall the original stress memory and give another rating on the distress scale. The client is deemed cured if they give a low or zero rating. If the distress rating remains high, the client gets more of the same.

Early on, EMDR practitioners hypothesised that eye movements might activate processes related to rapid eye movement dreaming. In 1992, Shapiro characterised the EMDR process as accessing 'nodal points' in neural memory networks where information from a stress event is located.[13] She has also portrayed the process as akin to the client's adult perspective connecting with the previously dissociated memory to relieve its affect and negative meaning.[14]

The EMDR procedure is just as effective without the eye movements, and practitioners do the things that most other therapists do.[15,16] EMDR therapists ask clients to repeatedly bring stress memories to mind, and they make lots of ratings on scales. However, unlike most other therapies, during EMDR, the client keeps their eyes open. This means that, when they recall a stress memory, clients simultaneously see the therapist's moving finger and the surrounding environment. As we've discussed, this dual attention process likely reduces the vividness of the client's imagery, thereby softening the emotional impact of the stress memory.

The final therapies we'll review help clients process avoidant stress responses by working with their bodies.

Somatic Psychotherapies

In the 1970s, Pat Ogden and Peter Levine developed the related approaches of 'sensorimotor psychotherapy'[17] and 'somatic experiencing'[18] to treat traumatic stress reactions. Practitioners of both therapies believe that if it's blocked during a stress event, the fight-flight-freeze response can become stuck in a person's body and nervous system. This suppressed reaction subsequently manifests as distressing physical or emotional symptoms. For example, if an assailant pins down a young victim, the child cannot enact fight-flight-freeze responses. Thus thwarted, the energy of this physical and psychological activation cannot dissipate, so it becomes locked in the body, where it remains latent. Therapists from both approaches help clients release the problematic energy by re-channelling it into an active behaviour. This usually involves them completing the previously blocked stress response. Practitioners believe this freed-up energy becomes available for the person to use in health-promoting ways.

Ogden's sensorimotor psychotherapy progresses through stages. The therapist sets up a safe environment where the client can focus on their trauma-related bodily movements, sensations, impulses, gestures and breathing. When the client is ready, the therapist asks them to recall the lead-up to the trauma, rather than the trauma itself, and notice any attendant emotional changes or bodily responses. The therapist then helps the client integrate these responses into a coherent recollection of the initial stress.

In Levine's somatic experiencing therapy, clients track their 'bodily felt sense' and gradually work to discharge the locked-in energy. A client's ability to self-regulate their emotions improves as they better understand their bodily sensations. Peter Levine likens the therapeutic process to chemical titration, in which chemicals that would explode if they were brought together suddenly only fizzle and eventually neutralise when you add them one drop at a time.[19] Bodily sensations, imagery and muscle movements are used to access and free up the locked-in protective responses. To control high levels of affect, the therapist doesn't ask the client to recall or discuss the original stress event. Rather, therapists indirectly approach the stress memory by focussing on what occurred just before or after the incident. When clients have improved control over their stress reactions, they complete the previously blocked physical reactions and work out how they can protect themselves in the future.

This concludes my review of popular psychological treatments for severe stress and trauma-related anxiety. The therapies we've examined might offer ideas that you can adapt as tools for riding stress waves.

Before I discuss how you might choose between these approaches should you wish to seek professional help, we need to consider what it means to say that a therapy works or that it's evidence-based.

The Evidence-Based Approach

The evidence-based approach is now the cornerstone of psychotherapeutic practice and is used to decree what works and what doesn't. Psychologists everywhere believe this approach makes sense. After all, basing practice on evidence has to be a good thing, doesn't it? What's the alternative? 'Hunch-based' practice doesn't sound right.

Psychology was, and still is, a fractured enterprise that lacks the unifying paradigms needed for a theory-based evaluation of treatments. When psychological therapies proliferated in the 1960s and 70s, there was an urgent need for evidence of efficacy. To solve the problem, clinical psychologists looked to another profession. Medical science has protocols for testing new medications, so why not use similar procedures to sort genuine from ineffective psychological treatments?

In 1972, epidemiologist Archie Cochrane introduced the evidence-based approach when he argued that properly designed studies could evaluate new medications, and the most reliable evidence comes from experiments known as 'randomised controlled trials'.[20] The essential feature of this method is the 'double-blind' comparison of a medication with a 'placebo' (a treatment that only works because a subject expects it to). In a double-blind experiment, neither the subject nor the experimenter knows whether the pill is a placebo or a medication.

The placebo has to be identical to the medication, except for the absence of the active drug being tested. It even has to taste the same and produce the same physiological reactions when ingested. If and only if you satisfy these conditions, can you conclude from your results that a medication is more effective than a placebo.

Unfortunately, you can't use the evidence-based approach to evaluate psychological treatments. Designing a proper control condition that equates to a placebo is impossible. Comparing two pills that look and taste exactly alike — a necessary condition for testing a medication — has no counterpart in psychology. How could you construct a control that resembles, say, cognitive therapy in every respect except for the active ingredient? What is the active ingredient? Unlike a medication, psychological therapies are not discrete, definable things.

Psychology fudged a solution to the control group problem by doing away with the double-blind test requirement. They decreed that a therapy could be considered evidence-based if subjects who receive the treatment do better than others waiting to be treated. Consequently, a variety of well-marketed therapies now satisfy criteria as evidence-based treatments for phobia, anxiety, depression and post-trauma stress. These practitioners do the same things that all other therapists do, but they promote their method as unique by highlighting differences and ignoring similarities with other therapies. Unfortunately, the evidence-based approach tells us little about the relative strengths, limitations or potential for causing harm of different approaches.

I'll share a couple of instructive cases that caution against giving too much weight to a treatment's evidence-based status.

Cautionary Cases

Therapists and researchers use clients' distress ratings as an outcome measure: the numbers are taken as evidence that a treatment works. A war veteran client, who had undergone eye movement desensitisation and reprocessing (EMDR) before I saw him, told me, 'You learn pretty quickly that you have to lower the number to stop the bloody finger'. He'd figured out that he could end the session by deceptively decreasing his distress ratings, whereas his therapist interpreted his lowered scores as meaning that the treatment worked. "Anne", whom I saw for a medico-legal assessment, told a similar story. Eight months after a motor vehicle accident, Anne had received EMDR for PTSD from a psychiatrist who wrote in a medical report that Anne 'made good improvement' and 'reported no recurrences of images of the accident'. When I saw her two years after the treatment, Anne said that she 'hated' the process and had given the treating psychiatrist low ratings to stop the moving finger.

In an early 1970s lecture, psychiatrist "Dr Allen" told us undergrads how he relieved a 10-year-old boy's symptoms of anxiety and obsessive-compulsive disorder by performing a frontal lobotomy. Dr Allen had pushed a needle behind the boy's eyeball, through his skull, up into the frontal lobes of his brain and wriggled the needle back and forth. The procedure worked in the sense that the boy lost his presenting problems. In those days, lobotomies were performed in Australia as often as anywhere else in the world, and Dr Allen was pleased he'd helped the boy.

If lobotomised children had lower anxiety scores than those waiting for brain surgery, would that make lobotomy an evidence-based treatment? And if it did, would that tell us how we should treat anxious children?

You can only believe lobotomy is a good idea if you restrict your thinking to the simple, linear relationship between symptom, treatment and outcome; the boy was anxious, the doctor cut his brain and now he's not anxious. The problems with this train of thought become obvious when you consider the effects of the surgery on the boy's overall physical, mental and social well-being.

A lobotomy damages the brain's frontal lobes, affecting a patient's ability to plan, foresee the future and carry out sequences of thought and action. Hence the reduction in the lobotomised boy's anxiety; he couldn't worry about something that he couldn't anticipate or imagine. The treatment might have ended the boy's anxiety, but the doctor-induced brain injury also crippled the boy's prospects for a happy, healthy life. Even if you believe that the benefits of lobotomy outweigh the costs, that doesn't mean that there aren't better ways to treat anxiety. It's obvious now, but it wasn't back then.

So where to now that I've raised doubt about the significance of claims that a therapy is evidence-based?

Choosing a Therapy

If you pursue professional psychological treatment for stress and anxiety, I recommend that you look beyond the evidence-based status of your provider's preferred modality. That's worth knowing, but it says nothing about a therapy's potential risks and benefits, how the treatment compares to others, why it works when it does, who it's suitable and unsuitable for, or how many clients drop out or are harmed by the intervention.

As a potential consumer of psychological services, how can you make an informed choice if psychologists can't give conclusive proof that a treatment works? I offer the following advice based on my clinical experience. I know the processes and the skills we've worked with in this book have helped many people update avoidant coping responses that troubled them. I've witnessed many inspiring outcomes and know the therapeutic usefulness of these interventions. I'll share one story.

A few years back, I had the rare pleasure of catching up with a client I treated long ago. "Peter" was 47 years old when I saw him in 1992. Conscripted as a National Serviceman, Peter had witnessed the death of friends during combat in the Vietnam War. When I first met Peter, he was severely traumatised and contemplating suicide. Across a dozen sessions, Peter's treatment included reformulating his traumatic memories to update his old stress responses and hypnotherapy for a phobia of hospitals and surgery.

Over lunch, I audio-recorded Peter's opinion of the work we did together over a quarter of a century previously. I asked, 'Was it worthwhile?' Peter replied, 'Most definitely, most certainly. It was a turning point in my life. I was walking around with feelings of dread. I got to the stage where I didn't want to open the mail. I'd become a hermit. And we did a session to prepare me for (gallbladder) surgery and recovery. That worked out just so well, and it's been there ever since because I had a thing about dentists as well because I had a traumatic experience with dental treatment in Vietnam. And there were so many pluses. That's when I gave up smoking as well'.

Let me be clear: there is no one psychological treatment that works for everyone and every stress reaction. If you went to a doctor you felt was not helping you, you'd look for another doctor. Similarly, if you attend psychological therapy and you're not comfortable with the treatment or you don't relate well with that therapist, seek help elsewhere. Don't give up. And please never think you're responsible if therapy doesn't suit you. Every person and every problem is unique. No one can know what will work for you. The therapist's job is to help you find the keys that unlock your potential and see you on your way to optimal mental health.

And, of course, you've now got this book.

In *Part 3*, I'll present three case studies illustrating the art of riding stress waves in action. One concerns a stress wave that began long ago, another deals with a more recent threat and the third addresses how we can respond to the stress tsunamis that'll come our way in the future.

Part 3

Art in Action

Chapter 17

Dealing with the Past

Life is divided into three terms — that which was, which is, and which will be. Let us learn from the past to profit by the present, and from the present, to live better in the future.
William Wordsworth (1770–1850)

TRACKING DOWN SOME MEMORIES of childhood stress can be easy. To discover why we're anxious about something, we often only have to look for the first memory that has anything to do with why we feel that way. This is how it is with my memory of Miss Dowdy, the teacher who terminated my singing career before it began; if I want to, I can still recall what happened that day and how it affected me. But sometimes, we need help locating an early memory of an event that still generates stress waves. This is how it was for Joan, who, during therapy, remembered her brother holding her underwater when she was six years old. Other stressful memories, especially from very early childhood, can stay hidden until we uncover them with hypnosis or some other method that enlists the assistance of the deep mind.

"Nora", a wife and mother of three young boys, asked me to help her prepare for major surgery. Nora was a confident, assertive woman. She described herself as a 'tomboy' who liked to rough it with her sons; she said she'd never worn a dress.

During our work together, Nora located an unexpected memory of a stress event that occurred very early in her life. When I asked Nora's deep mind to find a memory related to her current concerns, in her mind's eye, Nora witnessed what appeared to be her birth. Nora's mind chose the scene; my request was non-specific. As she looked on as an observer, Nora saw her family members recoil in shock and disappointment when, as she was born, they realised that she was a girl. Nora later explained that, in her family's impoverished Irish community, boys were preferred, and the birth of a girl was unwelcome.

In therapy, Nora uncovered a previously unknown memory of a very early stress event that affected how she felt about herself and how she related to other people. Nora had coped with the stress of being born an unwanted girl, not by feeling inferior or weak, but by becoming a strong, determined person. Her stress response underpinned a personal strength, but it also limited her as an adult woman. Nora's mental processing of the uncovered memory allowed her to explore previously inaccessible aspects of her personality, and during the months Nora waited for transplant surgery, she took to wearing dresses and enjoyed her newfound femininity.

Over decades of practice, Nora was one of a few clients who spontaneously recalled their birth during work with stress-related memories. Most of us can only remember back to a few years after our birth. Nonetheless, I've discovered that even though we can't consciously remember what happened, the stress we cope with as newborn babies and during infancy can affect our entire lives. And the stresses that left a mark on me also affect many others of my generation.

A Personal Case Study

Susan and I have been married for 50-plus years. When we were raising our family and running a farm and clinical practice, we had some emotional meltdowns at times of high stress. It was many years since we'd had such an episode but, a few years ago, Susan and I again overreacted to a relatively minor stress. Riding this stress wave, we discovered much about ourselves and each other that we didn't know before.

We were looking forward to a family gathering, and Susan was concerned about planning a week's worth of meals. At the same time, an unforeseen threat was impacting our farm. The pasture was lush, but two years of La Nina rains had leached nutrients from the soil, and our cattle rapidly lost condition. Unbeknownst to me, Susan was very anxious about the cattle, but she hid her feelings because, as she later explained, she didn't want to bother me while we were entertaining visitors. Days passed, the cattle became weaker, Susan became more anxious, and I remained oblivious to what was going on.

When I told Susan I'd bring the cattle down to the front of the farm, she panicked and said she was very concerned that our visitors would judge her harshly if they saw the cattle. I couldn't understand why Susan hadn't told me about her anxiety, and I felt more let down than made sense. Anyway, we fed the cattle, and they regained their condition. We weren't alone; cattle across the region had lost condition due to the soil leaching. Our responses to this stress had unnecessarily turned what should have been a routine challenge into a big problem. Over the coming weeks, we figured out how and why we did that.

Our mental processing began with the insight that our problematic stress reactions revolved around the food-related issues of catering for people and feeding cattle. We could see that Susan's thinking was affected by an avoidant strategy of not telling other people things that might upset them or cause them to think negatively of her. But I still didn't know why this made me feel so angry and abandoned. Then we began to remember and talk about things we'd always vaguely known about, but never fully comprehended, until now.

I recalled how, a couple of weeks before her death, my mother cried hot tears as she apologised for what she'd done to me when I was a baby. I was the firstborn, and my then-young mother had listened to male doctors instead of her natural maternal instincts. Mum relived traumatic memories of resisting the urge to comfort me as she left me to scream in hunger until the next scheduled feed time. Mum had told me about this a few times before, but it never made much impression on me, not even when she again talked about it before she died. But now, this story about my infancy seemed deeply significant, and the memories and reflections it stirred up had much to teach me that I needed to understand. Susan also began to recall and learn from stories about her birth and early childhood, which like me, had to do with food and the stress of hunger and being left to cry alone.

Susan, an only child, was born in a country doctor's office in rural California after a traumatic 23-hour labour in which her mother re-broke her previously injured tailbone. For months after the birth, Susan's mother was in a body cast, and Susan was bottle-fed on a rigid schedule as recommended by doctors. Adding to baby Susan's stress, her mother got the formula wrong, and again like me, for the first months of her life, Susan was underfed and hungry. Susan also recalled her father's volatile temper and her mother's stories about her father reacting to baby Susan's crying by banishing her and her mother to a guest cabin on their property. Susan remembered that, as she was growing up, her parents would boast that she never misbehaved and never talked back to them. She had learnt to avoid stress by keeping silent and not making trouble. For the first time, we could see how coping with protracted stress at so vulnerable an early age had affected the way Susan and I relate to each other, to other people and to the world around us.

I now understand why some stresses disturb me. In certain situations, when I feel abandoned, some of the anxiety and desperation that I must have experienced as an infant plays out in my now-adult mind and body. I also realised why I felt so frustrated that Susan didn't immediately feed the cattle. Starvation is an existential threat to all living things, especially when they're young and dependent on others for survival. For me, the cattle issue seemed personal; from my baby self's perspective, there's nothing more important than people and animals having enough food to eat.

Susan now knows that, in particular social situations, her go-to strategy for coping with stress has been to ignore her feelings, focus on what she imagines other people want and keep her head down until the stress wave passes. This all made sense for an only child growing up with a domineering father and a submissive mother. The strategy worked back then, but it produces less-than-optimal results for Susan as an adult.

A Generation's Shared Stress

Susan and I are 'baby boomers'. Born in the early 1950s, we came into a world bewitched by the exploding power of science and industrial technology. Influential men in white coats pushed material progress as they denigrated Nature and the emotional and spiritual side of life. Male doctors championed scientific medicine, usurped the role of women midwives and stigmatised home birth. They transformed birthing from a natural experience into a medical drama played out in a brightly lit hospital ward. Caesarean sections, episiotomies, forceps deliveries and induced labour became commonplace. Doctors routinely medicated mothers during delivery, so it was normal for babies to arrive so doped that they had to be held upside down and slapped to make them cry and induce their first breath.

After World War II, the medicalisation of birth wreaked havoc with the bonding and attachment processes that underpin the mother-child relationship. Doctors discouraged breastfeeding, promoted factory-produced formulas and mandated strict feeding schedules. They decreed that the crying of hungry babies was 'good for their lungs'. In those days, a mother rarely got to cuddle her newborn before the baby was whisked away to a nursery, wrapped in constricting blankets and left to cry alone. Denied skin-to-skin contact, infants bonded with the material things they could touch; hence, the family stories of my 'sucky rug', Susan's 'little pillow', my youngest sister's bedraggled cloth rabbit, and all the other things that stressed, skin-contact-denied infants cling to for comfort when they're left alone. And the stress didn't end there.

When a mother and her newborn baby left the hospital, behavioural psychologists took up the campaign against natural, compassionate parenting. When Susan and I were born, Western psychology was dominated by the doctrine known as behaviourism. American psychologists devised a stunning avoidant strategy to resolve their stress at not knowing how to study the mind scientifically: they decided to lose their minds. Seriously. The behaviourists took the psyche out of psychology. They banished subjective experience and tolerated no talk of the mind. Psychology was to only concern itself with observable, measurable things and behaviour. They tried to objectively define what happens to the organism (the 'stimulus') and how it reacts (the 'response') without considering the interaction's context and meaning. They relegated everything inside the mind — all our emotions, imaginations, memories, plans and dreams — to a 'black box' that was not to be opened. The behaviourists set the stage for some awful ideas that mislead parents and harm children to this day.

If, like the behaviourists, you believe that attending to a distressed baby reinforces crying behaviour, then you will not respond quickly to an infant's cries. You might even adopt the delusional belief that the baby is trying to manipulate you. With this mindset, parents let their baby 'cry itself out', believing this will make them less clingy and more independent. In reality, such neglect has the opposite effect. But if you understand that a baby can only tell you it needs something by crying and moving its arms and legs, you'll likely respond promptly and affectionately. You'll trust the baby's motives and not attribute manipulative intent to the innocent's stress response.

I can't imagine what it was like for baby Susan, baby Wayne and all the other infants who have to cope with protracted periods of hunger and a lack of nurturing contact. Our two daughters were more fortunate. Our parenting guide was Joseph Chilton Pearce's 1977 book, *Magical Child: Rediscovering nature's plan for our children*.[1] And in our small rural town, the Kyogle Hospital's matron, Bridie Gregory (1923–2017), established the first natural birthing centre outside of Sydney. Bridie was a friend who was there when our daughters were born, wide-eyed and alert, into a welcoming, supportive world. We trusted the natural birthing process and figured that Nature knew how to bring new souls into this world. We assumed that when our infant daughters cried, they needed something.

Susan and I were able to process stress responses that were established during the earliest days of our lives. We now understand the origin of the emotional punch when our old, automatic reactions get triggered; as adults, we re-experience some of our baby-self's suffering. Neither of us can recall any visual or auditory imagery from that time. Nonetheless, our mental processing of what happened has transformed our old stress responses. We now understand why we react as we do, and without being able to say how we've done it, we both feel that we've resolved much of the original stress. We've changed how we think about ourselves, and the future seems safer because we're primed to recognise and deal with provocative situations before the old stress reactions can get out of control.

Chapter 18

Healing Nature

> What you do makes a difference, and you have to decide what kind of difference you want to make.
> *Jane Goodall (1934–)*

THERE ARE TWO POSSIBLE theatres of engagement if we want to directly take on the stress tsunamis being whipped up by humanity's impacts on the natural environment: we can work to heal Nature and fortify her against the shock of future stress, or we can try to change the thinking of those who are responsible for the damage being done. In this book, I'll discuss what we can do to heal Nature. For reasons I'll explain later, I'll leave the stresses that confront political and environmental activists for another time.

In *Chapter 10*, I told you how Susan and I developed a systems model that identified lantana as the key factor responsible for the dieback in our native forests. We had worked out why our forests were sick, but we didn't know how to remove the lantana from the hundreds of hectares of steep, rugged forests we're responsible for. We understood the problem, but had no solution. I'll share an improbable story about the role that persistence, good luck, hope and an openness to new information can play when we take on a big stress wave.

Luck and Improbable Events

When Susan and a neighbour attended a local National Park meeting to ask about the dying trees and cacophony of bell miner calls in our forests, the rangers initially denied that there was a problem. But the questioning didn't let up, so they flicked the matter on to their senior ecologist, John Hunter. When John returned from a helicopter flight over our valley, he reported, 'It looks as if a bomb has gone off'. John saw a landscape of dying trees surrounded by a sea of lantana.

John Hunter's report led to the government setting up a working group and convening a national dieback forum. This produced a review of the scientific literature on the dieback.[1] The conference proved vital for two reasons. The science helped us understand the problem, but Susan's extraordinary good luck led us to a solution to our lantana problem.

Susan was sitting with a small group in a side room at the conference when John Hunter told a story about a visit to his family's farm in Queensland. John's father and his neighbours had heard about an old forestry practice of splashing small lantana bushes with a potent dose of the herbicide glyphosate mixed with water. When they applied their solution, the lantana died to its roots. The implications of John's story hit me straight away. I took the nozzle off a cattle drench gun so it squirted a jet of large droplets, made up a mix, put some on a lantana hedge and it worked a treat. We could kill hedges of lantana with what was, in effect, a water pistol.

John Hunter heard about what we'd done and organised scientific trials of the method. Over subsequent years, we adapted the technique to treat large areas of lantana. We could kill lantana in rugged country as fast as we could walk. There's minimal chemical runoff, so native plants quickly regenerate through the lantana carcasses. Years on, we've reduced the herbicide concentration and treated hundreds of hectares of affected native forest on our property.

HEALING NATURE

After the lantana is removed, it takes a couple of years for the bell miners to disappear. As the bell miners lose their protected nesting sites and end their natural lifespan, other birds and insect predators move in to eat the sap-sucking insects that kill the trees. When these forest areas recover their natural structure and canopy, they're protected from further lantana or bell miner invasion. You'll find more information on dieback and forest regeneration in the references for this chapter.[2,3]

We wouldn't have a cure for dieback if there'd been any break in the sequence of events that began with Susan pestering rangers, their bringing in John Hunter, John visiting his parents' farm, John's father trying out a new method, the dieback conference, Susan hearing John's story, her sharing the story with me and my trying out the method. But discovering how we could remove lantana from our forests doesn't mean that this weed-associated stress wave has, or ever will be, resolved. This brings us to some attitudes and beliefs that can block us from taking on the stress of restoring Nature to health.

Costs and Benefits of Solutions

The bush regeneration work on our property continues, and as news spreads that you can free landscapes from lantana's suffocating grip, others are taking up the challenge to save their eucalypt forests. But no matter what we do, the threat of forest dieback is immense and growing, and the damage inflicted on native plants, animals and ecosystems remains generally unrecognised and unaddressed. We protect our forests and have, thus far, managed to keep out many invasive weeds. But we've been unable to repel such exotic intruders as giant devil's fig (*Solanum chrysotrichum*) and cane toads (*Rhinella marina*).

While we're able, we'll take on the threats and challenges that come our way and continue our work to protect Nature. We accept that we can never eliminate all threats, but we still do what we can to improve things. We don't blame ourselves for not being able to save all forests. There are only two of us, and we know that we can never fully restore even the forests under our care.

As more severe stress waves come our way, a fearless accounting of costs and benefits will become essential. Our friend, "Kate", strongly objects to our killing lantana with glyphosate because it's a poison. For Kate, the only acceptable solution would be to pull out the lantana by hand, a genuinely herculean task when you've got mountains of the stuff. Kate's critique raises an important issue. In our industrialised world, 'pure' actions are rarely possible; nothing we do to heal Nature will likely result in unalloyed success free of compromise and adverse consequences.

Fossil fuel technology — in the form of machinery and chemicals — bestows undoubted benefits. It's what we do with the technology that causes problems. Our friend Kate has good grounds for arguing against the use of glyphosate. The herbicide is dangerous and must be handled with care. Susan and I don't want glyphosate used in public places, and we avoid genetically modified crops that have been sprayed with the chemical. We want to use as little chemicals as possible on our land. Still, we have no alternative to glyphosate and splatter gun technology for removing lantana in our forests.

Susan and I understand that, no matter how long we live, we'll never see our forests grow to maturity; that'll take hundreds of years. Our task is to protect our young forest from an existential threat, nurture it back to health and see it on its way towards a sustainable future. We think of glyphosate as a life-saving medicine for ailing forests; a treatment you administer only a couple of times and stop using when the patient recovers. In many areas, we've used splatter gun once for a good, permanent result and follow-ups now mainly involve pulling lantana seedlings out by hand. The dappled shade of our regrowth forests will keep the lantana from ever again dominating.

Logging scarred our bush with tracks and clearings, which

became chock-full of lantana. Humans created the stress with fossil fuel technology, and now, the native forests cannot rid themselves of this invasive weed without our help.

Using glyphosate in splatter guns to regenerate native forests is like producing solar panels to generate renewable energy. Both processes depend on fossil fuel technology, involve dangerous substances and come with a carbon footprint and a pollution debt. When we use solar panels, we accept the environmental cost of the pollution created by their manufacture, transport and ultimate disposal. It takes a few years to pay off the carbon and pollution debt owed on our solar panels, but then we have clean, sustainable energy. As with our use of solar panels, we use glyphosate to regenerate dying forests because the benefits outweigh the costs.

In coming decades, clean water, air and soil will be the most precious commodities in the world, bar none. Forests are Nature's irreplaceable and priceless gift. The leaves of trees transform sunlight into life. Healthy forests are the planet's lungs; they inhale carbon dioxide and exhale oxygen. Forests support biodiversity, filter precious water, prevent erosion and sequester carbon. A healthy forest is self-sustaining, potentially forever. If we don't repair our forests, the environmental cost will be incalculable.

With effort and the right mindset, after even catastrophic stress waves, we can find opportunities to make things better. For example, bushfires take much, but they temporarily clear weed-infested forests, thereby eliminating much of the heavy work involved in bush regeneration. A year or so after a fire, it's easy to pull out lantana seedlings by hand. If we were to follow up bushfires by keeping incendiary lantana out until the canopy heals, we'd simultaneously resolve the stress created by this invasive weed and reduce the intensity and impacts of future bushfires.

If we turned this process of post-fire bush regeneration into an organised community activity, we could also assist trauma-affected people. Can you imagine a community coming together, a year or so after a disastrous bushfire, to pull lantana seedlings out by hand as they walk through a recovering forest? Such an event would confer a dual benefit: people could resolve their stress as they create a healthy, fire-resistant forest buffer around where they live.

Next, we'll discuss how we might manage the coming stress waves as we face the future on our fragile, beautiful planet.

Chapter 19

Facing the Future

> Life is a shipwreck, but we must
> not forget to sing in the lifeboats.
> *Voltaire (1694–1778)*

IN THE PAST, HUMANITY'S POTENTIAL to harm didn't matter much. Nature was bountiful, there weren't too many of us and we didn't have the means to cause serious trouble. The planet could accommodate us, and each generation left a healthy enough environment for their descendants. But nowadays, there's no safe harbour, no reliable shelter from the stress waves being whipped up by humanity's impacts on climate and other natural systems.

The late-18th century's industrial revolution harnessed the power of coal and steam to drive machines that disrupted everything. In the early 19th century, industrialisation accelerated with the advent of the petroleum industry, the internal combustion engine and the rise of corporations. After World War II, we entered a phase of rapid economic growth that shows no sign of letting up. As people moved from the country to towns and cities, we traded our traditional agrarian past — with its spiritual, physical and emotional connections to Nature — for more exciting, urbanised lifestyles and the pursuit of profit and pleasure. There was work and wages to be had, and thanks to industrialised agriculture, there was plenty of food. Like most species, humanity responded to the good times by breeding up its numbers; that's when we baby boomers arrived. I and my cohort have enjoyed steady improvements in health and material well-being. Still, a quarter of the way through the 21st century, the industrial revolution looks like a Faustian bargain. And the shift from improving lifestyles to the development of planet threatening technologies is recorded forever in the ground.

We've already survived the radioactive aftermath of hydrogen bombs. Nuclear tests left an indelible line in the geological record that marks the onset of the Anthropocene period in which human activity became a dominant influence on the planet. Australians barely remember the fallout that dusted us when I was a child. My great-aunt lived in Coffs Harbour, and the 'black clouds' that she vividly recalled were probably from British hydrogen bomb tests in South Australia. In 1956, radioactivity from the first bomb crossed the east coast, and rain deposited fallout from Brisbane to Lismore. Clouds from the second bomb also crossed the east coast about a day after detonation. The third bomb sprinkled radioactive dust over South Australia, Victoria and New South Wales. The fourth bomb dispersed contamination widely from Darwin to Newcastle.

Every living thing affects the world it inhabits, but the relationships between Mother Nature and her offspring are usually balanced and mutually maintained. We humans — the self-named 'wise person' (*Homo sapiens*) — are the exception. We're the only creatures that thoughtlessly, and sometimes deliberately, damage the natural systems we depend on.

In lockstep with our ballooning population — from about two and a half billion in 1950 to more than eight billion as I write this — the impacts of mining, farming and industrial development have intensified. The ongoing pursuit of wealth and progress comes at an ever greater cost. We can drink water from a plastic bottle, but we're finding micro-plastics just about everywhere, even in mothers' breastmilk. As the industry slogan put it, we enjoy 'better living through chemistry', but we're exposed to hormone-disrupting chemicals that cause illness and birth defects. We can transport ourselves and goods around the globe, but fossil fuel mining, processing and burning create pollution and pump greenhouse gases into the atmosphere. Herbicides transformed agriculture as farmers put aside their ploughs for 'no-dig' cropping. But now, agribusiness uses glyphosate to ripen crops for human consumption, and we find traces of the herbicide in human blood. Such are the trade-offs between benefits and costs in this age.

So how will we live well as we respond to the stress waves coming our way? We must first decide whether we'll engage with the stress or try to avoid it.

The Avoidance Option

The future will play out differently for you, me and everyone else. Nonetheless, whatever personal challenges lie ahead, we must all decide what we'll do about the coming stress tsunamis generated by social, economic, environmental and political crises. If we opt for avoidance, we'll be subject to the usual flaws and features of this strategy for dealing with stress. And if we decide to take on the challenge, the basic principles and practices for riding stress waves will apply.

Many will try to ignore, dismiss or otherwise avoid the coming threats and challenges. Avoidance would save us the onerous task of having to resolve some awful threats, and the strategy could work if we're unlikely to be affected by extreme events. Two downside risks come with this approach. If a catastrophe does occur, we'd be unprepared and especially vulnerable to harm. Further, as the portents of disaster become more frequent and difficult to ignore, our deep minds are likely to ramp up episodes of anxiety and fight-flight-freeze. The alternative approach of engaging with the stress entails more work initially, but would improve our prospects of surviving and thriving as the future plays out.

If our regular stress scans detect persistent anxiety and we can't ignore the looming threats, we will need to mentally process the stress and work out how to respond. For most people, the best option will be to focus on what I call the 'home front'; this is where we have the greatest responsibility to act and a reasonable prospect of making a difference.

Taking Care of the Home Front

> Even if I knew that tomorrow the world would
> go to pieces, I would still plant my apple tree.
> *Martin Luther (1483–1546)*

As it is for most folk, whenever I confront a new stress wave, my first impulse is to protect my family, friends and local community. In my life, I've concentrated on my professional psychological practice, raising a family, farming, regenerating native forests and protecting rural Australia from gas-field industrialisation. In any demanding undertaking, success depends on our ability to sustain effort for a potentially long time. To effectively ride big stress waves, we need to sort out what we can realistically achieve, and ration our mental, physical and emotional resources accordingly. If we spread ourselves thin by caring about too many people and issues, we risk burnout and being unable to help anyone. So our first duty is to care for ourselves and our families. This is the foundation on which we can build our efforts to help others.

Dear Reader, you and I are but two among more than eight billion human souls living on this planet, and we'll do our share if we leave the world a little better for our having lived in it. There are many ways to help our family, friends, community, Nature and the entire planet as we take care of the home front. Each of us has to work out what makes sense in our circumstances. To give you examples of what I'm referring to, I'll share some of what

Susan and I are doing to ready our home front for the coming climate-crisis-generated stress waves.

We manage our animals, orchards and gardens to produce as much of our food as we can. We're not 'preppers' (people who prepare for a catastrophe they believe will happen soon), but we aim to be self-sufficient in essential supplies and equipment. We practise holistic farming and rotational grazing; our cattle do well, and our soils become more fertile as their carbon content increases. We've installed sprinklers on our buildings and are ready to fight the inevitable bushfires. Removing lantana has increased biodiversity and reduced the flammability of our forests. When our regenerated forests burn, they'll release fewer particulates and less carbon into the atmosphere than lantana-infested bushland. But, for my readers who don't live on farms, there are many other ways to take care of your home front.

When you take on the challenge and get your executive and deep minds onto the job, you'll find creative ways to respond to the future. You might rediscover Nature or explore the practices of nature therapy, therapeutic farming or 'forest bathing'.[1,2] Hours spent by a creek, walking in the bush or exploring the universe at the bottom of your garden don't cost much. Connect with others and your community; fellowship, friendship and family are important for our well-being. Do what you can to stay fit and healthy by eating well, exercising and enjoying warm, intimate relationships.

Shrinking your carbon and pollution footprints is time and effort well spent. You might support some worthwhile environmental cause by donating money, signing petitions, voting for Nature-friendly politicians or even by becoming involved in the political process yourself. Along the way, you might discover your 'totem'.

Indigenous Australian children are traditionally assigned a totem to protect throughout their lives. The totem links the child to all living creatures and the spiritual world of The Dreaming.

A totem might be an animal, a plant, a place or a natural feature. If, for instance, your totem is the goanna, then it's on you to protect goannas and everything they rely on to survive. If your totem is a creek, it's your duty to prevent anything that compromises the quality and flow of its water. Importantly, people who share the same totem have a ready-made, special relationship with each other. When you find your totem, you might also discover your deep connection to life and to other people who share your passion.

If we focus primarily on the home front, we still have to reconcile ourselves to harsh realities and accept that there's much we cannot change. The stress tsunami isn't going away, and there's no hiding from the fact that the day might come when we lose everything. But today is not that day, and it's up to us to choose what we'll do with the time that's available to us. If your stress scans detect persistent anxiety, dig deep and often into your kit of tools and techniques for riding stress waves. When you've done all you can to take care of your home front, your responsibility is to enjoy your life.

We're caught up in a drama that affects everyone and everything. You and the many people who care are humanity's best hope for the future. This is a time to take on challenges, practice the art of riding stress waves and get on with playing our part. The adventure's far from over, and we have good reasons to be hopeful.

On Hope

> I am an optimist. It does not seem
> too much use being anything else.
> *Winston Churchill (1874–1965)*

The human mind creates our perils and our prospects. How we think and act will determine the future. We have the mental ability to meet the coming challenges creatively, and hope is the emotion that can drive our efforts to improve things. For without hope, nothing much gets done. Hope is the antidote to helplessness and despair; it gives us a reason to act.

Predicting apocalypse has always been popular, and nowadays, there are plenty of potential calamities to worry about. If you list all the ways the world could end, extinction seems like a done deal. But despairing fatalism won't help us ride the coming stress waves. In all great human endeavours, intent, hard work, sacrifice, persistence and good luck are essential for victory. I'll give you my argument for why we can be hopeful. Let's begin by examining how good we humans are at predicting the future.

We don't have to go far back in time to find unlikely, unanticipated events that changed the course of history for the better. Throughout my teenage years in the 1960s, nuclear war between the superpowers seemed imminent, but the world didn't blow up, thanks, in part, to Stanislav Petrov. In 1983, Lieutenant Colonel Petrov defied Soviet military protocol when, despite signals of an incoming missile attack, he refused to launch a nuclear counter-strike. A series of crucial events during World War II still seem incredible: The Battle of Britain, Winston Churchill's speeches to the British people, Alan Turing inventing the digital computer while riding his push-bike and then helping to crack the Nazi's enigma code, and Hitler's suicide.

No one predicted history-making events that improved people's lives, such as Nelson Mandela ending apartheid in South Africa or the fall of the Berlin Wall. Nor did anyone foresee such disruptive incidents as the 9/11 attacks on New York's World Trade Towers, the COVID-19 pandemic or — except for an episode of *The Simpsons* — Donald Trump's presidencies.

Do you remember the Y2K fracas as the world approached New Year's Day 2000? Contrary to the unanimous predictions of legions of experts, the clock struck midnight, and nothing untoward occurred. History teaches us to be cautious about assuming we know what will happen in the future. And that opens the door for hope.

We can find grounds for optimism even further back, millennia before written history. We humans have already survived climate disasters. For example, modern humans reached Australia more than 50,000 years ago.[3] For ten millennia, from about 30,000 years ago, the country was cooler and drier than it is now. Sand dunes dominated the interior and ice covered central Tasmania and the southern highlands of New South Wales. These conditions promoted Australia's exceptional biodiversity by forcing humans, animals and plants into the isolated refugia of gullies and other protected places.

Then, about 20,000 years ago, the global climate warmed, ice sheets collapsed and sea levels rose quickly. Some 8,000 years ago, rising waters separated Tasmania from the mainland, and Australia's climate settled into the pattern of drought and flooding rains that we're familiar with. When Europeans arrived, a million or more indigenous First Peoples from 250 language groups called the Great South Land home. Theirs is a story of survival through multiple climate crises. With only stone and wood technologies, our First People's success was founded on thousands of generations of stories, communities in balance with Nature and a deep knowledge of Country. Never bet on the demise of humanity; we're survivors across deep time.

It's impossible to know what's coming as humanity responds to the climate crisis and its associated stress tsunamis. History only reads like a story when we look back. When the future is yet to play out, we're involved in an unscripted drama with plenty of plot twists to come. No one can predict the tipping points in public opinion, technology, political will or who knows what else that might change how humanity relates to nature and accelerate the repair of natural systems. We know that Earth's trajectory of environmental decline can be reset. Before the COVID-19 pandemic, no one thought they'd ever see blue skies over New Delhi, clear waters in Venice's canals and skies free of aircraft contrails. And these were just a few effects of a virus.

I'm a baby boomer; my youngest granddaughter is a 'Gen Alpha'. Born between 2013 and 2025, the name Gen Alpha was chosen to denote a 'new start'. I like that. A new start is what we need, and the future belongs to the young. A recent survey asked a sample of Australians whether they thought humans had the right to 'use nature for their benefit, even if it impacts on the needs of other creatures'.[4] It didn't surprise me that 62 percent of the baby boomers thought humans should always take priority. But thankfully, only 21 percent of Gen Z — those born between 1997 and 2012 — agreed with that attitude. Gen Alphas, like my grand-daughter, were too young for the survey, but I reckon they'll continue the trend of increasing compassion and respect for Mother Nature. The finding that almost 80 percent of young people don't believe that humanity has the right to use Nature selfishly gives me hope.

We can count on unpredictable helpful events as humanity responds to the oncoming stress tsunamis. We won't know what these will be until they occur, but we can look forward to some exciting times. To despair and do nothing because we believe there's no hope would only make the future we fear more likely to come about. There's bad news aplenty, but if you look for them, there are also plenty of positive signs.

I recommend that you adopt a rural perspective when considering the future. A farmer plants a tree now for the shade and shelter it will provide down the track. A bush regenerator plants trees that'll take hundreds of years to reach maturity. We need to act now to create the future we want, even though we're unlikely to personally see how things turn out.

Humans might not be as fast or as strong as other animals, but we have the stamina and resilience to keep going regardless of what we face. People can recover from the worst traumas and ride the most savage stress waves to find renewed purpose and peace.

At this point, it might seem appropriate for me to address the second possible theatre of engagement with the coming stress tsunamis: leaving our home front for the front-line confrontation with the people and organisations responsible for the assault on Mother Nature. But I'm not going to do this. I'll explain why.

What I have to say about political and environmental activism would only interest a few readers. In this book, I've advised you to focus on stress waves that you can do something about. There's no reason for you to know about the extraordinary stresses that activists have to deal with unless you've fallen, or are about to fall, down the activist rabbit hole. I'm planning to write a supplementary book for our courageous protectors.

It's time to recap our journey together and bring this book to a close.

Chapter 20

Bringing It All Together

> You chose the best among us — a strong man:
> For where he fixt his heart he set his hand to
> do the thing he willed, and bore it through.
> *Alfred Lord Tennyson (1809–1892)*

IN *PART 1*, WE DISCUSSED the nature of stress and how we respond to life's challenges. You learnt about the structure of the human psyche and how the executive and deep minds work together — like an aeroplane's pilot and crew — to protect us in stressful times. We saw how natural coping strategies that avoid or engage with stress give us two alternative options for dealing with threats and challenges. Each approach entails costs and benefits, and depending on the circumstances, both strategies can work well. But for more complex and severe threats, an avoidant approach is unlikely to yield optimal results and can leave us with persistent anxiety. Some of these avoidant stress reactions can attract diagnoses of mental disorders even though they arise from our psyche's attempts to protect us.

You also learnt in *Part 1* that you can update old, suboptimal, avoidant reactions by engaging with the stress, enlisting both your executive and deep minds, and bringing your key mental processes to bear on the task.

In *Part 2*, we examined tools, tips and techniques for updating old stress responses, riding stress waves and achieving optimal mental health. You worked with tools that utilise the creative potential of your key mental processes. Along the way, you might have identified some blocks that affect how you deal with stress. We also reviewed psychological therapies for treating severe stress reactions. And we talked about perhaps the greatest stress waves of all: our fear of death and our grief for what we've lost.

The case studies in *Part 3*, illustrated how the art of riding stress waves plays out in the real world. We saw how we can resolve stress reactions that we adopted as infants, even when we can't remember what happened to us. We discussed the stress of working to heal Nature and what's involved in caring for our home front. I argued for hope and an optimistic engagement with the challenges of our time.

Your task now is to practice what you've learned about riding stress waves. Over time, engaging with stress, learning what you need to learn, resolving the threat and working out how to better protect yourself in the future will become easier and more natural for you. As you develop your skills, be prepared for setbacks. It takes time and effort to learn new ways of thinking and acting. Habits resist change until you update them.

Use your new knowledge and skills to identify and counter anything that blocks you from practising your art. Harness the power of your executive and deep minds to the task. Remember that your conscious attention is limited, and much goes on in your psyche that you're unaware of. Reflect on the way that your perception creates the reality you see. Take control of your imagination and memory to learn from the past and plan for the future. Free yourself from limiting beliefs and take on attitudes that foster success. Break word spells that harm, mislead and restrict. Choose your words carefully and use language respectfully to influence yourself and others. Appreciate your emotions and listen to what they tell you. Stay with your anxiety until it guides you to a problem's source and solution. Get used to thinking things through and driving a train of thought that has more than one carriage. Respect and listen to the ancient, intuitive wisdom that doesn't speak in words. Change what you can and accept what you can't. Do all these things, and you'll be richly rewarded.

Congratulations, Dear Reader. You've made it to the end of the book. If you picked up some useful ideas and can better ride the stress waves in your life, then, for me, our journey together was well worth it.

References

Chapter 2 – Stress and Stress Responses

1. Albrecht, G.A. 2005. Solastalgia: A new concept in human health and identity. *PAN (Philosophy, Activism, Nature), 3,* 41–55.

2. American Psychiatric Association. 2022. *Diagnostic and statistical manual of mental disorders, 5th edition*, APA.

3. Creamer, M., Burgess, P. & McFarlane, A. C. 2001. Post-traumatic stress disorder: Findings from the Australian National Survey of Mental Health and Well-Being. *Psychological Medicine, 31,* 1237-1247.

4. Rosenman, S. 2002. Trauma and posttraumatic stress disorder in Australia: Findings in the population sample of the Australian National Survey of Mental Health and Wellbeing. *Australian & New Zealand Journal of Psychiatry, 36,* 515-520.

5. Mills, K.L., McFarlane, A.C., Slade, T., Creamer, M., Silove, D., Teesson, M. & Bryant, R. 2011. Assessing the prevalence of trauma exposure in epidemiological surveys. *Australian and New Zealand Journal of Psychiatry, 45(5),* 407–15.

Chapter 3 – The Structure of Mind

1. Miller, G. A. 1956. The magical number seven, plus or minus two: Some limits on our capacity for processing information. *Psychological Review, 63,* 81–97.

Chapter 4 – Avoidance Strategies

1. Jung, C. G. 1992. *Experimental researches (Collected works, Vol. 2)*. London: Routledge.

2. American Psychiatric Association. 2022. *Diagnostic and statistical manual of mental disorders, 5th edition*, APA.

3. Somerville, W. R. & Jupp, J. J. 1992. Experimental evaluation of a brief 'ideodynamic' hypnotherapy applied to phobias. *Contemporary Hypnosis, 9*, 85–96.

4. Ohman, A. & Mineka, S. 2001. Fears, phobias, and preparedness: Toward an evolved module of fear and fear learning. *Psychological Review, 108(3)*, 483–522.

Chapter 5 – The Engage Strategy

1. Breuer, J. & Freud, S. 1893. On the psychical mechanism of hysterical phenomena: Preliminary communication. In A. Richards (ed.). 1974. *Studies on hysteria: The Pelican Freud Library, Vol. 3*. Great Britain: Penguin Books.

2. Watkins, J. 1949. *Hypnotherapy of war neuroses: A clinical psychologist's casebook*. New York: Ronald Press.

3. Silove, D. 1998. Is posttraumatic stress disorder an overlearned survival response? An evolutionary-learning hypothesis. *Psychiatry, 61*, 181-90.

4. Foa, E. B. 1997. Trauma and women: Course, predictors, and treatment. *Journal of Clinical Psychiatry, 58*, 25-28.

5. Foa, E. B. & Kozak, M. J. 1986. Emotional processing of fear: Exposure to corrective information. *Psychological Bulletin, 99*, 20-35.

6. Horowitz, M. J. 1993. Stress-response syndromes: A review of posttraumatic stress and adjustment disorders. In J. P. Wilson & B. Raphael (Eds.), *International handbook of traumatic stress syndromes* (pp. 49–60). Plenum Press.

7. Erickson, M. H. & Rossi, E. L. 1979. *Hypnotherapy: An exploratory casebook*. New York: Irvington Publ.

8. Erickson, M. 1948. Hypnotic psychotherapy. *The Medical Clinics of North America*, 571–583.

9. Erickson, M. H. 1980. Self-exploration in the hypnotic state: Facilitating unconscious processes and objective thinking. In E. L. Rossi (Ed.), *The collected papers of Milton H. Erickson on hypnosis, Vol. 4*, pp. 393-396). New York: Irvington.

10. Barnett, E. A. 1981. *Analytical hypnotherapy: Principles and practices.* Canada: Junica Publishing Co.

11. Somerville, W. R. & Jupp, J. J. 1992. Experimental evaluation of a brief 'ideodynamic' hypnotherapy applied to phobias. *Contemporary Hypnosis, 9*, 85–96.

12. Rachman, S. 1980. Emotional processing. *Behaviour Research and Therapy, 18*, 51–60.

13. Rachman, S. 2001. Emotional processing, with special reference to post-traumatic stress disorder. *International Review of Psychiatry, 13*, 164–171.

Chapter 7 – Attitudes and Beliefs

1. Dyer, F. & Martin, T. 1910. *Edison: His Life and Inventions.* The Project Gutenberg EBook, 2006.

2. Van der Kolk, B. A. 2015. *The body keeps the score: Brain, mind, and body in the healing of trauma.* New York, New York: Penguin Books.

Chapter 8 – Emotions

1. Covey, S. 1989. *The 7 habits of highly effective people.* N.Y.: Simon & Schuster.

2. Rose, J. 2014. *The Literary Churchill: Author, reader, actor.* New Haven & London: Yale University Press.

3. Tolkien, J.R.R. 1991. *The lord of the rings*. Harper Collins.

4. Churchill, W. 1940. *First Speech as Prime Minister to House of Commons*, May 13, 1940.

5. Roland, D. 2020. *The Power of Suffering: Growing through life crises*. Simon and Schuster.

6. Calaprice, A. 2005. *The new quotable Einstein*. Princeton University Press.

7. World Wildlife Fund. 2020. *Australia's 2019–2020 bushfires: The wildlife toll. Interim Report*. World Wide Fund for Nature Australia.

Chapter 9 – Language

1. Ellis, A. 1997. Must musturbation and demandingness lead to emotional disorders? *Psychotherapy: Theory, Research, Practice, Training, 34*(1), 95–98.

2. Shakespeare, W. 1993. *Romeo and Juliet*. Dover Publications.

3. Mitchell, J. T. & Everly, G. S., Jr. 1995. Critical incident stress debriefing (CISD) and the prevention of work-related traumatic stress among high risk occupational groups. In G. S. Everly, Jr. & J. M. Lating (Eds.), *Psychotraumatology: Key papers and core concepts in post-traumatic stress* (pp. 267–280). Plenum Press.

4. Seery, M., Silver, R., Holman, E., Ence, W. & Chu, T. 2008. Expressing thoughts and feelings following a collective trauma: Immediate responses to 9/11 predict negative outcomes in a national sample. *Journal of Consulting and Clinical Psychology, 76(4)*, 657–667.

5. Pennebaker, J. W. 1993. Putting stress into words: Health, linguistic and therapeutic implications. *Behavior Research Therapy, 31*, 539-548.

6. Pennebaker, J. W. 2014. Expressive writing can help your mental health, Interview, *Speaking of Psychology*, American Psychological Association, Episode 277.

Chapter 10 – Thinking and Reasoning

1. Wardell-Johnson, G., Stone, C., Recher, H. & Lynch, A. 2006. Bell Miner Associated Dieback (BMAD) independent scientific literature review: A review of eucalypt dieback associated with Bell miner habitat in north-eastern New South Wales. *Australia Occasional Paper DEC 2006/116*. Department of Environment and Conservation (NSW).

2. Somerville, S., Somerville, W. & Coyle, R. 2011. Regenerating native forest using splatter gun techniques to remove Lantana. *Ecological Management & Restoration, 2(3)*, 164.

3. Savory, A. & Butterfield, J. 2016. *Holistic Management: A commonsense revolution to restore our environment. 3rd edition.* Amazon Books.

Chapter 13 – Memory and Imagination

1. Bartlett, F. C. 1932. *Remembering*. Cambridge, Eng.: Cambridge Univ. Press.

2. Laor, N., Wolmer, L., Wiener, Z., Reiss, A., Muller, U., Weizman, R. & Ron, S. 1998. The function of image control in the psychophysiology of posttraumatic stress disorder. *Journal of Traumatic Stress, 11*, 679-96.

3. Finke, R. A. 1980. Levels of equivalence in imagery and perception. *Psychological Review, 87(2)*, 113–132.

4. Van der Kolk, B. A. 2015. *The body keeps the score: Brain, mind, and body in the healing of trauma*, New York, New York: Penguin Books.

5. Bandler, R. 1985. *Using your brain — for a change*. Moab, Utah: Real People Press.

6. Somerville, W. 2004. Cognitive Control Therapy for PTSD. *Doctor of Psychology dissertation*. Department of Psychology, Bond University, Gold Coast, Queensland.

7. Nigro, G. & Neisser, U. 1983. Point of view in personal memories. *Cognitive Psychology, 15*, 467-482.

8. Brewer, W. F. & Pani, J. R. 1996. Reports of mental imagery in retrieval from long-term memory. *Consciousness and Cognition, 5*, 265-87.

9. White, A. & Hardy, L. 1995. Use of different imagery perspectives on the learning and performance of different motor skills. *British Journal of Psychology, 86*, 169-80.

10. Spiegel, D. & Cardena, E. 1990. New uses of hypnosis in the treatment of posttraumatic stress disorder. *Journal of Clinical Psychiatry, 51*, 39-43.

11. Hossack, A. & Bentall, R. P. 1996. Elimination of posttraumatic symptomatology by relaxation and visual-kinesthetic dissociation. *Journal of Traumatic Stress, 9*, 99-110.

12. Marks, D. F. 1972. Individual differences in the vividness of visual imagery and their effect on function. In P. W. Sheehan (Ed.), *The function and nature of imagery* (pp. 83-108). New York: Academic Press.

13. Andrade, J., Kavanagh, D. & Baddeley, A. 1997. Eye-movements and visual imagery: A working memory approach to the treatment of post-traumatic stress disorder. *British Journal of Clinical Psychology, 36*, 209-23.

14. Barnett, E. A. 1981. *Analytical hypnotherapy: Principles and practices*. Canada: Junica Publishing Co.

15. Somerville, W. R. & Jupp, J. J. 1992. Experimental evaluation of a brief 'ideodynamic' hypnotherapy applied to phobias. *Contemporary Hypnosis, 9*, 85-96.

16. Watkins, H. H. 1993. Ego-state therapy: An overview. *American Journal of Clinical Hypnosis, 35*, 232-240.

17. Jackman, R. 2020. *Healing your lost inner child: How to stop impulsive reactions, set healthy boundaries and embrace an authentic life*. Practical Wisdom Press.

18. Bandler, R. & Grinder, J. 1979. *Frogs into princes*, NLP. Moab, Utah: Real People Press.

19. Rusch, M., Grunert, B., Mendelsohn, R. & Smucker, M. 2000. Imagery rescripting for recurrent, distressing images. *Cognitive & Behavioral Practice, 7*, 173-182.

20. Covey, S. 1989. *The 7 habits of highly effective people*. N.Y.: Simon & Schuster.

21. Stanton, H. E. 1988. Relaxation, deepening, and ego-enhancement: A stress reduction 'package'. *Australian Psychologist, 23*, 315-322.

22. Grossman, D. 1996. *On killing: The psychological cost of learning to kill in war and society*. Little, Brown and Co.

23. Eisenberg, N. & Cohen Silver, R. 2011. Growing up in the shadow of terrorism: Youth in America after 9/11. *Amer. Psychologist, 66(6)*, 468–481.

24. Holmes, E. A., Creswell, C. & O'Connor, T. G. 2007. Posttraumatic stress symptoms in London school children following September 11, 2001: An exploratory investigation of peri-traumatic reactions and intrusive imagery. *Journal of Behavior Therapy and Experimental Psychiatry, 38*, 474–490.

Chapter 14 – Sleep, Dreams and Daydreams

1. Kleitman, N. 1982. Basic rest-activity cycle — 22 years later. *Journal of Sleep Research and Sleep Medicine, 5(4)*, 311–317.

2. Rossi, E. & Nimmons, D. 1991. *The 20-minute break: Using the new science of ultradian rhythms*. Los Angeles, CA: Jeremy P. Tarcher, Inc.

3. Freud, S. 1900. *The interpretation of dreams*, S.E. Vol. IV.

4. Somerville, W. 1976. Falling asleep: Mental activity and the effects of pre-sleep stimuli. *Empirical thesis for Bachelor of Arts Honours degree*. Macquarie University.

5. Ekirch, A.R. 2005. *At day's close: Night in times past*. New York: W.W. Norton & Co.

6. Somerville, W. 1976. Falling asleep: Mental activity and the effects of pre-sleep stimuli. *Empirical thesis for Bachelor of Arts Honours degree*. Macquarie University.

7. Freud, S. 1913. *The interpretation of dreams. Third edition*, translated by A. A. Brill. New York: The Macmillan Company.

8. Krakow, B., Kellner, R., Pathak, D. & Lambert, L. 1995. Imagery rehearsal treatment for chronic nightmares. *Behavior Research and Therapy, 33*, 837-843.

Chapter 15 – Intuition

1. Van der Kolk, B. A. 2015. *The body keeps the score: Brain, mind, and body in the healing of trauma*, N.Y., New York: Penguin Books.

Chapter 16 – Therapies for traumatic stress

1. Baddeley, A. D. & Andrade, J. 2000. Working memory and the vividness of imagery. *J. of Exper. Psychology: General, 129*, 126–145.

2. Kavanagh, D. J., Freese, S., Andrade, J. & May, J. 2001. Effects of visuospatial tasks on desensitization to emotive memories. *British Journal of Clinical Psychology, 40*, 267-280.

3. Reynolds, M. & Tarrier, N. 1996. Monitoring of intrusions in posttraumatic stress disorder: A report of single case studies. *British Journal of Medical Psychology, 69*, 371-379.

4. Bowen, G. R. & Lambert, J. A. 1986. Systematic desensitization therapy with post-traumatic stress disorder cases. In C. R. Figley (Ed.), *Trauma and its wake. Vol. 2: Traumatic stress theory, research, and intervention* (pp. 280-291). New York: Brunner Mazel.

5. Williams, J. M. G., Teasdale, J. D., Segal, Z. V. & Soulsby, J. 2000. Mindfulness-based cognitive therapy reduces overgeneral autobiographical memory in formerly depressed patients. *Journal of Abnormal Psychology, 109*, 150–155.

6. Williams, M., Russell, I. & Russell, D. 2008. Mindfulness-based cognitive therapy: Further issues in current evidence and future research. *J Consult Clin Psychol. 2008 Jun; 76(3)*: 524–529.

7. Becker, C. B. & Zayfert, C. 2001. Integrating DBT-based techniques and concepts to facilitate exposure treatment for PTSD. *Cognitive & Behavioral Practice, 8*, 107-122.

8. Somerville, W. R. & Jupp, J. J. 1992. Experimental evaluation of a brief 'ideodynamic' hypnotherapy applied to phobias. *Contemporary Hypnosis, 9*, 85-96.

9. Smucker, M. R., Dancu, C., Foa, E. B. & Niederee, J. L. 2002. Imagery rescripting: A new treatment for survivors of childhood sexual abuse suffering from posttraumatic stress. In R. L. Leahy & T. E. Dowd (Eds.), *Clinical advances in cognitive psychotherapy: Theory and application* (pp. 294-310). New York: Springer Publ.

10. Rusch, M., Grunert, B., Mendelsohn, R. & Smucker, M. 2000. Imagery rescripting for recurrent, distressing images. *Cognitive & Behavioral Practice, 7*, 173-182.

11. Craig, G. & Fowlie, A. 1995. *Emotional freedom techniques: The manual.* Sea Ranch, CA: Gary Craig.

12. Callahan, R. J. & Callahan, J. 1996. *Thought Field Therapy (TFT) and trauma: Treatment and theory.* Indian Wells, California: Callahan Techniques.

13. Shapiro, F. (Speaker). 1992. *Eye movement desensitization and reprocessing* (Cassette Recording No. E297-6AB). Phoenix, Arizona: The Milton H. Erickson foundation, Inc.

14. Shapiro, F. & Maxfield, L. 2002. Eye movement desensitization and reprocessing (EMDR): Information processing in the treatment of trauma. *Journal of Clinical Psychology, 58,* 933-946.

15. Hyer L. & Brandsma, J. M. 1997. EMDR minus eye movements equals good psychotherapy. *Journal of Traumatic Stress, 10,* 515-22.

16. Cusack, K. & Spates, C. R. 1999. The cognitive dismantling of Eye Movement Desensitization and Reprocessing (EMDR) treatment of Posttraumatic Stress Disorder (PTSD). *Journal of Anxiety Disorders, 13,* 87-99.

17. Ogden, P. & Fisher, J. 2015. *Sensorimotor psychotherapy: Interventions for trauma and attachment.* (D. Del Hierro & A. Del Hierro, Illustrators). W W Norton & Co.

18. Levine, P. 2008. *Healing Trauma: A Pioneering Program for Restoring the Wisdom of Your Body.* Sounds True. Kindle Edition.

19. Payne, P., Levine, P. A. & Crane-Godreau, M. A. 2015. Somatic Experiencing: Using interoception and proprioception as core elements of trauma therapy: Corrigendum. *Frontiers in Psychology, 6,* Article 423.

20. Cochrane, A. 1972. *Effectiveness and efficiency. Random reflections on health services.* London: Nuffield Provincial Hospitals.

Chapter 17 – Dealing with the past

1. Pearce, J.C. 1977. *Magical child: Rediscovering nature's plan for our children*. E. P. Dutton.

Chapter 18 – Healing nature

1. Wardell-Johnson, G., Stone, C., Recher, H. & Lynch, A. 2006. Bell Miner Associated Dieback (BMAD) independent scientific literature review: A review of eucalypt dieback associated with Bell miner habitat in north-eastern New South Wales. *Australia Occasional Paper DEC 2006/116*. Department of Environment and Conservation (NSW).

2. Somerville, S., Somerville, W. & Coyle, R. 2011. Regenerating native forest using splatter gun techniques to remove Lantana. *Ecological Management & Restoration, 2(3)*, 164.

3. Somerville, W. & Somerville, S. 2019. *Curing Bell Miner Associated Dieback: Bush regeneration on Creek's Bend, Kyogle.* YouTube video. https://www.youtube.com/watch?v=s4zINkKPESU

Chapter 19 – Facing the future

1. Hansen, M., Jones, R. & Tocchini, K. 2017. Shinrin-Yoku (Forest Bathing) and Nature Therapy: A State-of-the-Art Review. *Int J Environ Res Public Health, 14(8)*: 851.

2. Elsey, H., Bragg, R., Brennan, C., Elings, M., Murray, J., Richardson, Z., Wickramasekera, N., Hucklesbury, A. & Cade, J. 2014. *The impact of care farms on quality of life among different population groups: protocol for a systematic review.* https://doi.org/10.1002/CL2.121

3. Cane, S. 2013. *First footprints: The epic story of the first Australians*. Allen and Unwin.

4. Readfearn, G. 2023. Seismic shift: Younger Australians reject idea humans have right to use nature for own benefit, survey shows. *Guardian, Australia, 23 Jun 2023*, Guardian online.

Index

Names in double quotation marks indicate stories about people.
Page numbers for all graphics are in the Illustrations.

2019 drought, 106
2019–20 bushfires
    impact on author, 21–22, 59, 106
    impact on scientists, 109
    PM's one-thought solution, 33–34
    post-fire recovery, 233–34
9/11 (WTC), 126, 173, 241

A

abreaction and catharsis, 53
acceptance, 105–6, 207
acceptance & commitment therapy, 207
ACT. *See* acceptance and commitment
activism, 243–44
addiction process, 82–83
addictive substances, 82
Adelson, Edward, 145
aeroplane analogy, 28, 45–46
agoraphobia and panic disorder
    beliefs, 42–43
    breathing, 43
alcohol, 82, 202
alpha waves, 176
analytical hypnotherapy, 56–57, 165
"Andrew" (family therapy), 134–35
anger, 92–93
"Anne" (EMDR), 215
Anthropocene, 123, 236
anxiety
    addictive substances, 82–83
    anxiety disorders (DSM), 36–48
    as signal of danger, 3, 86–87
    as symptom, 3
    courage and, 98–99
    history of treatment, 53–57
    imagery perspective, 157–58
    letting go unnecessary, 91–92
    lobotomy for, 215
    media, 172–74
    medications for, 2–4, 202
    memory, imagination and, 149–51
    mental processing of, 57–59
    need to keep, 74–77
    protective function of, 3
    quit smoking and anxiety, 119–20
    rationing emotional energy, 89–91
    stress and, 17–19
    stress scan, 87–89
    tape over warning light, 3
    treatments for, 202–13
anxiety disorders (DSM), 36–49
apartheid in South Africa, 241
apnoea, 178–79
Aragorn's speech (*Lord of the Rings*), 99
art as skilled endeavour, 13–15
art of riding stress waves
    aim, 15
    background history, 53–57
    basic formula, 60–61
    essential knowledge, 14–15
    skills for, 15
attention, 24–27, 141–42, 200, 211
attitudes and beliefs
    addictive substances, 82–83
    agoraphobia, role in, 42–43
    chronic illness & disability, 80–81

cognitive therapy and, 206–7
healing Nature, 232
learning & making mistakes, 70–71
need to keep stress reaction, 74–77
optimism and pessimism, 72–73
others and the world, 77–79
physical pain, 79–80
PTSD, role in, 44
self-efficacy, 69–70
Socratic questioning of, 132–34
stress responses, 73–74
therapy, role in, 53–55
avoidant personality disorder, 38
avoidant strategies
agoraphobia & panic disorder, 42–43
avoidant personality, 38
effective use of, 33–34
Laing, R.D., quote, 31
let it go through to the keeper, 31–32
"Ms Dowdy" (teacher), 35
obsessive-compulsive disorder, 41–42
one-thought solution, 32–34
politicians, use of, 33–34
posttraumatic stress disorder, 44–48
preferences and personality, 35–36
protective nature of, 31–32
separation anxiety, 37–38
social anxiety disorder, 42
specific phobia, 39–41
when causes trouble, 34–48
awareness, 25–27
ayahuasca, 202

B

baby boomers, 225–26, 236, 243
balancing emotions. *See* rationing ...
Bandler, Richard, 155
Barnett, Edgar, 57
barrier of amnesia, 176

"Barry" (dentist chair), 206
basic rest-activity cycle, 175–76, 181
Beecher, Henry Ward, quote, 175
begin with end in mind, 170
behaviourism. *See* behaviourist ...
behaviourist psychology
exposure, 54
habituation, 54
parenting, impacts on, 226–27
phobia treatments, 54
beliefs. *See* attitudes and beliefs
Bell miner associated dieback (BMAD)
bush regen as therapy, 233–34
costs/benefits of solutions, 231–33
ecosystem collapse, 135
family therapy for forests, 136–37
fossil fuel technology, 232–33
glyphosate, 230–31
Hunter, John, 230–31
John Hunter's father, 230
"Kate" (anti-glyphosate), 232
lantana associated dieback, 121–22
lantana invasion, 135
lantana, role in, 230–31
lerps, 137
model of forest dieback, 136–37
naming BMAD, 121–22
national dieback forum, 136
National Parks meeting, 230
psyllid insects, 137
review of scientific literature, 230
splatter gun, 230
value of forests, 233
working group, 230
benzodiazepines, 5, 107
Berlin Wall, fall of, 241
"Bill" (WWII veteran), 155–56
bio-computer analogy, 5–6
birthing experience, 224
black humour, 161–62
Blake, William, quote, 143
Blyton, Enid, 183

INDEX

BMAD. *See* Bell miner associated ...
Bodhisattva. *See* meditating bodhisattva
book parts, 7
brain
    brain injuries, 5
    electrical activity in, 176
    frontal lobotomy, 215–16
    relationship to mind, 5–6
tobacco addiction, 82–83
breathing
    anxiety, effects on, 43–44
    agoraphobia, role in, 43
    sleep apnoea, 178–79
    ultradian break, 181–82
Breuer, Josef, 53
broken glass story, 105
burning out, 90–91
bushfires (2019)
    grieving over, 106
    impact on author, 21–22, 59
    impact on scientists, 109
    PM's holiday during, 33–34
bush regeneration. See Bell miner ...

C

cane toads, 231
cannabis, 202
carbon footprint, 233
"Carl" (exposure therapy), 204–5
"Carol" (guilt), 97
cartoon voices, 154, 161
catastrophic thinking, 130–31
catharsis, 53, 57
cautionary cases, 214–15
chakra (centre of energy), 209
"Charles" (9/11), 173
chequer board illusion, 145–47
Chevreul, Anton, 192–93
Chevreul's pendulum, 192–93
Ch'i, 209
choosing a therapy, 216–17
Churchill, Sir Winston, 98, 240

chronic illness and disability, 80–81
cinematic analogy (memory), 167
circle of concern, 89–90
circle of influence, 89–90
circus monkey, 154, 161
CISD. *See* critical incident ...
climate, 1, 102, 122–23, 235, 242
climate change. *See* climate
climate crisis. *See* climate
climate destabilisation. *See* climate
clinical psychology. *See* psychology
Cochrane, Archie, 213
cognitive behaviour therapy, 206–7
cognitive control training, 155
cognitive therapy, 206–7
colour
    chequerboard illusion, 145–47
    colour/b&w, 153, 158–59
    new car, 33
computers
    hardware, 5–6
    human bio-computer, 6
    programs, 5–6
    software, 5–6
Confucius quote, 65
conscription, 101
contemplation, 142
control group problem, 213
conversion disorder, 53
cooperation, 77, 90
costs/benefits of solutions, 232–33
courage, 98–99
Covey, Stephen, 89–90
COVID-19 pandemic, 1, 241
crafting the future, 169–70
Craig, Gary (EFT), 209
critical incident stress debriefing, 126

D

"David" (phobia of heights), 194–96
da Vinci, Leonardo, quote, 86
day in court. *See* virtual day in court

day's residue, 177
DBT. *See* dialectical ...
dealing with the past, 221–25
death. *See* fear of death
deep mind
    aeroplane analogy, 28
    deep mind at work, 27–28
    ego defences, 28
    habits, 28
    intuition, 27
    learning to drive a car, 23
    Susan's driving story, 23–24
    working with the, 191–94
depression, 93–94
dialectical behaviour therapy, 207
dieback. *See* Bell miner ...
discounting the positive, 132
distance in imagery, 153, 159–60
Doctor of Psychology degree, 156
double-blind comparison, 213–14
"Dr Allen" (lobotomy), 215
Dr Beer, 82
dreams and dreaming. *See* sleep
dream interpretation, 187–88
DSM (diagnostic manual), 36–48
Dutch courage. *See* courage

E

ecstasy (MDMA), 202
Edison, Thomas, quote, 71
EFT. *See* emotional freedom techniques
ego defence mechanisms, 28
ego state therapy, 165
Einstein, Albert, 104
Ellis, Albert, 115
emotional freedom techniques, 209–10
EMDR. *See* eye movement ...
emotional impact of imagery, 151–62
emotional processing
    aeroplane analogy, 57–58
    enactive mastery, 58

    outside of awareness, 194–97
    meridians, 209
emotions
    anger, 92–93
    "Carol" (guilt), 97
    courage, 98–99
    depression, 93–94
    fear and anxiety, 86–88
    fear of death, 100–6
    grief, 107–11
    guilt and shame, 94–97
    hope, 115, 200, 240–43
    humour, 161–62
    "James" (guilt), 97
energy psychology, 209
energy system (EFT), 209
engage strategy, 51–61
ego defence mechanisms, 28
enactive mastery, 58
environmental activism. *See* activism
Erasmus, Desiderius, 177
Ericksonian hypnotherapy, 57
Erickson, Milton, 56–57
everyday trance, 175
evidence-based approach
    cautionary cases, 214–16
    Cochrane, Archie, 213
    control group problem, 214
    double-blind, 213–14
    limitations of, 216
    lobotomy as, 215–16
    placebo, 213
    randomised trials, 213–14
executive mind
    aeroplane analogy, 28
    conscious awareness, 24–27
    nature of, 24–26
exposure therapy
    assumptions & procedure, 203–6
    "Carl" (exposure therapy), 204–5
    caveats and risks, 205–6
    distractions during, 205

INDEX

expressive writing. *See* Pennebaker, J.
eye movement desensitisation and reprocessing
    "Anne" (EMDR), 215
    development & procedure, 210–11
    rating scales in, 211

F

facing the future
    activism, 244
    avoidance option, 237–38
    human/Nature relationship, 235–36
    industrial revolution, 235–36
    on hope, 240–43
    taking care of home front, 238–40
fallacy of hindsight & 'what ifs', 130–31
falling asleep, 183–84
false memories, 149
family therapy
    "Andrew", 134–35
    for forests, 135–36
    systemic family therapy, 57, 135
Faustian bargain, 236
fear and anxiety, 86–92
fear of death
    acceptance of, 105–6
    avoiding the dying, 102
    mental processing of, 100–2
    suicide, 102–3
    unity of all things, 103–4
fear of public speaking, 35, 51–52
"Felice" (storm phobia), 76–77
fields
    consciousness, 6
    electromagnetic and quantum, 6
fight-flight-freeze response
    2019–20 bushfires, 21–22
    mind and body effects, 20
    other animals, 20–21
    snakes, 21
filtering, 131–32

first and second sleeps, 180–81
first atomic reactor, 241
first-person perspective. *See* memory and …
flawed reasoning
    discounting the positive, 132
    filtering, 131–32
    mind reading & fortune telling, 132
    personalisation, 131–32
    polarised thinking, 131
Foa, Edna, 54
Foa, Edna and Kozak, Michael, 54–55
forensic assessment of guilt, 96
forest bathing, 239
forest dieback. *See* Bell miner associated…
fossil fuel technology, 232–33
Frankenstein. *See* Shelley, Mary
Frankl, Viktor, quote, 199
Freud, Sigmund
    abreaction and catharsis, 53
    day's residue, 178
    dreams, 187
    ego defence mechanisms, 28
    hypnosis and stress memories, 53
    libido, 209
    process of association, 53
    projection, 28
    quote, 23
    repression, 28
frontal lobotomy, 215–16
functional equivalence, 150

G

Gandhi, Mahatma, quote, 92
Gen Alpha, 243
generalisations, 114
generation's shared stress. *See* baby …
Gen Z, 243
gestalt psychology, 147
giant devil's fig, 231
giving up tobacco, 82–83, 119–20

global warming. *See* climate change
glyphosate herbicide, 230–233
Goodall, Jane, quote 229
good memories, 168–169
Gregory, Bridie, 227
grief
    author's great-aunt, 107
    ceremonies, 107–9
    "Harry's" funeral, 108
    Kerri's funeral, 108
    resolving grief, 107–110
guided imagery
    disposing of unwanted things, 171
    removing barriers, 171
    the pond, 171
guilt and shame
    "Carol" (abuse), 97
    forensic assessment of guilt, 96
    function of, 94
    "James" (broken promise), 97
    "Jan" (soup kitchen guilt), 97
    "Rob" (veteran guilt), 95, 97

H

habits, 28
habituation, 54, 206
"Harry's" funeral, 108
head injuries. *See* brain injuries
healing nature
    improbable events, 230–31
    lantana problem, 230–31
    theatres of engagement, 229
    use of glyphosate, 230–33
Heraclitus quote, 185
Hitler, Adolf, 241
Hobart, Tasmania, 23
holistic farming, 137–38
holistic thinking, 134–39
hope
    as a noun, 115
    as a verb, 115
    grounds for, 240–44

hope and try, 114–15
    role in therapy, 200
Horowitz, Mardi, 55
human bio-computer analogy, 5–6
humour, use of, 154, 161–62
Hunter, John, 230–31
hypnagogia, 176, 183–84
hypnagogic imagery. *See* hypnagogia
hypnopompic imagery, 177
hypnosis and hypnotherapy
    Chevreul's pendulum, 192–93
    Ericksonian hypnotherapy, 56–57, 203
    hypnotherapy for phobia, 208
    ideomotor signalling, 192
    ideosensory signals, 192
    induction of, 191
    new hypnosis, 56
    outside of awareness, 194–97
    Sorcerer's Apprentice suggestion, 83
    styles of, 203
    "Sylvia" (hypnotherapy), 196–197
    "Terry" (self-hypnosis), 118
    tobacco addiction, 82–83
    use of 'yes' effect, 32–34

I

ideodynamic hypnotherapy, 165, 208
ideomotor signalling, 192, 195
ideosensory signals, 192
illusions. *See* perceptual illusions
imagery. *See* memory and imagination
imagery perspective & anxiety, 157–58
imagery rescripting therapy, 165, 207–9
imagination. *See* memory and imagination
importance of ceremonies, 107–9
Indigenous Australians
    climate crises, 242
    history of survival, 242
    the dreaming, 239

INDEX 267

totem, 239–40
industrial revolution, 235–36
inner child work, 165
inner mind. *See* deep mind
insomnia, 179–81
intuition, 27, 191–97

J

"James" (guilt), 97
James, William, quote, 51
"Jan" (soup kitchen), 97
Janet, Pierre, 168
"Jenny" (weight loss), 175–177
Jesus' death, 101
"Jim and Claire" (PTSD), 46
"Joan" (deep water), 40
Johnson, Wendell, quote, 114
journey metaphor, 170
Jung, Carl, 34, 168, 187–188

K

Kabat-Zinn, John, quote, 13
"Kate" (anti-glyphosate), 232
Kekule, August (dream), 183
Kerri's funeral, 108
key mental processes
    awareness and, 24–27
    defined, 24–25
    operation of, 24–25

L

labels. *See* names and labels
Laing, R.D., quote, 31
language
    critical incident debriefing, 126
    generalisations, 114
    hope and try, 114–15
    motivation style, 119–20
    must and should, 115–17
    names and labels, 120–25
    negative language, 117–18
    talking with others, 125–27

    troublesome words, 114–20
    writing, 127–128
lantana, 121–22, 135–37, 230–31
lantana associated dieback, 122
Lao Tzu quote, 70
Lara Croft game, 172–73
learning and making mistakes, 70–71
lerps (sugary coatings), 137
letting go unnecessary anxiety, 91–92
Levine, Peter, 211–12
libido, 209
Lincoln, Abraham, quote, 72
lobotomy, 215
logs on road illusion, 144–45
London, Jack, quote, 113
LSD-25, 5, 202
lucid dream (father's death), 109–10
Luther, Martin, quote, 238

M

Macbeth, 1
magic mushrooms, 202
Magical Child, 227
Mandela, Nelson, 98, 241
Martina Reynolds. *See* Reynolds
Master of Clinical Psychology, 57
Maury, Alfred, 183
MBCT. *See* mindfulness based …
MDMA (ecstasy), 202
media prescription, 174
media stress
    9/11 attacks, 173
    Lara Croft game, 172–73
    mental health impacts, 173–74
    US school shootings, 173
medical model of mental health
    logic of, 2–3
    physicalism, 3–5
    'tennis ball' experiment, 2–3
medications for mental health problems
    argument for use, 2–3
    riding stress waves, 3–4, 202–3

    relapse with use of, 4
    separation anxiety disorder, 37–38
meditating bodhisattva, 105
meditation, 141–42
memory and imagination
    add support, 154, 161
    anxiety due to, 149–51
    better ending, 95
    brightness, 153, 158–59
    cartoon voice, 154, 161
    circus monkey, 154, 161
    colour vs. black/white, 153, 158–59
    controlling emotional impact, 151–62
    distance, 153, 159–60
    functional equivalence, 149–50
    media stress, 172–74
    memory as reconstructions, 149
    perspective, 153, 157–58
    self-statements, 154, 162
    size, 153, 160
    training memory criteria, 152
    volume, 154, 160
memory complexes, 34
mental disorders (DSM)
    agoraphobia and panic, 42–44
    avoidant personality disorder, 38
    definition in DSM, 36
    obsessive-compulsive disorder, 41–42
    posttraumatic stress disorder, 42–48
    separation anxiety disorder, 37–38
    social anxiety disorder, 42
    specific phobia disorder, 39–41
mental exercises and thought experiments, 7–8
mental processing, 57–59
metacognition, 142
"Michael" (hypnagogia), 184
mind
    awareness, 24–27
    bio-computer analogy, 5–6
    cup of tea example, 4–5
    levels of explanation, 4–5
    relationship with brain, 2–6
    structure of, 23–29
mind reading and fortune telling, 132
mindfulness-based cognitive therapy, 207
"Miss Dowdy" (teacher), 35
"Mitch", 151
model for BMAD, 136
motivation style, 119–20
movie metaphor for memories, 167
must and should, 115–17
musturbation, 115

N

names and labels
    'A rose by any other name...', 120
    Bell miner associated dieback, 121–22
    Biblical names, 120
    climate change, 122–23
    'natural', 124–25
    using middle initial, 121
native forest dieback. *See* Bell miner ...
natural trance, 100–1
nature therapy, 239
need to keep a stress reaction, 74–77
negative language, 117–18
neuro-linguistic programming, 57, 165
new endings for memories, 166–68
new hypnosis, 56–57
Nicolas Tarrier, *See* Reynolds...
nightmares, treatment of, 189
NLP. *See* neurolinguistic ...
"Nora" (birth memory), 221–22
Northern Rivers, 1

O

obsessive-compulsive disorder, 41–42
OCD. *See* obsessive-compulsive ...

INDEX

Ogden, Pat, 211–12
one-thought solution
    definition, 32–34
    effectiveness of, 33–34
    Scott Morrison example, 33–34
    use by politicians, 34
    'yes' effect, 33
opportunity costs, 51, 233
optical illusions. *See* perceptual illusions
optimism and pessimism, 72–73

P

Pearce, Joseph Chilton, 227
Pennebaker, James, 127
perception
    perceptual illusions, 144–47
    reality as a dashboard, 144
    seven senses, 143
    vision, 143–44
perceptual illusions
    chequerboard, 146–47
    logs on road, 144
    old woman/young woman, 145
personal case study, 222–27
personalisation, 130–32
perspective in imagery, 153, 157–58
"Peter" (veteran client), 216–17
Petrov, Lieutenant Colonel, 241
Peyote, 202
phobia
    agoraphobia, 42–44
    behavioural treatment of, 54
    characteristics of, 39
    "David" (heights), 194–96
    evolution of, 41
    "Felice" (storm phobia), 76–77
    "Joan" (deep water), 40
    "Peter" (medical), 216–17
    protective nature of, 39–41
    social phobia, 42
    Somerville and Jupp, 57, 208
    specific phobia disorder, 39–41
photovoltaics. *See* solar panels
physical pain, 79–80
physicalism, 5
placebo, 213–14
polarised thinking, 131
population explosion, 236
post-trauma growth, 103
posttraumatic stress disorder (PTSD)
    aeroplane analogy for, 45–46
    as protective stress response, 44–45
    case studies, 46–47
    characteristics of, 44–45
    cognitive control training, 155
    delayed-onset, 150–51
    Doctor of Psychology study, 156
    effects of reliving stress, 150
    EMDR, 210–11, 215
    functional equivalence, 149–50
    hysteria, 53
    "Jane" (bank teller), 46–47
    "Jim" and "Claire" (veteran), 46
    Macbeth quote, 1
    near misses, 150–51
    new endings for memories, 165–68
    nightmares, treatment of, 189
    "Peter" (former client), 216–17
    resolution of, 47–48
    talking about trauma, 125–26
    vicarious traumatisation, 78–79
power naps, 181
preppers, 239
process of association, 53
programs (computer), 5–6
projection (Freud), 28
psychedelics, 5, 202–3
psychoactive medications. *See* medications for…
psychological therapies. *See* therapies for…

psychology
    cognitive psychology, 134
    evidence-based approach, 213–14
    impacts on parenting, 226–27
    psychological perspective, 2–7
    psychology and psychiatry, 2–7
    psychonaut, 202
psyllids, 137

Q
quit smoking and anxiety, 119–20

R
"Rachael" (learning), 71
Rachman, Jack, 57
radical vs. conservative, 123–24
radioactive fallout, 236
randomised controlled trials, 213–14
rapid eye movement (REM)
    day's residue, 177
    frequency, 186–87
    interpretation, 187–88
    nightmare treatment, 189
    partial paralysis during, 185
    sleep cycle, 177
rating scales
    how to use, 8
    severity of stress, 19
    stress scan, 87–89
    training memory scale, 152
    use in therapy, 200–1, 205, 207, 210–11, 214–15
rationing emotional energy
    caring for assets, 90
    circle of concern, 89–90
    circle of influence, 89–90
    letting go of anxiety, 91–92
real and perceived danger, 91–92
reasoned thought, 132–34
reciprocal inhibition, 204
relapse, 4
repression, 28

resolving grief
    author's great-aunt, 107
    author's lucid dream, 109–10
    ceremonies, 107–9
    "Harry's" funeral, 108–9
    Kerri's funeral, 108
    "Reverend Judy" sermon, 108
resolving stress memories
    movie metaphor, 166
    rescripting memories, 165–68
    transfer adult resources, 163–65
respectful communication, 193–94
Reynolds and Tarrier, 201
"Rhonda" ('must'), 117
"Richard" (MVA survivor), 75
"Rick" (child protection), 79
"Rob" (veteran guilt), 95
"Robert" (agoraphobia), 43
Romeo and Juliet (a rose…), 120

S
Sacks, Oliver, quote, 105
sand play, 208–9
Savory, Allan, 137–38
self-efficacy, 69–70
Selye, Hans, quote, 17
Seneca quote, 103
sensorimotor psychotherapy, 211–12
separation anxiety disorder, 37–38
set and setting, 202
Shakespeare, William
    Macbeth quote, 1
    Romeo and Juliet quote, 120
    The Tempest quote, 100
Shapiro, Francine, 210–11
Shelley, Mary, 185
Shelley, Percy, 185
'should', 115–17
sleep. *See* sleep, dreams and …
sleep apnoea, 178–79
sleep, dreams and daydreams
    alpha waves, 176

author's lucid dream, 109–10
barrier of amnesia, 176
basic rest-activity cycle, 175
day's residue, 177
everyday trance, 175
first and second sleeps, 180–81
hypnagogia, 176, 183–84
hypnopompic imagery, 177
"Michael" (hypnagogia), 184
natural trance, 181–83
rapid eye movement, 177, 185–88
ultradian break, 175
sleep onset experiences, 183–84
sleep stages, 176–77
sleep onset experiences, 183–84
sleep onset study (author), 183–84
sleeping well
    insomnia, 179–81
    sleep apnoea, 178–79
    temperature and noise, 178
social anxiety disorder, 42
Socrates quote, 132
Socratic questioning, 132–34
solar panels, 233
solastalgia, 19
solution-focused therapy, 57
somatic experiencing, 211–12
somatic psychotherapies, 211–12
Somerville, Susan
    2019 bushfires, 21–22, 59, 106
    bush regen, 10, 121–22, 136–37, 230–31
    driving to Hobart, 23–24
    facing the future, 239
    personal story, 222–25
Somerville, Wayne
    author's great-aunt, 107
    avoidance of singing, 35
    Doctor of Psychology degree, 156
    family therapy for forests, 136–37
    father's death, 109–10
    giving up tobacco, 119–20
    grief over dying forests, 106
    hypnotherapy for phobia, 208
    lucid dream, 109–10
    Master of Clinical Psychology, 57
    sister's funeral, 108
    sleep apnoea, 178–79
    sleep study, 179–180
    Somerville & Jupp study, 57, 183–84
    taking care of home front, 238–39
    tinnitus story, 80–81
specific phobia disorder. *See* phobia
Spinoza, Baruch, quote, 85
splatter gun (BMAD), 233
Stanton, Harry, 170
stereotyping and prejudice, 77
stimulus & response. *See* behaviourist...
stress
    forms and intensity, 18–19
    good and bad, 18
    past, present and future, 18
    positive role of, 18
    stress and anxiety defined, 17–18
    stress waves, 1
    threats and challenges, 18
stress and anxiety, 17–19
stress scan, 87–89
stress responses
    eco-anxiety, 19
    environmental grief, 19
    solastalgia, 19
stress waves, 1, 60
subconscious mind. *See* deep mind
subjective units of distress scale, 200–1
SUDS. *See* subjective units ...
suicide, 102–3
supporting younger self, 164, 195, 208
surf board riding
    art of, 13–15
    basic knowledge and skills, 13–15
    breakers, 13

rips, 13
stress-wave metaphor, 14
sustainable agriculture. *See* holistic farming
"Sylvia" (repressed memory), 196–97
systematic desensitisation, 203–4
systemic family therapy, 57
systems theory, 136–39
Szasz, Thomas, quote, 34

T

talking about trauma, 125–27
talking with others, 124–27
television news, 172, 174
Tennyson, Alfred, quote, 245
"Terry" (self-hypnosis), 118
The Simpsons, 241
therapeutic farming, 239
therapies for traumatic stress
    acceptance/commitment therapy, 207
    cognitive behaviour therapy, 207
    cognitive therapy, 206–7
    dialectical behaviour therapy, 207
    dual attention in therapy, 200
    emotional freedom techniques, 209–10
    exposure therapy, 204–6
    eye movement desensitisation ..., 210–11
    hypnotherapy, 203
    ideodynamic hypnotherapy, 208
    imagery rescripting therapy, 207–8
    medications, 202–3
    mindfulness-based cognitive ..., 207
    sensorimotor psychotherapy, 211–12
    shared processes in therapy, 199–201
    somatic experiencing, 211–12
    systematic desensitisation, 203–4

thinking and reasoning
    fallacy of hindsight/'what ifs', 130–31
    flawed reasoning, 131–2
    holistic thinking, 134–38
    reasoned thought, 132–34
    thinking styles, 129–30
thinking styles
    field-dependent/independent, 129–30
    principle-based & emotion-focussed, 130
third-person perspective. *See* memory and ...
Thoreau, Henry David, quote, 119
thought field therapy (TFT), 209–10
tinnitus, 81
tobacco, giving up, 82–83, 119–20
Tolkien, J.R.R., 98–99
"Tom" (van der Kolk patient), 75
"Tom" and "Alicia" (cancer), 99
totem, 239–40
training memories criteria, 152
training memory exercise, 152–55
trauma
    definition, 19
    incidence of, 19
    types, 19
troublesome words
    generalisations, 114
    hope and try, 114–15
    motivation style, 119–20
    must and should, 115–17
    negative language, 117–18
Trump, Donald, 241
Turing, Alan, 241
Tutu, Desmond, 115
Twain, Mark, quote, 103

U

ultradian break, 175
unconscious mind. *See* deep mind

unity of all things, 103–5

V
van der Kolk, Bessel, case, 75
van der Kolk, Bessel, quote, 151, 191
vicarious traumatisation, 78–79
Virgil quote, 69
virtual day in court, 96–97
Voltaire quotes, 141, 235

W
Watkins, John G., 53
Watts, Alan, 102
"Wendy" (dream), 186
'what ifs'. *See* fallacy of hindsight…
Wordsworth, William, 221
working with good memories, 168–69
World War II, 241

Y
Y2K, 241
'yes' effect, 32–34
Yin-Yang symbol, 104
Yogananda quotes, 129, 149, 157
young woman illusion, 145–46

About Dr. Wayne R. Somerville

Wayne has practised for more than 35 years as a clinical psychologist and trauma specialist. He has helped many people overcome anxiety, stress and trauma, and taught them to ride the stress waves in their lives with joy and style. On their rural property, Wayne and his wife, Susan, have farmed, worked horses and developed a treatment for forest dieback. Wayne and Susan campaign against the gas field industrialisation of rural Australia.

Wayne holds the degrees of Bachelor of Arts with 1st Class Honours in Psychology, Master of Clinical Psychology and Doctor of Psychology. He has researched therapies for phobia and posttraumatic stress disorder, published a paper on hypnotherapy for phobia, and presented workshops, seminars and training programs on psychological therapies for stress and trauma. With his wife, Susan, Wayne co-authored a journal paper on the treatment of forest dieback and has presented workshops and seminars on bush regeneration.

At *www.ridingstresswaves.com.au* you'll find information about upcoming seminars and workshops. You can also download audio recordings of Wayne reading the mental exercises and thought experiments from *The Art of Riding Stress Waves*.

Please leave your honest review on an Amazon books website. You can email Wayne at: drwaynesomerville@gmail.com.

www.ingramcontent.com/pod-product-compliance
Lightning Source LLC
Chambersburg PA
CBHW031236290426
44109CB00012B/322